Shrub Roses
and
Climbing Roses

PAUL'S HIMALAYAN MUSK, *a beautiful strong Rambling Rose seen here growing over the stump of an old tree. This is an ideal Rambler to grow into old fruit trees that contribute little in the way of fruit. It can also be encouraged to thread its way through shrubs and over hedges, or be grown on pergolas and arches.*

Shrub Roses
and
Climbing Roses

with HYBRID TEA and FLORIBUNDA ROSES

DAVID AUSTIN

Antique Collectors' Club

To my wife Pat

Parts of this book first appeared in *The Heritage of the Rose* by David Austin, 1988, revised 1990, reprinted 1993

Cover photograph by Graham Stuart Thomas

Printed in England by the Antique Collectors' Club Ltd., Woodbridge, Suffolk IP12 1DS on Consort Royal Satin paper supplied by the Donside Paper Company, Aberdeen, Scotland

David Austin is head of the firm of David Austin Roses of Albrighton, where he grows nearly one thousand different varieties of rose and maintains one of the most beautiful rose gardens in Britain. He has left his mark on the development of the rose by creating an entirely new class of rose — the English Rose — one that combines the charm, form of flower and fragrance of the Old Roses with the free and continuous flowering of the Hybrid Teas.

It can therefore be said that he is in a unique position to write about roses. His writing is both clear and lively and his enthusiasm and love of his subject will soon become obvious.

In the successful companion volume to this book, *Old Roses and English Roses*, David Austin discussed the Old Roses and their modern successors — his own English Roses. He now writes about the beautiful Shrub and Ground-cover Roses, the dainty Species Roses and the many lovely Climbing and Rambling Roses. In addition, he writes at length on the popular Hybrid Teas and Floribundas, as well as the numerous small Patio and Miniature Roses that have recently arrived on the garden scene.

In this book the author describes some 560 roses in detail: bud and flower formation and development, shape and size of plant, foliage, colour, fragrance, date of introduction and breeder. Cultivation and pruning advice is given for each main grouping of roses.

Born in 1926, David Austin began his working life as a farmer and has always lived and worked in Shropshire. His wife is the sculptress Pat Austin, and they have a daughter and two sons. His son David and daughter Claire are both engaged in the business.

THE FAMOUS FRENCH *rose garden at Roseraie du Parc de Bagatelle, Paris, showing roses planted in borders in a formal style, and growing up free-standing pillars which give height to a border and provide a point to attract the eye.*

Contents

Acknowledgements

I wish to express my thanks to a number of people who have helped me in the production of this book.

Graham Stuart Thomas for reading the manuscript and making numerous helpful suggestions.

Barry Ambrose of the Royal Horticultural Society, Wisley, for much help, encouragement and practical advice, including suggestions for plants for association with roses.

Diane Ratcliff and Doreen Pike for typing the scripts and much other help.

8

Photographic Acknowledgements

David Knight, A.B.I.P.P., A.R.P.S., A.S.I.A. (Art and Design), of the School of Art and Design, The Polytechnic, Wolverhampton.

Michael Warren, A.B.I.P.P., A.M.P.A., who specialises in horticultural photography and has a large library of pictures.

Vincent Page, Picture Editor of *The Sunday Times Colour Supplement,* who possesses one of the largest collections of rose pictures, and who gave extensive and valuable assistance in the editing of photographs.

Claire Austin, B.A. (Hons.), who assists the author at his nursery, specialising in hardy plants.

Graham Stuart Thomas, O.B.E., V.M.H., D.H.M., V.M.M., formerly Garden Adviser to the National Trust and author of many books on gardening.

Professor G. Fineschi, Italy, whose garden in Florence contains one of the finest collections of roses in Europe.

Other photographs are from R.C. Balfour, Harry Smith's Horticultural Photographic Collection, Paul Edwards, garden designer, and the following nurseries/nurserymen: Cants of Colchester, James Cocker & Sons, Dickson Nurseries Ltd., Fryer's Nurseries Ltd., R. Harkness & Co. Ltd., Le Grice Roses, John Mattock Ltd., Wisbech Plant Co. Ltd. and B.J. Tysterman.

NOZOMI, *a small Ground-cover Rose seen here falling towards a pool. Its naturally creeping habit makes it an ideal rose to grow in a hanging basket.*

WEDDING DAY *(back), a strong Rambling Rose which can be used for growing into a large tree.* ROSA PAULII *(right) is a Species Hybrid which will grow in partial shade. It is also excellent for covering large areas of ground. On the right the Gallica Rose Officinalis.*

Introduction

In the companion volume to this book, *Old Roses and English Roses*, I discussed the various groups of roses up to the advent of the Hybrid Tea Roses, and included with these the natural successors of the old varieties – the English Roses – which are very similar in character to the Old Roses.

In this volume I cover the Hybrid Teas and their close relations, the Floribunda Roses, as well as a great variety of hybrids of these roses, which are usually known as Modern Shrub Roses. Together with these, I describe the great variety of Climbing and Rambler Roses which are so useful in the garden. Finally I include a number of wild Species Roses and their immediate hybrids – many of which are excellent garden shrubs.

Nearly all of these roses have been introduced in the present century and this illustrates very well the enormous development that has taken place during this period. A great deal, though not all, of this has been for the best. The rose has evolved from the Old Roses – which were very beautiful shrubs – and has become a flower capable of fulfilling almost any function in the garden – from the tiniest Miniature Rose to the popular Hybrid Tea bush, through to large border shrubs and Climbing Roses and even to giant Ramblers that will climb up sizeable trees. It is all these roses that I write about in this book.

CHAPTER 1
Shrub Roses of our Time

By 1920 most of the wild species roses of the world had arrived in Western Europe and there had already been a huge proliferation of garden roses. It was the crossing of certain of these species and their hybrids with garden varieties that gave rise to the roses discussed in this chapter. That is to say the Hybrid Musks and the Modern Shrub Roses, as well as the more recent so-called Ground-cover Roses. The garden roses used were, in the main, Tea Roses, Hybrid Perpetuals, and more particularly the Hybrid Teas. The resulting roses are usually quite large shrubs, perhaps 5 or 6ft. in height, although they are frequently much smaller, and at times larger.

The roses in this chapter usually inherit something of the modern garden roses' ability to repeat flower, and are thus very useful garden shrubs, flowering as they do when most shrubs of other genera have finished, often continuing late into the summer. Being taller, they have a grace of growth not found in the shorter Bush Roses — it requires some length of stem to make this possible. At the same time it is difficult, if not impossible, for Shrub Roses to rival Bush Roses in continuity of bloom. It seems that the maintenance of a large shrub leaves less energy for recurrent flowering. The flowers generally do not have the bud formation of the Hybrid Tea, nor do they have the full open flower of the Old Rose, but tend to be semi-double and informal, producing a mass of colour. Having said this, it is important to stress that they are usually in no way gaudy, but provide the gentle colour effects so suitable to the rose.

Recent years have seen the appearance of certain varieties that are in effect no more than very large Floribundas. These are usually the by-products of some hybridist's Floribunda breeding programme which have turned up something too large in growth for that class. Such roses are, in my opinion, seldom very desirable.

DENTELLES DE MALINES *(left), a Shrub Rose which also makes a good Climber for lower walls. It is also good as a Ground-cover Rose.* LÉONTINE GERVAIS *(right) is a Rambling Rose suitable for growing on pergolas, arches, pillars (as here) and other structures.*

BUFF BEAUTY, *an excellent Hybrid Musk Rose, seen here with herbaceous plants.*

Hybrid Musk Roses

This is rather a misleading name for a group of roses that are only remotely connected with the Musk Rose via the Noisettes. It is, however, a pleasant name and conveys a more accurate feeling for the class than any other we are likely to come up with. These roses do, in fact, usually have a strong fragrance which is similar to that of the Musk Rose with its ability, in the words of Francis Bacon, to 'carry on the air'.

The Hybrid Musks are usually shrubs of 5 or 6ft. in height, although there are a few smaller varieties which are often of less value. The flowers are generally of small to medium size and held in sprays. Given adequate growing conditions they repeat flower well, sending up strong stems from the base to provide a second crop in late summer. It may be said that they are to the Shrub Roses what the Floribundas are to the Hybrid Teas, producing as they do an excellent massed effect. It is there that the analogy ends, for their growth is more graceful than that of a Bush Rose and their flowers are usually of soft colouring. Both growth and foliage are close to that of the Modern Rose, with its smooth, shiny texture.

The history of the Hybrid Musks begins in Germany in 1902, when Peter Lambert sowed what he believed to have been self-fertilised seed of a Rambler called 'Aglaia' and raised a variety that he named 'Trier'. 'Aglaia' was itself a cross between *Rosa multiflora* and the buff-coloured Noisette 'Rêve d'Or'. 'Trier', a 6ft. shrub or short Climber bearing sprays of small, nearly single white flowers tinged with cream and pink, had the great advantage that it was both repeat flowering and shrubby in growth. Lambert saw the possibilities of this variety and used it in the development of a number of roses he called 'Lambertiana'. Most of these were, in fact, of little merit, being not much more than rather large Polyantha Roses.

It was not long before the Reverend Joseph Pemberton took a hand. He lived in a village in Essex with the picturesque and appropriate name of Havering-atte-Bower, and here he raised a series of varieties we now call Hybrid Musks. These were the result of crosses between 'Trier' in particular, but also between certain Polyanthas and Noisettes, with a variety of different Hybrid Teas, Tea Roses and Noisettes. They were introduced by a nurseryman called J.A. Bentall, who also bred a few varieties himself, notably 'Buff Beauty' and 'Ballerina'.

There the story ends, for little more work has been done on the Hybrid Musks since that time. The problem seems to have been exactly the same as with the Rugosas (see *Old Roses and English Roses*), for in many cases the Hybrid Musks are also the result of crossing diploids with tetraploids, thus leading to varieties that are sterile and inhibiting further progress. Alternatively, it may be that no one has thought it worthwhile proceeding further. If this is so, I think it is a mistake, for it is possible to visualise many good things coming out of these roses and the problem of sterility can be overcome.

The Hybrid Musks require good cultivation and adequate manuring if they are to reach their full potential. Well treated they will form graceful shrubs, bearing an abundance of bloom in summer and again in autumn. Being repeat flowering, pruning is important. Take out the old and weak wood as the shrub matures, and prune back the strong main shoots by one third to encourage new growth. Be careful to leave sufficient strong growth to enable the shrub to build up its structure, otherwise it may remain short.

In recent years a number of new roses have been introduced that seem to come very close to the Hybrid Musks in the nature of their growth. I am thinking mainly of the roses that I list as Ground-cover Roses, which are often not so much ground cover as sprawling shrubs. These new roses are usually without fragrance, but in growth are not dissimilar to Hybrid Musks, and the time may come when it will be convenient to place all these together in one class. Perhaps the linking factor would be that they all have some connection with the ramblers of the Synstylae family.

AUTUMN DELIGHT. As the name suggests this rose is notable for its display of flowers late in the season. These have considerable charm, being almost single and of cupped formation, yellow in the bud, creamy-yellow when open with contrasting dark stamens, and fading almost to white with age. The early blooms are held in small sprays, but later large heads are produced on shoots from the base of the plant. It grows to little more than 3ft. in height. Bred by Bentall (U.K.), introduced 1933.

BALLERINA. This is by no means a typical Hybrid Musk, being much more like a very large Polyantha, but do not let this deter you, as it is, in fact, a beautiful rose. Its small single Polyantha blooms held in many-flowered clusters are of a soft pink with a white centre. 'Ballerina' flowers with remarkable continuity, and combines this with quite exceptional toughness and reliability. It forms a tight, rounded shrub of 4ft. in height by almost as much across, while the flowers are held in close trusses, slightly reminiscent of a hydrangea. A mass planting of this rose can provide a pleasing effect, the flowers mingling attractively with its light green foliage. It is also excellent when grown as a standard. Slight fragrance. The parents are not recorded. Bred by Bentall (U.K.), introduced 1937. See page 18.

BUFF BEAUTY. One of the finest of the Hybrid Musks, bearing flowers of a lovely rich apricot-yellow and having a strong Tea Rose fragrance. They are semi-double to double, of medium size and held in small or large clusters on a well-balanced arching shrub which may be 5 or 6ft. in height and as much across. It has large, thick, dark green leaves, and its smooth stems are tinted with brown. When well grown, the whole plant has an appearance of almost tropical lushness. The breeding has not been recorded nor, so far as I know, has the breeder. Although I am well aware it is fruitless to surmise on such matters, I would hazard a guess it has 'Lady Hillingdon' as one of its parents, for its colour, growth and scent all seem to point to this. It is reliably recurrent flowering. One of the finest of the rather small number of yellow shrub roses available to us. See page 15.

CALLISTO. This is a small shrub of 4ft. in height, but quite broad and

BALLERINA, *Hybrid Musk Rose. Perhaps the most reliable of all repeat-flowering Shrub Roses.*

bushy. The flowers are small, rambler-like and held in tight sprays, and of a pleasing yellow shade, fading with age almost to white. Strong fragrance. A seedling from 'William Allen Richardson', it is thus probably a pure descendant from a Noisette Rose. Raised by Pemberton (U.K.), introduced 1920.

CORNELIA. A vigorous shrub bearing sprays of small, formal rosette-shaped flowers with three or four rows of petals. Their colour is apricot-pink at first, becoming creamy-pink with a distinct boss of yellow stamens at the centre. 'Cornelia' forms a fine, shapely shrub with quite small foliage. In the autumn large sprays of bloom are produced on the strong new stems from the base of the plant. There is a strong fragrance that carries far. 'Cornelia' will grow to about 5ft. in height and spread to 6ft. The parents are not recorded but it appears to be closely related to 'Trier'. Bred by Pemberton (U.K.), introduced 1925.

DANAË. A small shrub, 3 to 4ft. in height, bearing sprays of small, fragrant, deep yellow rambler-like flowers that fade to white as they age. 'Trier' x 'Gloire de Chédane-Guinoisseau'. Pemberton (U.K.), 1913.

CORNELIA, *Hybrid Musk Rose, seen here with* Rosa *'Paulii' behind.*

DAYBREAK. A small shrub of about 3ft. in height with sprays of loosely formed semi-double flowers of pale yellow fading to ivory, and with dark yellow stamens. The foliage is tinted brown at first, later becoming dark green. Strong Musk Rose fragrance. 'Trier' x 'Liberty'. Pemberton (U.K.), 1918.

FELICIA. A strong and reliable shrub flowering very freely both in summer and autumn. Its parents were 'Trier' by the Hybrid Tea 'Ophelia', and the flowers, though small and held in large sprays, have something of the character of the latter rose about them. They begin as somewhat pointed apricot-pink buds, and open to rather informal blush-pink flowers with a strong aromatic fragrance. The foliage, too, leans towards the Hybrid Tea, both leaf and flower having rather more substance than is usual among the Hybrid Musks. It will form a broad, shapely, branching plant of 5ft. in height. A first class, practical shrub, that will also make a good hedge. Bred by Pemberton (U.K.), introduced 1928. See page 22.

FRANCESCA. A large, graceful shrub of 6ft. in height, with broad, arching growth. It is well clothed with foliage, the individual leaves being long and pointed. The long pointed buds of slim, Tea Rose elegance open to quite large, semi-double flowers which are nicely poised in well spaced sprays and coloured apricot-yellow fading to pale yellow. Strong Tea Rose scent. From 'Danaë' x 'Sunburst'. Raised by Pemberton (U.K.), introduced 1922.

MOONLIGHT. This is the result of a cross between 'Trier' and the early Tea Rose 'Sulphurea', although it leans heavily towards the former. The individual flowers are small, semi-double and white with yellow stamens, and are held in medium-sized sprays, followed by very large sprays late in the summer. 'Moonlight' is useful where a tall shrub is required as it will reach 8ft. or more in height, although it is more upright than broad and has been known to ascend up to 15ft. in trees. The stems are tinted mahogany, and the foliage dark green. Strong Musk Rose fragrance. Bred by Pemberton (U.K.), introduced 1913.

NUR MAHAL. One of the few red Hybrid Musks. The result of crossing the old dark crimson Hybrid Tea 'Château de Clos Vougeot' with an unspecified Hybrid Musk seedling. It is not so widely grown as many of the Hybrid Musks, which I think is unfortunate, for it is a rose of some character. The flowers are medium sized, crimson at first, opening wide and turning to mauve-crimson with contrasting yellow stamens. They have an evenness of outline that gives them a pleasing formality. The growth is wide and branching, about 4ft. in height and rather more across. Fragrant. Bred by Pemberton (U.K.), introduced 1923.

PAX. A cross between 'Trier' and 'Sunburst' resulting in a shrub rather similar to 'Francesca' which, in fact, shares 'Sunburst' as one of its parents. The growth is tall, broad and elegantly arching, with brown stems and dark green leaves. The flowers start as long pointed buds and open to large, loosely formed and semi-double white flowers with golden stamens and a pleasing fragrance. They are held in sprays of medium size which have a delicacy and natural charm the equal of any of this group. Further, often massive sprays follow late in the season. Height 6 to 8ft. Bred by Pemberton (U.K.), introduced 1918.

PENELOPE. This is usually regarded as one of the most reliable of Hybrid Musk Roses, indeed of all Modern Shrub Roses, and has for many years been widely used both in private gardens and for amenity planting. It forms an excellent full branching shrub of about 5ft. in height and a little more across. The flowers, which are of medium size and borne in large clusters, show some affinity to its mother parent, the Hybrid Tea 'Ophelia'. Coppery-salmon tinted buds open blush-pink and semi-double, soon becoming almost white, the overall effect being pale pink. They have a strong musky fragrance and are followed by pleasing coral-pink hips — a rare bonus in a repeat-flowering rose, although it may be preferable to remove the earliest of these when the petals fall to encourage further bloom. Bred by Pemberton (U.K.), introduced 1924. See page 23.

PINK PROSPERITY. Not, as the name might seem to suggest, a sport from 'Prosperity', but quite a different rose, with small tight-petalled, pompon flowers of clear pink and with a strong fragrance. It is robust and healthy and of rather upright habit. Overall, in both flower and growth, it lacks the softness and grace of other roses in this class. The breeding is not recorded — it is probably not of the usual Hybrid Musk origin and is more likely to be a Polyantha cross. Height 5ft. Bred by Bentall (U.K.), introduced 1931.

PROSPERITY. A cross between the creamy-blush Polyantha Rose 'Marie-Jeanne' and the Tea Rose 'Perle des Jardins', 'Prosperity' is, therefore, of rather different origin from most Hybrid Musks, being a hybrid of a Polyantha, and this shows up in its growth. However, the Tea Rose parent brings a softness and shrubbiness that renders this variety quite in keeping with the class. The growth is strong, bushy and rather upright, about 5ft. in height and slightly less across, with shiny, dark

FELICIA, *a fine example of this Hybrid Musk Rose, seen against a background of foliage.*

green foliage. The flowers are creamy-white, flushed with pink at first, later becoming ivory-white tinged with lemon at the centre. They are quite small and held in many flowered trusses. Good fragrance. Bred by Pemberton (U.K.), introduced 1919.

THISBE. A small shrub of moderate vigour, carrying clusters of small, semi-double buff-yellow flowers soon paling to creamy-buff. It has a

PENELOPE, *one of the best Hybrid Musk Roses and always reliable.*

Left: VANITY, *a really beautiful tall single Hybrid Musk Rose.*

Right: PROSPERITY, *one of the best Hybrid Musk Roses.*

strong and pleasing fragrance. The breeding is the same as for 'Prosperity', see above, but this time we have a rose that is much closer in character to its Polyantha parent. Height 4ft. Bred by Pemberton (U.K.), introduced 1918.

TRIER. The foundation rose of the class described in the introduction to this section. It is not in itself a particularly outstanding variety, forming a rather upright shrub of 6 or 8ft. in height, with sprays of small, single white flowers tinted with blush and with a hint of yellow at the base. Thought to be a self-seedling from 'Aglaia'. Bred by Lambert (Germany), introduced 1904.

VANITY. A tall shrub of 8ft. in height, bearing large, almost single, light crimson flowers which are held widely spaced in open sprays. In late summer, long, strong shoots appear, often bearing huge many-flowered heads of bloom. The whole effect is one of light and airy grace. Due perhaps to its size, the branches are not plentiful and this often results in lop-sided and very open growth. For this reason it is a good idea to plant closely in groups of two or three bushes, so that they grow together to give the appearance of one fine shrub. 'Vanity' is ideal for the back of a large border, where its dainty flowers look very beautiful when seen above other plants. The foliage is dark green and rather sparse, a feature that seems only to add to its attraction by exposing its glaucous green stalks. There is a strong and pleasing fragrance. A cross between 'Château de Clos Vougeot' and unnamed seedling. Bred by Pemberton (U.K.), introduced 1920. See page 23.

WILHELM ('Skyrocket'). In 1927 Pemberton introduced a crimson Hybrid Musk called 'Robin Hood', the result of a cross with the crimson Polyantha 'Edith Cavell'. 'Robin Hood' is a rather dull variety showing a strong Polyantha influence, and in 1934 Kordes crossed it with the red Hybrid Tea 'J.C. Thornton' to produce 'Wilhelm'. The result of all this work is a rose that is rather far removed from what I would consider to be a true Hybrid Musk. It is modern in character, with rather upright growth similar to that of a large Floribunda. For all this, 'Wilhelm' provides a fine splash of colour, with a mass of small semi-double dark crimson flowers in large clusters. It repeats reliably and there are long-lasting orange-red hips in the autumn. There is only a slight fragrance. Height 5 to 6ft.

WILL SCARLET. A scarlet sport of 'Wilhelm', similar in every way except colour and providing a brilliant display. Light fragrance. Introduced by Hilling (U.K.), 1947.

Modern Shrub Roses

We group under this heading a large number of Shrub Roses of widely varying origins, nearly all of them bred during the last fifty years. Perhaps the most important thing they have in common is that all but a few have some Hybrid Tea in their make up, a fact that often shows up in their appearance, both in flower and growth. They might well be said to be hybrids of the Hybrid Teas or Floribundas. The other side of their parentage may come from any one of a variety of species and classes, resulting in many widely differing shrubs.

It would be easy to draw the conclusion that these roses are a pretty ordinary lot and little more than overgrown Hybrid Teas or Floribundas. Indeed this sometimes is the case, and many of the new Shrub Roses passing through the various trial grounds fit the description perfectly. If, however, we select carefully, we can find what are undoubtedly some of the best Shrub Roses of this century. It is these that I have tried to include in my list.

Nearly all these roses are easily grown and very robust. More often than not they are recurrent flowering. They are, therefore, highly suitable for the average garden, and as this group includes some of the best known of all Shrub Roses, many of them are easily obtained at local garden centres. Most are extremely showy, producing masses of bloom. Local authorities buy them in large numbers, and no wonder, for there cannot be many shrubs of any kind that produce so much colour.

The name of Kordes occurs again and again among these roses, and it should be said that this firm has contributed more than any other to their development. Kordes was interested in breeding hardy Shrub Roses for the North European climate. Some of these may appear a little coarse, no doubt due to the pursuit of hardiness, to the exclusion of other qualities, but we have only to mention such varieties as 'Frühlingsmorgen', 'Fritz Nobis' and 'Cerise Bouquet', to realise how beautiful many of them are.

Cultivation is no problem. Good feeding and adequate pruning will yield a better performance and greater continuity of flowering, but due to the great diversity of habit of this class, it is not possible to be specific as regards pruning. Usually it is best to thin out weak wood and cut back the remaining growth by about a third, but a little imagination is called for here — where the growth is closer to the wild species greater freedom should be allowed and less pruning done.

Many of these shrubs are equally good as Climbers, perhaps for a wall, fence or pillar, and the majority of the taller kinds are suitable for growing in this manner.

ALCHEMIST. A vigorous upright shrub of 6ft. in height with plentiful, glossy foliage. The flowers, a mixture of yellow and yolk-yellow, are unusual among Modern Shrub Roses in that they are of typical Old Rose rosette shape, opening flat — in fact rather similar to those of the English Rose 'Charles Austin', though less cupped in shape. They have a strong fragrance, but there is no second crop. 'Alchemist' can equally well be grown as a shrub or a Climber, when it might grow to 10ft. or more. This variety is the result of a cross between the Hybrid Tea 'Golden Glow' and a *Rosa eglanteria* hybrid. Bred by Kordes (Germany), introduced 1956.

THE ALEXANDRA ROSE (Ausday). This is an interesting new rose, which is closely related to the Alba Roses (see *Old Roses and English Roses*). It was originally bred with the objective of improving the English Roses, but now and again a beautiful rose appears in our breeding field which seems to be more in place amongst the Modern Shrub Roses than with the English Roses. It bears dainty, single 'wild rose' flowers in an

FRÜHLINGSGOLD, *one of the most widely planted Modern Shrub Roses.*

ALCHEMIST, *a Modern Shrub Rose or Climber with Old Rose flowers.*

attractive coppery-pink, with pale yellow at the centre and pretty stamens. The growth too is attractive, with thin stems and dainty, rather Alba-like leaves, providing a light, airy appearance. Flowering continues with remarkable regularity throughout the summer months; indeed, I can think of few garden shrubs to compare with this rose in this respect. We would expect it to be extremely hardy and disease-resistant. Height, 4½ ft. Breeding, 'Shropshire Lass' x 'Heritage'. This variety was introduced in aid of the Alexandra Rose Day — a charity that helps a number of very worthwhile causes. Austin (U.K.), 1992.

ALOHA. I have just described 'Alchemist' as being unusual among Modern Shrub Roses for its Old Rose flower formation; here we have another variety of which the same might be said.

When the once-flowering Rambler Rose 'Dr. Van Fleet' sported to produce the repeat-flowering rose 'New Dawn', the way was open to breed new and more reliably repeat-flowering Climbers. 'Aloha' is one of the results of such endeavours. However, since it is very short in growth, it is much better treated as a recurrent-flowering shrub, although it can be used as a Climber of 6ft in height. As a shrub it forms a rather floppy plant, its branches laden down with masses of heavy blooms. These are very double, deeply cupped in form and much like those of an old Bourbon Rose, while the colour is rose-pink, deeper on the outside of the flower. There is a strong fragrance. The foliage is glossy, leathery and disease resistant. If you have a low retaining wall, this rose can be planted on top and allowed to trail downwards with the most pleasing effect. 'Mercedes Gallart' x 'New Dawn'. Bred by Boerner (U.S.A.), introduced 1949.

AUTUMN FIRE ('Herbstfeuer'). An arching shrub bearing sprays of semi-double, fragrant, dark red flowers. In spite of its name, I have not found it to be particularly good in autumn, but it does have excellent, very large orange-red hips — perhaps it is to these that the name refers. Height 6ft. Kordes (Germany), 1961.

BLOOMFIELD ABUNDANCE. A miniature-flowered rose with tiny, pale pink Tea Rose buds of perfect scrolled formation. These are so like those of the rose 'Cécile Brunner', see Chapter 5, as to be almost indistinguishable at first sight. This is no doubt partly because the flowers are so small, but nevertheless the similarity is quite remarkable. The real difference is that 'Bloomfield Abundance' forms a shrub of some 6 or 8ft. in height, whereas 'Cécile Brunner' seldom grows to more than 4ft. The individual blooms can easily be recognised by one characteristic: on 'Bloomfield Abundance' the lobes of the calyx are unusually long and leafy for the size of the flower, trailing down as it opens; on 'Cécile Brunner' these are short.

'Bloomfield Abundance' is a tall, airy shrub, producing its blooms singly and in small clusters on long, wiry stems. Later in the year long shoots appear from the base of the plant in the manner of a Hybrid Musk Rose, and these produce dozens of widely separated flowers. It is a very reliable shrub, the result of a cross between a *Rosa wichuraiana* hybrid called 'Sylvia', and the Hybrid Tea Rose 'Dorothy Page-Roberts'. Bred by George C. Thomas (U.S.A.), 1920.

BONN. A strong, upright shrub of 6ft. in height and rather ungainly habit. The flowers are semi-double, orange-scarlet, becoming tinged with purple as they age. This rose is perhaps a little coarse, but repeats quite well and there are dark red hips in the autumn. Fragrant. 'Hamburg' x 'Independence'. Bred by Kordes (Germany), 1950.

CERISE BOUQUET. A unique rose that is difficult to compare with any other. It is the result of a cross between *Rosa multibracteata* and the Hybrid Tea Rose 'Crimson Glory'. The growth is tall and gracefully arching, 6 to 8ft. in height by as much across though examples of up to 12ft. are not uncommon and, when allowed to trail through other shrubs, up to 15ft. The flowers are quite small and surrounded by attractive, leafy grey-green bracts. Starting as prettily scrolled buds, they open semi-double and flat to expose their stamens and are of a pleasing cerise-crimson colour. The particular charm of this rose lies in the fact that the individual blooms are held on long, leafy, hanging stems fanning out in the most graceful manner from an already bending branch. The foliage is small, greyish-green and attractive. Although it can be a little tempera-mental when first planted, I can think of no faults. It has a rich, fruit-like fragrance. There is only one period of flowering, but then it is one of the most beautiful shrubs in the garden. I understand this rose will make a good Climber, and can well imagine that it would be very fine when so grown. Bred by Kordes (Germany), introduced 1958. See page 39.

CLAIR MATIN. A rose of modern appearance, bearing dainty, pale pink, semi-double flowers of medium size with a slight fragrance. It has branching, slightly arching growth of 7ft. in height and about 6ft. across. The foliage is deep green and leathery. Perhaps its greatest virtue is that it repeat flowers with remarkable reliability. 'Clair Matin' may equally well be grown as a Climbing Rose, when it will achieve a height of 12ft. 'Fashion' x ('Independence' x 'Orange Triumph') x 'Phyllis Bide'. Bred by Meilland (France), 1960.

COMPLICATA. See Rosa Complicata, Chapter 6.

DENTELLE DE MALINES. Some years ago I received a number of new roses from Mr. Louis Lens of the well-known Belgian firm of rose specialists. All were bred by himself. I had them for a number of years before appreciating how good they were. They turned out to be exceptionally strong-growing shrubs, bearing masses of small rambler-like blooms in big trusses, and I selected from these three varieties which seemed to me to be the best. They were 'Dentelle de Malines', 'Pleine de Grâce' and 'Running Maid', all three of which are ideal for the larger garden or for mass planting in public places — indeed I can think of no roses that make a more impressive show. They are also beautiful and have attracted attention from visitors to the gardens at our nurseries. 'Dentelle de Malines' is a hybrid between *Rosa filipes* 'Kiftsgate' and an unspecified rose. It is particularly attractive, with the tiny, very cupped flowers of *R. filipes,* and of a lovely, soft clear pink colouring. The growth is elegantly arched and covered with shapely sprays of bloom. It is not recurrent flowering.

EDDIE'S JEWEL. A cross between the early light crimson Floribunda 'Donald Prior' and a hybrid of *Rosa moyesii*, this rose forms a shrub of 8ft. tall and 6ft. across. The growth and foliage bear some resemblance to *R. moyesii*, but the flowers, which are deep red, are semi-double. It will frequently produce some flowers in late summer. There are no hips. Bred by Eddie (Canada), 1962.

ERFURT. A well-formed shrub of branching, slightly arching growth with good foliage. The flowers, which are borne in small clusters, are of medium size, semi-double, and slightly cupped, their colour being rosy-pink with a prominent contrasting white centre and a boss of golden stamens. 'Erfurt' is not a glamorous rose, but it is reliable and repeats well. It has a light fragrance. Height 5ft. 'Eva' x 'Réveil Dijonnais'. Bred by Kordes (Germany), 1939.

FOUNTAIN. An upright shrub, 5ft. in height, bearing large blood-red typically Hybrid Tea flowers with shapely buds. They are of particularly pure colouring and have a strong fragrance. There is ample deep green disease-resistant foliage. It is nice to see a Hybrid Tea flower on a good shrub. Parentage unknown. Bred by Tantau (Germany), introduced 1970.

FRANK NAYLOR. Sprays of medium-sized, dusky-crimson semi-double flowers against complementary dusky, dark green foliage. A shrub of excellent branching habit, producing its flowers with quite exceptional continuity. This would be a good rose in every way were it not for its susceptibility to mildew, but it is worth growing in areas where this disease is not a problem. Bred by Harkness (U.K.), 1978.

FRED LOADS. A cross between two Floribundas, 'Orange Sensation' and 'Dorothy Wheatcroft', this rose will reach 6ft. in height, sending up long, strong, upright growth from the base. It is very much the giant Floribunda, but flowers freely and continually, providing a mass of semi-double flowers of orange-vermilion. The foliage is bright green, disease resistant and plentiful. Fragrant. Bred by Holmes (U.K.), 1968.

FRITZ NOBIS. A cross between the strong growing Hybrid Tea Rose 'Joanna Hill' and 'Magnifica', the latter being a direct descendant of the Penzance Sweet Brier 'Lucy Ashton'. It is remarkable how 'Fritz Nobis' has caught the strong, bushy growth of the Sweet Brier, and managed to combine this with the most charming Hybrid Tea-like flowers. The whole shrub remains in balance, growing to about 6ft. in height and the same across. The flowers start as perfect pointed buds and open to shapely semi-double flowers of a clear pink. Add to this a delicious clove scent, and we have one of the best Modern Shrub Roses. There are few

MARGUERITE HILLING, *a Modern Shrub Rose with all the virtues of its parent 'Nevada'.*

Right: FRITZ NOBIS, *a very good Shrub Rose.*

Below: FRÜHLINGSMORGEN, *Modern Shrub Rose. One of the most beautiful single roses.*

roses capable of such a fine display. It is unfortunate this occurs only in early summer, but to ask more would, perhaps, be too much, and we do have the compensation of its dark red hips that last long into the winter. The foliage is large and dark green. Bred by Kordes (Germany), introduced 1940.

FRÜHLINGSANFANG. W. Kordes introduced a number of Shrub Roses with the prefix 'Frühlings' or, in English, 'Spring', all of which are hybrids of one or other of the Pimpinellifolia group, and I list what I regard as the three best. These all flower early in the season, before most other garden roses appear. 'Frühlingsanfang' is a cross between 'Joanna Hill' and *Rosa pimpinellifolia* 'Grandiflora', and forms a large shrub, of species-like appearance, 9ft. in height by as much across. The flowers are large and single, ivory-white, opening flat, with yellow stamens, and are followed in autumn by maroon-red hips. Introduced 1950. See page 35.

FRÜHLINGSGOLD ('Spring Gold'). This is one of the most widely planted of all Shrub Roses, both in gardens and public places. The reason for this is not hard to explain, for no garden rose is more hardy, so reliable, or so easily grown, even under difficult conditions. The flowers are creamy-yellow in colour, fairly large, semi-double, with rich yellow stamens, and although they are rather untidy in form this does not matter in the mass. They have a strong fragrance that carries across the garden. There is only one period of bloom, early in the season, but what a magnificent flowering it is — the whole shrub is covered with flowers! It usually grows to about 7ft. high by as much across, although sometimes, if permitted, it will grow much larger. A hybrid of 'Joanna Hill' and *Rosa pimpinellifolia hispida*. Bred by Kordes (Germany), introduced 1937. See page 26.

FRÜHLINGSMORGEN ('Spring Morning'). The third member of this series is one of the most delicately beautiful of all single roses. The flowers are large, slightly cupped and perfectly formed. According to the strength of the sun, they can vary in colour from cherry-pink to clear rose-pink, paling a little towards the centre, and they have the most attractive, long and elegant maroon-coloured stamens. The growth is not quite so unfailingly robust as in the case of the two varieties above, but it will grow to about 5 or 6ft. in height and the same across. It cannot be said to be recurrent flowering, though there are frequently a few further blooms later in the year. The foliage is of a dark and leaden green. There is a slight fragrance. Breeding ('E.G. Hill' x 'Kathrine Kordes') x *Rosa pimpinellifolia* 'Grandiflora'. Bred by Kordes (Germany), introduced 1942. See page 31.

GOLDBUSCH. A low-growing, spreading bush with coral-tinted buds opening into semi-double or double ochre-yellow flowers with yellow stamens. These have a Tea Rose fragrance and there is a second crop later in the summer. The foliage is abundant, glossy and light green. Height 4ft. spreading to 5ft. Perhaps a little ordinary, but there are not too many Shrub Roses of this colour. Bred by Kordes (Germany), introduced 1954.

GOLDEN WINGS. It is rather surprising that good, repeat-flowering single roses are rare among Shrub Roses of garden origin, in spite of the fact that the rose is, of course, single flowered by nature. This variety does, however, have single flowers. They are large, perhaps 4 or 5ins. across, sulphur-yellow, fading slightly with age, with attractive brown stamens. They open from long, pointed buds and have a sweet fragrance. With these attractions goes a genuine ability to flower throughout the summer. 'Golden Wings' is a beautiful rose, with something of the charm of a wild species. If it has a fault, it is the fact that its growth is rather open, stiff and stick like, though this can be improved by careful pruning to encourage more branching growth. Its breeding is both complex and interesting: Hybrid Tea 'Soeur Thérèse' x (*Rosa pimpinellifolia* 'Grandiflora' x 'Ormiston Roy'). 'Ormiston Roy' was *R. pimpinellifolia* x *R. xanthina.* 'Golden Wings' is thus closely connected with two species of the Pimpinellifolia group. See page 35.

JACQUELINE DUPREZ (Harwanna). An exciting new Shrub Rose which is related to the Scottish Roses, although this is perhaps more apparent in the flowers than in the growth. It bears dainty, semi-double, blush-white flowers of about 4 inches across. These are most attractively set off by prominent golden stamens. The growth is vigorous and bushy and it flowers regularly. There is a light musky fragrance. It may be expected to reach 6ft. It appears in every way an excellent Shrub Rose. Breeding, Harkness (U.K.), 1989.

JAMES MASON. This is the result of hybridizing 'Scarlet Fire' and the Gallica Rose 'Tuscany Superb'. 'Scarlet Fire' is itself partly Gallica, so 'James Mason' is an interesting cross and a good example of what the breeder can do with Old Roses. The flowers are of a rich crimson colouring and have something of the formality and restraint of a Gallica. They are semi-double with two rows of petals and contrasting yellow stamens. There is abundant foliage of near Gallica appearance, which can at times obscure the flowers. Fragrant. Raised by Peter Beales (U.K.), introduced 1982.

NEVADA, *one of the best Modern Shrub Roses, growing to 8ft. and covered in bloom.*

FRÜHLINGSANFANG, *a robust Modern Shrub Rose that will grow in poor conditions.*

GOLDEN WINGS, *an excellent repeat-flowering Modern Shrub Rose.*

KARL FÖRSTER. A cross between 'Frau Karl Druschki' and *Rosa pimpinellifolia* 'Grandiflora', with pointed buds opening into double pure white flowers with a slight scent. The growth is vigorous, up to 7ft. in height, with attractive greyish-green foliage showing signs of Pimpinellifolia influence. It should, I suppose, be considered together with the 'Frühlings' series, but it is rather different in character and is recurrent flowering. Bred by Kordes (Germany), introduced 1931.

KASSEL. A vigorous upright shrub of 6ft. in height, bearing semi-double cherry-red flowers in Floribunda-like clusters. It has a little more character than 'Bonn', see above, to which it is rather similar, but is still rather coarse. Slight fragrance. 'Kassel' may also be grown as a 12ft. Climber. Breeding 'Hamburg' x 'Scarlet Else'. Kordes (Germany), 1957.

LAVENDER LASSIE. Often described as a Hybrid Musk, this rose really has little in common with that group. It is more like a tall Floribunda, growing to about 4ft. in height and rather narrow. The flowers are 3ins. across and have something of the character of an Old Rose, with numerous small petals in rosette formation. The colour is a pale lavender, which is useful as there are few truly repeat-flowering Shrub Roses of this shade; it is, however, variable in this respect, sometimes being nearer to a lilac-pink shade. It is fragrant, repeats well and is free from disease. Bred by Kordes (Germany), introduced 1960.

LITTLE WHITE PET. This must be one of the best small Shrub Roses for sheer garden value. It is, in fact, a dwarf sport from the excellent old Sempervirens Rambler, 'Félicité et Perpétue'. The flowers are exactly like those of its parent, being pure white, very small, of near pompon shape, with many petals, and held in large clusters. The plant grows into a perfectly symmetrical mound of about 2ft. in height and at least 2½ft. across, and is very free flowering. Perhaps the most remarkable thing about this rose is that in spite of the fact its parent does not repeat flower it does, and does so more continuously than most others. This does seem to happen on the rare occasions that we have a dwarf sport of a Rambler. In fact, this rose is not repeat flowering in the manner of, say, a China Rose — it is more that each spray of flowers continues over an extended period by the production of further branches just beneath it. It is hardy, disease resistant and has a light but pleasing fragrance — indeed it has all the virtues! What a pity, then, that it has defied all attempts of the hybridiser to use it for breeding. It might have been discussed together with the Polyanthas, for which it can easily be mistaken, but it has a softness that we do not usually associate with those roses, and is much more of a shrub. Discovered by Henderson (U.S.A.), 1879.

MAGENTA. Like 'Lavender Lassie' this rose has flowers in the Old Rose formation. They are not exactly magenta in colour, being perhaps better described as a mixture of lilac-pink and mauve. They are of medium size, full petalled, opening flat and rosette shaped, with the strong myrrh fragrance we usually associate with the English Roses. It forms a shrub of about 4ft. in height with rather straggly growth. A reliable rose, but perhaps a little coarse in appearance, it is the result of a cross between a yellow Floribunda seedling and 'Lavender Pinocchio'. Kordes (Germany), 1954.

MÄRCHENLAND. A cross between the Hybrid Tea 'Swantje' and the Hybrid Musk 'Hamburg', resulting in what is, in fact, a large Floribunda of upright growth, about 4ft. in height. Although seldom grown, I include it here for the simple charm of its large, wide semi-double flowers and clear pink colouring. These are fragrant and recurrent and are held in small and occasionally large clusters. Bred by Tantau (Germany), 1951.

MARGUERITE HILLING ('Pink Nevada'). A sport from 'Nevada', see below, to which it is entirely similar except for the colour of the flowers which is a deep pink paling a little towards the centre. It sometimes seems that this rose has been overshadowed by its famous parent, and if this were so it would be unfortunate, as I think it is better in pink than in cream, although cream is a less common colour in roses. The sport occurred in three different places over a period of years: at Sunningdale Nurseries, in Mrs. Nancy Steen's garden in New Zealand, and in the garden of a Mr. Sleet who, it seems, first discovered it. It will frequently sport back and produce a branch bearing the flowers of 'Nevada', and such branches should be cut away. Height 8ft. 'Marguerite Hilling' is always one of the major attractions in our garden. First marketed by Hilling's Nurseries (U.K.), 1959. See page 31.

MARJORIE FAIR. A hybrid between 'Ballerina' and 'Baby Faurax', this rose is similar to 'Ballerina', with closely packed Polyantha-like sprays, but its single flowers are of a deep carmine with a white eye at the centre. It forms a small bushy shrub of 3ft. by as much across, and is reliably repeat flowering, hardy and disease resistant, but not, I think, so beautiful as 'Ballerina'. Bred by Harkness (U.K.), introduced 1978.

MARTIN FROBISHER. I have recently received a number of Rugosa hybrids from the Agricultural Research Station, Ottawa, where they have been breeding roses to withstand the Canadian winters. These promise to be interesting, but I am not sufficiently acquainted with them to discuss them here. This is one of these hybrids which I happened to acquire some years previously. It was derived from open-pollinated seed from the Rugosa 'Schneezwerg', and we do not, therefore, know the other parent. Whatever this may have been, we have here a rose that bears little resemblance to a Rugosa. The flowers are charming: small, double, rosette shaped, of Old Rose appearance and soft pink in colour, the general effect being a little like that of an Alba Rose, while the foliage bears some resemblance to that of *Rosa pimpinellifolia,* although there are almost no thorns. The leaves are small and of a dull metallic green. It is regularly recurrent flowering. Fragrant. Height 4 or 5ft. Introduced 1968.

MÜNCHEN. The result of the same cross as 'Erfurt': 'Eva' x 'Réveil Dijonnais', and from the same raiser, Kordes, in 1940. The growth is very similar to 'Erfurt', about 5 by 5ft., strong and healthy with shiny, dark green foliage. The flowers are semi-double, medium sized and garnet-red with occasional streaks of white. They are held in clusters and repeat well. Almost no fragrance.

NEVADA. For many years one of the most popular Shrub Roses, and not without justification. It is the result of a cross between 'La Giralda', an extremely strong and large flowered Hybrid Tea Rose, and a form of *Rosa moyesii,* probably *R. moyesii* 'Fargesii'. It exhibits many of the characteristics of its *R. moyesii* parent, forming a shapely shrub of dense growth with long, arching, almost thornless branches. These are smothered all along their length with large creamy-white, semi-double flowers opening flat with yellow stamens. They are sometimes tinged with pink, particularly in warm, dry weather. Although a little untidy when taken individually, in the mass the blooms give a show that is hard to beat among flowering shrubs of any kind. There is a second crop late in the summer and occasional flowers at other times. It is completely free from mildew but can be affected by blackspot, although no more so than many other modern shrub roses.

'Nevada' and its sport 'Marguerite Hilling', see above, are almost unique in their ability to repeat flower while still retaining their graceful, near species-like growth and it is this that makes them so special. Most Shrub Roses that repeat flower do so by producing long shoots from the base of the plant after the first flush of bloom. These usually produce large heads of flowers as is the case with the Hybrid Musks. 'Nevada' also sends up such branches in order to renew its growth, but they do not provide the bulk of the later flowers — these come from small side shoots along the branch. In this way 'Nevada' is better able to retain the grace of its growth. Unfortunately there is a price to be paid. When the shrub is perhaps eight or ten years old it often

CERISE BOUQUET, *Modern Shrub Rose. A typical spray of bloom of this large and elegant shrub.*

begins to become ragged and lose its shapely form as well as some of its vigour, and it is for this reason it has sometimes been said the variety has deteriorated. This is not, in fact, the case; it is the individual plant that has deteriorated. Such a decline can be avoided by the regular removal of old wood to encourage the new. Blackspot may be a problem and spraying is worth while. When deterioration occurs, it may be a good idea to prune the shrub almost to the ground and start again, at the same time providing a liberal dose of manure. Height about 8ft. by as much across. Bred by Pedro Dot (Spain), introduced 1927. See page 34.

NYMPHENBURG. One of the best of Kordes' hybrids, introduced in 1954, from a cross between the Hybrid Musk 'Sangerhausen' x Floribunda 'Sunmist'. Its semi-double flowers are rather similar to those of a Floribunda, and are held in small clusters. They are pale pink at the edges, shading to yellow at the centre and have a strong fruit-like scent. The growth is very vigorous, upright but slightly arching, usually 8ft. high by 6ft. across, and it may be used as a pillar rose. For so large a shrub it repeats well. Big, glossy, dark green foliage. A tough, reliable variety.

PEARL DRIFT. An interesting rose from the breeders' point of view. For many years they have tried to obtain crosses with the beautiful Climber 'Mermaid', but these have nearly always proved sterile. The aim has been to produce more Climbers with the very good qualities found in 'Mermaid' — its refined beauty, its ability to climb and repeat flower well, and an almost complete resistance to disease. After so many years, this is the first such rose to appear on the market, although I have heard of other seedlings. 'Pearl Drift' is a cross with the Modern Climber 'New Dawn'. No doubt the breeder was looking for a Climber, but in this case it has turned out to be a shrub with nice compact sprawling growth of 3ft. in height and about 4ft. across. The flowers are large, semi-double, tinted with pink in the bud, opening white shaded with peachy-pink. These are held in clusters and are produced very freely and continuously over a long period. The foliage is a glossy light green and has good disease resistance. It will be interesting to see how it develops. Bred by Le Grice (U.K.), introduced 1983.

PLEINE DE GRÂCE. An exceptionally strong rose; I know of few other Shrub Roses that can match it in this respect. It might well be regarded as a Rambler, for it will cover a large area when so grown, at least the equivalent of the larger Ramblers. It was, however, sent to me as a shrub, and is of such excellence when so grown, that I think it should, first and foremost, be regarded as such. It will grow to 8ft. in height and 12ft. across, probably considerably more, and forms a well-rounded mound of arching branches which are covered with huge sprays of small blooms forming a deluge of white. This magnificent display is followed by a positive mist of small orange-red hips in the autumn. If you have a wild spot with plenty of space, this is the ideal variety with which to fill it. Bred by Lens (Belgium), introduced in England 1985. See page 42.

ROUNDELAY. A 5ft. shrub of upright growth, flowering freely and producing trusses of medium-sized, full-petalled, cardinal-red flowers that open flat and have a strong fragrance. The growth is robust and healthy. 'Charlotte Armstrong' x 'Floradora'. Bred by Swim (U.S.A.), introduced 1953.

SALLY HOLMES. A bushy recurrent-flowering shrub of 5ft. in height, bearing large, creamy-white semi-double flowers with a light fragrance. These can be very beautiful, but those produced on the strong main stems tend to be packed together much too closely, forming a clumsy head of bloom. When they appear on side branches it is quite a different matter, for here we have fewer flowers which can show off their delicate refinement to perfection. It might be worth while cutting off the larger heads before they flower in order to encourage branching. The parents were 'Ivory Fashion' x 'Ballerina'. Bred by Holmes (U.K.), a successful amateur breeder, introduced 1976.

SCARLET FIRE ('Scharlachglut'). A tall, vigorous shrub of graceful, slightly arching growth, with plentiful foliage. The flowers are single and a brilliant scarlet-crimson with contrasting yellow stamens. Although these appear only in the summer, they are followed by fine, large pear-shaped, orange-scarlet hips in the autumn, lasting well into the winter. Little or no fragrance. An excellent shrub, providing a brilliant splash of colour without being in any way crude. It has Old Rose connections, the result of a cross between 'Poinsettia' x a Gallica called 'Grandiflora'. Bred by Kordes (Germany), introduced 1952.

SCINTILLATION. A cross between *Rosa* 'Macrantha' and the Hybrid Musk 'Vanity', this rose forms a low, sprawling shrub of open growth, about 4ft. in height and perhaps 6 or 8ft. across. The flowers are medium to large, semi-double and of the palest lilac-pink, opening wide to show their stamens. They are held in large sprays. 'Scintillation' blooms only once in the summer, but then for a long period, the overall effect being one of daintiness and grace. The foliage, like that of its parent 'Vanity', is rather sparse. A group of two or three plants can provide a beautiful effect. Bred by Austin (U.K.), 1968.

THE FAIRY. This rose might properly have been included with the Polyanthas, as its flowers are of exactly their type. It is, however, a shrub rather than a bush with low arching growth spreading out in an almost fan-like manner, 2ft. in height by 3ft. across. The flowers are small, soft-pink in colour and borne in great quantities in broad, flat sprays. Flowering starts very late, but continues throughout the summer almost without a break, providing colour when many other roses have passed their peak. The foliage is tiny, almost like that of box. This rose has always been regarded as a sport from the Rambler 'Lady Godiva', but Peter Beales suggests it was, in fact, the result of a cross between the Polyantha 'Paul Crampel' and 'Lady Godiva'. Looking at the plant, this would seem possible, although as far as I know its breeder, Bentall, did not record his crosses. Introduced 1932.

ZIGEUNERKNABE ('Gipsy Boy'). A variety that would look entirely at home among the Old Roses, and indeed is sometimes classified with the Bourbons, a position to which it has little claim. It is, in fact, a seedling from a rose called 'Russelliana', which was itself probably a seedling from *Rosa setigera*. Its other parent is not known, but might have been a Rugosa. The growth is exceptionally strong and bushy, at least 7ft. in height and almost as much across, with many strong thorns. It has rough, dark green, Rugosa-like foliage. The flowers are a little more than

PLEINE DE GRACE. *This superb Modern Shrub Rose will produce a greater mass of bloom than any other I know. It may also be used as a Rambler.*

medium sized, cupped in shape at first, opening flat and almost double, while the colour is a dark crimson-purple with a little white at the centre. The blooms appear only in early summer and are followed by small orange-red hips. This rose is not unlike 'Chianti' in appearance, though the flowers held in small, tight sprays, are not of the same quality and lack fragrance. It is, however, one of the toughest of roses and ideal for a difficult position in the garden. Bred by Lambert (Germany), introduced 1909.

Ground-Cover Roses

In recent years there has been a swing towards what are known as Ground-cover Roses. That is to say roses which tend to form a mass of low growth rather than growing into a bush or shrub. A few of these roses have been with us for some time, 'Max Graf' and 'Raubritter' are obvious examples, but there are now so many varieties becoming available that they warrant a section to themselves. Ground-cover plants in general have become very popular, and a new type of rose has been bred with this market in mind.

The idea behind the use of ground-cover plants is that they save labour, and this is considered particularly important for public planting, because it is intended that these roses should form a thicket of growth which will smother all weeds. They have a rather tidy appearance in contrast to the often rather unruly growth of other Shrub Roses.

RUNNING MAID, *Ground-cover Rose. It is a mass of colour when in bloom, but has one season of flowering only.*

If weeds are a problem, it will be necessary to get rid of them before planting, for if they get a hold before the rose has grown it may be the weeds will control the rose, rather than the rose control the weeds! Moreover, it is very difficult to remove weeds or suckers from among prickly growth. For this reason, these roses are frequently grown on their own roots from cuttings, and this can be a distinct advantage.

Whether or not we favour ground-cover planting, we have here an interesting new group that brings another dimension to roses. Furthermore, Ground-cover Roses do not necessarily have to be used only for ground cover, for their growth is pleasing in itself and they can be used in the same way as any other Shrub Rose.

All are very hardy and easily grown, and bring with them a Rambler-like charm. Some of them are recurrent flowering, but even those that are not bloom over an extended period.

BONICA (Meidomonac). This is one of the most successful of the Ground-cover Roses — particularly in northern Europe, where it has been planted on a very large scale. It bears sprays of small, double flowers of soft pink, paling towards the edges. The growth is broad and bushy and, unlike many Ground-cover Roses, it flowers intermittently throughout the summer. It is a tough and hardy rose with dark, disease-resistant foliage. Altogether, one of the best of this group. It will make a good Standard. Height, 2½ft., spreading to 4ft. or more. Breeding *(R. sempervirens* x Mlle. Marthe Carron) x Picasso. Meilland (France), 1982.

FAIRYLAND. The parentage of this rose was 'The Fairy' x 'Yesterday', a promising cross that has produced a good Ground-cover Rose. It bears sprays of small, cupped, rosy-pink, semi-double flowers on dense spreading growth. It will spread to about 5ft. while reaching little more than 2ft. in height. There is a strong fragrance, and it is repeat flowering. A hardy, reliable rose of considerable charm. Bred by Harkness (U.K.), introduced 1980.

FERDY. Clusters of small, salmon-pink flowers on vigorous cascading growth of about 3ft. in height spreading to about 6ft. It has plentiful, healthy, light green foliage, and produces a mass of bloom in early summer followed by a lesser crop in autumn. Bred by Keisei (Japan), 1985.

GROUSE. The parents of this rose were 'The Fairy' x a *Rosa wichuraiana* seedling, and it has retained something of the Wichuraiana's prostrate growth. It will spread over an area some 10ft. wide, flowering freely in July and August but not later. The flowers are pale pink and single, with a dainty wild rose charm. Fragrant. Bred by Kordes (Germany), 1984.

MAX GRAF. Almost the original Ground-cover Rose and still one of the best. It is a Rugosa hybrid, and I have described it with those roses in the companion to this volume *Old Roses and English Roses*.

NORFOLK (Poulfolk). A useful Ground-cover Rose, if only for its yellow colouring. Its flowers are fully double and bright yellow — the growth neat and bushy. Perhaps a little nearer to a Shrub Rose than a Ground-cover Rose, as it grows to a height of 1½ft. and spreads to only little more than 2-2½ft. Unusually amongst these roses, it has a very strong fragrance. Poulsen (Denmark), 1990.

NOZOMI. A climbing Miniature Rose which, perhaps more importantly, also has the useful ability to creep and make good ground cover. It was bred in Japan by Onodera, and introduced in 1968. Indeed, it has an oddly Japanese appearance and it is easy to picture it growing in a Japanese garden. It has small glossy leaves and sprays of tiny pearly-pink flowers in midsummer, and will spread to perhaps 5ft. while remaining little more than 1ft. high. Although sometimes mixed with larger ground-cover roses this is not advisable, as it will look out of place and will almost certainly be swamped. When grown as a short Weeping Standard it can be effective, and is frequently exhibited in this form at the Chelsea Flower Show. Such Standards have to be forced under glass, and this gives the flowers an attractive delicacy they do not possess when grown outdoors. A useful, not entirely satisfying rose, but one of the few that looks at home in the rock garden, and I have seen it grown over rocks by water, providing a charming effect. The breeding was Floribunda 'Fairy Princess' x Miniature 'Sweet Fairy'.

PARTRIDGE. A rose from the same cross as 'Grouse' to which it is similar except that its flowers are pure white. It has the same wide-spreading prostrate growth and single flowers. It blooms in late July and early August. Kordes (Germany), 1984.

PHEASANT. The third rose in the 'Game Bird' series, this time with double flowers of deep rose-pink borne in large clusters. It has the same vigorous prostrate growth of about 2½ft. in height, spreading to perhaps 6 or 7ft. Some repeat flowering. Bred by Kordes (Germany), introduced 1986.

PINK BELLS. Large clusters of pretty soft pink, fully double rosette-shaped flowers of about 1½ins. across, held against shiny, dark green foliage. The growth is arching and spreading, growing to about 2ft. in

SMARTY, *a pretty modern Ground-cover Rose that repeats well.*

height and 4ft. across, providing a most charming effect. It flowers in late July and early August. Breeding 'Mini Poul' x 'Temple Bells'. Bred by Poulsen (Denmark), introduced 1980.

RAUBRITTER. A cross between 'Daisy Hill' and the Rambler 'Solarium', this rose forms a sprawling shrub of 3ft. in height and some 7ft. across, the growth developing into a low, spreading mound. The flowers are most charming: clear pink in colour, small, of a very definite cupped shape and held in clusters. It has the atmosphere of an Old Rose, although it is, in fact, quite different from any variety I know. The foliage is dark green like that of *Rosa* 'Macrantha'. Although it has some tendency towards mildew it should still be grown, for it is a most beautiful rose. Bred by Kordes (Germany), introduced 1936.

RED BELLS. Very like 'Pink Bells', but with light crimson-red flowers. Summer flowering only. Bred by Poulsen (Denmark), 1980.

RAUBRITTER, *a Ground-cover Rose bearing sprays of unique enclosed cupped flowers. At the back a good example of 'Roseraie de l'Hay', though not in full flower.*

RED BLANKET. A repeat-flowering Ground-cover Rose that forms a mound of growth 2½ ft. high and 5ft. or more across. It bears sprays of medium-sized, semi-double flowers of rosy-red colouring. Good, glossy, dark green foliage. Bred by Ilsink (U.K.), introduced 1979.

ROSY CUSHION. From the same breeder as the rose above, to which it is similar, with the exception of its flowers which are single and coloured pink with white at the centre. Good foliage, excellent habit of growth, repeat flowering. The breeding was 'Yesterday' x unnamed seedling. Introduced 1979.

RUNNING MAID. A low shrub of excellent dome shape and close twiggy growth bearing large, nicely spaced sprays of pretty little deep pink Rambler-like flowers. It blooms only in the summer, but is good in every way, whether used for ground cover or in the border. There are tiny orange-red hips in the autumn. Bred by Louis Lens (Belgium), introduced in the U.K. 1985. See page 43.

SMARTY. A third variety from the breeder of 'Red Blanket' and 'Rosy Cushion', and to my mind the best and most beautiful. It is a shrub of 2 or 3ft. in height, its spreading growth bearing sprays of single, soft pink flowers of Dog Rose appearance and providing a most charming effect. It is reliably repeat flowering, almost completely disease resistant, and has a light fruit-like fragrance. Bred by Ilsink (U.K.), introduced 1979. See page 46.

SNOW CARPET. A miniature creeping rose that I describe in Chapter 5, under Miniature Roses. Although a true ground creeper, it is much smaller than the roses in this class, and therefore fulfils a rather different role.

SURREY. A bushy shrub of 2½ft., spreading to 4ft. across and bearing masses of soft pink flowers intermittently throughout the summer.

SWANY. It is interesting that this rose has *Rosa sempervirens* as one of its parents, and therefore has a connection with the beautiful Sempervirens Ramblers. The other parent was a Wichuraiana Rambler called 'Mademoiselle Marthe Carron'. The result is a charming rose bearing sprays of small, very double, cupped, pure white flowers that open flat. The growth is truly prostrate and it will spread to 6ft. or more. The foliage is a glossy, dark green. It is completely hardy.

TEMPLE BELLS. A pretty little creeping rose bearing numerous small, almost single white flowers, its small, glossy green leaves adding to the picture. Bred from *Rosa wichuraiana* x the Miniature Rose 'Blushing Jewel', it has something of the character of *R. wichuraiana*. Bred by McGredy (New Zealand), 1976.

WHITE BELLS. The fourth, and perhaps the most attractive, of the 'Bells' series, this rose bears small, white rosette-shaped flowers in sprays. As with its three namesakes, it has excellent dense bushy growth, flowering in late June and early August. Bred by Poulsen (Denmark), introduced 1980.

CHAPTER 2
Climbing Roses

It is a remarkable fact that a genus that has been responsible for the production of so many garden shrubs — shrubs which, if considered alone, would be sufficient to make it the most important of garden flowers — should also provide us with what is, without doubt, the most important of all climbing plants, but such is the case. It is difficult to overestimate the value of Climbing Roses in the garden. They provide a feeling of abundance, particularly in more formal and architectural areas, which may be in need of softening and a sense of life. They bring height where it might otherwise be lacking and many of them flower intermittently throughout the summer. No plant can fulfil these functions better than the Climbing Rose.

All roses delight us, but perhaps a Climbing Rose, well grown and in full flower, more so than any other, and if not always in the individual flower, at least in the mass, although the individual flower is often particularly beautiful when seen looking down at us from the branch of a Climbing Rose. Perhaps it is the association of plant and architecture that gives Climbing Roses a certain advantage.

Before going further, it is necessary to explain that the Climbing Roses are divided into two main groups: the Climbers and the Ramblers. The division is an artificial one, for both are in reality climbing plants, but this division does help us deal with them more easily. A Climbing Rose usually has larger flowers such as we might find in the Old Roses or the Hybrid Teas.

The Rambler Roses usually have smaller flowers in larger clusters, and are often of more lax growth. They are also inclined to send up long, sometimes very long, stems from the base of the plant. In fact, they do just what their name suggests, ramble. The Climbers may be stiffer in growth, and although they, too, produce strong base shoots, they tend to build up gradually on past growth. Most Climbing Roses are repeat flowering; the Ramblers almost never are. This is a very arbitrary division, one type frequently overlapping with the other, but in spite of this, when we see these roses there is generally little doubt as to which group they belong.

DESPREZ A FLEUR JAUNE, *Noisette Rose, sometimes known as 'Jaune Desprez'.*

In this chapter we are concerned with the Climbing Roses: the Noisettes with their delicate refinement, the Climbing Tea Roses, the Climbing Hybrid Teas with their flowers of many colours, the Modern Climbers with their continuous abundance, as well as other sorts of other classifications or of none, which are often of great beauty. Perhaps the best and most frequent use for these roses is on walls, including house walls where, with the additional warmth that these provide, they are often the earliest garden roses to flower, thus making them particularly precious, and giving them plenty of time to make further growth and so flower again. In addition, no climbing plant is more suitable for growing over arches, on pillars, on trellises, pergolas and so on.

Annual tying and pruning is, of course, necessary with Climbers, and this can be a little more arduous than is the case with shrubs, but really need not be too great a task. All we have to do is to take away some of the long main growth where this is too plentiful, or is becoming old and worn out. This may not be required for a few years. Having done this, cut back the side shoots which have flowered in the previous year to 2 or 3ins., at the same time pruning away weak or dead shoots.

When attaching the young branches to a wall or length of trellis it is best, whenever possible, to train them, if not horizontally at least on a slant. This encourages them to break and form new flowering shoots all along the branch, and so provide far more flowers. Otherwise the rose will always be pushing upwards, producing its blooms only at the top, where they cannot be seen and leaving the lower parts bare. There is a special problem with pillars, for with these we have less latitude. This can be overcome by winding the growth around the pillar in spiral form.

Climbers sometimes take time to get going and a little persuasion may be necessary. A liberal quantity of some form of natural manure, mixed with the soil where they are to grow, will work wonders. If such material is readily available, it may be used very freely, and you will be amply rewarded in the years to come. Roses planted against walls may well require the most attention for such areas are usually very dry, due to the fact that the soil here is protected and may receive little or no rain. The rose will not begin to move until its roots have themselves moved out into more moist ground. A hosepipe can be useful in the first year or two. Give Climbers in such positions an occasional very heavy watering, one that will soak down deep into the soil. It is vital to avoid drying out early in the life of the rose.

Noisette Roses

Even before the China Rose was hybridized with various Old Roses to produce the first recurrent-flowering roses (described in Chapter 3 of the companion to this volume, *Old Roses and English Roses*), it was cross fertilized with the Musk Rose to give us the first repeat-flowering Climbing Roses. This is rather surprising, for it has never been easy to breed such Climbers. Credit for this innovation goes to John Champney, a rice planter of Charleston in South Carolina in the early 1800s. Champney produced a rose which was first named *Rosa moschata hybrida*, but later became known as 'Champney's Pink Cluster'. It is sometimes said he obtained this rose by crossing the then new 'Parsons' Pink China' with pollen from the Musk Rose, but it is more likely it was an accidental hybrid, as the deliberate cross fertilization of roses was not practised at that time.

Philippe Noisette, a nurseryman, also of Charleston, sowed seed from 'Champney's Pink Cluster' to produce a variety known as 'Blush Noisette' which, although not so tall in growth as its parents, was repeat flowering. Thus it was that the Noisettes were born. 'Blush Noisette' was later crossed with 'Parks' Yellow China', to give us yellow Noisettes. Noisettes were also freely crossed with the Tea Rose, further widening their range and improving their quality, and the Noisette Roses are, even today, some of the most beautiful and freely recurrent flowering of all Climbing Roses. These qualities they frequently combine with tall, rampant growth — something breeders still find very hard to achieve. In addition, the colour yellow was added to the repertoire of garden roses, and we are short enough of yellows among Climbing Roses even today.

The period of development of Noisettes was brief, and one cannot help feeling that here is a job not yet completed and with very considerable possibililties for further progress. Once again, as we found with the Hybrid Musks, the problem is that Noisettes are diploids and this tends to make further development difficult, most roses being tetraploid.

The Noisettes as a class include some of the most beautiful of all Climbers. They have a refinement and delicacy of appearance that would be hard to equal elsewhere. The flowers are in the true Old Rose tradition, with petals of a lovely silky texture, and nearly all have a good fragrance.

The winter hardiness of some of them is unfortunately a little questionable, but this should not prevent us from growing them in anything but the coldest positions. Given the protection of a warm wall, they will be perfectly safe. Some are, in fact, quite hardy.

AIMÉE VIBERT ('Bouquet de la Mariée', 'Nivea'). This rose, which was raised by Vibert of France in 1828, is not a typical Noisette, but a cross between a Noisette, probably 'Blush Noisette', and *Rosa sempervirens,* the 'Evergreen Rose'. It has the plentiful, long, graceful, rich green foliage of *R. sempervirens,* and bears open sprays of small, pure white, double flowers with yellow stamens. These have a simple charm that is hard to compare with any other Climber. There is a slight musky fragrance. From the Noisette it gains the ability to flower again, starting early and often continuing well into the autumn. It is somewhat tender, although it will survive most winters it is likely to encounter in the U.K. Early flower shoots are sometimes cut back by frost and this will delay flowering until July. It will climb to a height of 15ft. in a warm position and may also be grown as a large, sprawling shrub. Either way it is a most beautiful rose. We have here a variety that is, in fact, a perpetual-flowering Rambler of strong growth, and it is thus something very unusual. It might have been more accurately included with the Ramblers, but it is by ancestry a Noisette. The only comparable Rambler with this quality is 'Phyllis Bide', a shorter and less beautiful rose, a fact which should give the plant breeder some food for thought.

ALISTER STELLA GRAY ('Golden Rambler'). Bred by A.H. Gray, a Tea Rose enthusiast, this rose was introduced by George Paul in 1894. It bears small yolk-yellow buds of tightly scrolled formation which open into prettily quartered flowers, later fading to a creamy-white and remaining beautiful at all stages. The flowers have a silky texture and are held in small sprays on the ends of long, thin stems. Later in the year large heads of bloom appear. They have a delicious tea scent. This rose may be grown either as a Climber and will achieve 15ft. on a warm wall, or as a large arching shrub. A most charming rose. See page 54.

BLUSH NOISETTE. The first Noisette Rose, it is hardy, very tough and a great survivor, and still to be seen in old gardens where it may have been planted long ago. The flowers are almost double, small, Rambler like and cupped, and are held in tight clusters. They are of a lilac-blush colour with exposed yellow stamens and have a strong clove fragrance. Although of modest appearance, the flowers are pretty and produced in profusion, repeating well and creating a pleasing massed effect. This variety has a tendency to remain short and bushy, in fact it will form a good shrub. It needs the encouragement of a wall to achieve height, where it can grow to 12ft. Noisette (France), before 1817. See page 55.

BOUQUET D'OR. A seedling from 'Gloire de Dijon', and thus one of the

ALISTER STELLA GRAY, *Noisette Rose. Some of the most beautiful Climbing Roses are to be found among the Noisettes.*

roses sometimes known as Dijon Teas. The flowers are quite large and full petalled with a slight scent, their colour a coppery-salmon with yellow at the centre. It is hardy and fairly vigorous, growing to a height of 10ft. Bred by Ducher (France), introduced 1872.

CÉLINE FORESTIER. Although not a strong rose, this is one of the most beautiful, and given a warm wall and careful treatment it will do well. The flowers are fully doublé, neatly rounded, opening quartered with a button eye. Their colour is a pale yellow, the petals having a silky texture. There is a rich Tea Rose fragrance. Given time it will grow to about 8 or 10ft., perhaps more in a warm climate. A charming rose of delicate refinement. Bred by Trouillard (France), introduced 1842.

CLAIRE JACQUIER ('Mademoiselle Claire Jacquier'). Here we have a truly vigorous Noisette that will grow to as much as 30ft. but, as is often the case with Climbing Roses, what it gains in vigour it loses in its

BLUSH NOISETTE, *the first Noisette Rose, can be a short bushy Climber or strong Shrub.*

ability to repeat flower. A very good early flush of bloom is followed by only occasional flowers later. The individual flowers are rather loosely formed, rich yellow at first, paling with age to pale yellow, and with a delicious fragrance. They are held against plentiful light green foliage. Hardy. Bred by Bernaix (France), introduced 1888.

CLOTH OF GOLD ('Chromatella'). A self-sown seedling from 'Lamarque' and, like its parent, rather tender. If planted against a warm wall it can do well, and is very fine when grown under glass. The flowers are double and of a soft sulphur-yellow which deepens towards the centre. Fragrant. Height 12ft. Introduced by Coquereau (France), 1843.

DESPREZ À FLEUR JAUNE ('Jaune Desprez'). An excellent Climber blooming freely and with remarkable continuity. The flowers are quite small, opening flat, with many silky petals and a button eye, their colour a warm yellow shaded with peach, paling with age. They have a strong and pleasing fragrance. The growth is vigorous, reaching 20ft. on a warm wall. The result of a cross between 'Blush Noisette' and 'Parks' Yellow China'. Bred by Desprez (France), 1835. See page 50.

DUCHESSE D'AUERSTÄDT. A sport from 'Rêve d'Or', with large, cupped, full-petalled golden-yellow flowers, similar in form to those of 'Gloire de Dijon'. It has ample foliage and will grow to about 10ft. in height. Discovered by Bernaix (France), introduced 1888.

GLOIRE DE DIJON. A famous old Climbing Rose, once found in many a cottage garden, where it was often known as 'Old Glory'. There can be few roses that have given more pleasure to more people since its introduction in 1853. It is said to have been a cross between a Tea Rose, the name of which is not known, and the old Bourbon 'Souvenir de la Malmaison', and indeed its general appearance would seem to support this. It has large, globular, buff-yellow flowers that flatten and become quartered later, taking on pink tints, particularly in hot weather. They have a strong, rich fragrance. There is no doubt this is a much hardier rose than the typical Noisette, probably due to the fact that it is in part Bourbon. It is truly recurrent-flowering. The foliage is thick and heavy, more like that of a Hybrid Tea. Unfortunately, however, it appears to have lost some of its vigour in recent years, probably due to generations of propagation on a large scale. It might be worth making a search for a robust old plant of 'Gloire de Dijon' and to build up a new stock from this. It is still very widely distributed throughout the country, and it is unlikely that the whole stock would decline at once. Bred by Jacotot (France). See page 58.

LAMARQUE. Not, I am afraid, a rose for this country, except in the warmest areas, and even then it would be best to grow it on a south wall. Under glass it could, I am sure, be magnificent. The flowers are palest lemon-yellow (almost white), quartered and flat and of exquisite delicacy. It will grow to about 10ft., but I would expect much more in warmer climates. 'Blush Noisette' x 'Parks' Yellow China'. Bred by Maréchal (France), 1830.

LEY'S PERPETUAL. This rose was given to me by Mr. Wyatt, who for some time edited an excellent magazine called *The Rose*, which unfortunately ceased publication. A seedling from 'Gloire de Dijon', it has a great deal in common with that rose. The flowers are cupped, medium sized, and of a pleasing pale yellow colour, with a Tea Rose fragrance. It will grow to about 15ft. in height. A beautiful and worthwhile rose deserving more attention. I am not aware of the breeder, although I would expect it to be 'Ley', nor do I know the date of introduction.

MADAME ALFRED CARRIÈRE. If a very strong, reliable, repeat-flowering, white Climber is required, you need look no further than this variety. Even today, there is no white Climbing Rose to rival it in performance. The flowers are large, cupped and creamy-white with just a tint of pink, and have a Tea Rose fragrance. They cannot be said to be particularly shapely, and the growth is rather stiff and upright, though this stiffness can be overcome by careful training. It can be relied upon to give a magnificent display over a long period. The foliage is large and plentiful. Reliably hardy. Bred by Schwartz (France), introduced 1879.

MARÉCHAL NIEL. Until Pernet-Ducher introduced the blood of *Rosa foetida* into the Hybrid Teas at about the turn of the century, there was no rose of such a truly deep yellow, other than a few less developed varieties such as *R. hemisphaerica* and 'Persian Yellow'. 'Maréchal Niel' was, therefore, highly prized for this reason, as well as for the perfection of its large, pointed buds. In fact it was treated with near reverence. Its long, hanging, strongly fragrant flowers of pure yellow and perfect Tea Rose shape were unique at the time. The trouble was that it would not withstand our cold winters and damp summers, and for this reason the Victorians nearly always grew it under glass, indeed lean-to greenhouses were built with the main object of growing this rose. Whether it is worth going to such lengths today is rather doubtful, although there is still nothing finer than a perfect example of its waxy blooms. Unfortunately it does not always grow very well, and requires careful treatment if it is to thrive. Graham Thomas says it should be grown like a vine, with the

GLOIRE DE DIJON, *a hardy Noisette Rose, once seen in every cottage garden, it flowers well in summer and autumn.*

roots in the open soil and the growth trained into the house on a framework, under the slope of the glass. Given such conditions it may be expected to grow to up to 15ft. Believed to be a seedling from 'Cloth of Gold'. Bred by Pradel (France), 1864.

RÊVE D'OR ('Golden Chain'). A seedling from 'Madame Schultz', itself a seedling from 'Lamarque', this too is only for a warm wall. The flowers are semi-double, buff-yellow with pink shadings, paling with age, and of a rather informal shape. They are produced freely, and repeat particularly well. The foliage is plentiful and glossy. Little fragrance. A first class Climber. Bred by Ducher (France), 1869.

WILLIAM ALLEN RICHARDSON. This once famous rose was a sport of 'Rêve d'Or', to which it is similar except for the distinct yolk-yellow colouring at the centre of its flowers. Unfortunately the growth is rather weak, and it is probably not worth growing except by the collector. It requires a warm wall. Height 10ft. Bred by Ducher (France), introduced 1878.

58

Climbing Tea Roses

I have described the Tea Roses as bushes, but there are also a number that are, by nature, Climbers. These are nearly all sports from bush varieties. Although the bushes are usually too tender to warrant growing anywhere but in warm climates, a number of the Climbers are well worth a place in our gardens. This is partly because they can be grown on warm walls where they will withstand all but the hardest frosts. Also, many of the survivors of this group are at least remotely interbred with the Hybrid Teas which gives them added hardiness. Although some Climbing Teas are rather difficult to grow, two or three of them can be included among the most beautiful of Climbing Roses. 'Lady Hillingdon', 'Sombreuil' and 'Paul Lédé' are particularly fine.

As a class they tend to have silky or waxy petals, and some of them have long, pointed buds. The foliage and growth are similar to those of the Hybrid Teas, but they are perhaps a little less heavy and more

MRS. HERBERT STEVENS, *a beautifully formed Climbing Tea Rose that is comparatively hardy.*

refined in appearance. Most of them flower early, and continue late into the autumn if weather permits.

It is usually essential to plant them against a warm wall to avoid frost damage. As with bush Tea Roses minimum pruning is the rule, otherwise cultivation is the same as for other Climbing Roses.

DEVONIENSIS, CLIMBING. A sport from the bush variety discovered by Pavitt and introduced in 1858, the original bush having been bred by a Mr. Foster of Devonport, and introduced in 1838. 'Devoniensis' was the first Tea Rose to be bred in England, although due to the climate it is not surprising that very few were raised in the U.K. This variety is, in fact, quite hardy on a warm wall. Its flowers are creamy-white, attractively flushed with pink and apricot at the centre. At its best they are beautiful with a silky sheen and a strong Tea Rose fragrance. In the past this rose has been called the 'Magnolia Rose'. The parentage is not known.

FORTUNE'S YELLOW ('Beauty of Glazenwood', 'Gold of Ophir', 'San Rafael Rose'). This famous old rose was brought to England from China by the well-known plant collector Robert Fortune in 1845, having been discovered in the garden of a rich Mandarin at Ningpo. Its flowers are held either singly or in small clusters and are semi-double, bright coppery-yellow in colour, shaded with white. It will grow to about 4 or 5ft. in height, no doubt more in a favourable climate. It is not recurrent flowering, and is only suitable for the collector.

GENERAL SCHABLIKINE. A rose which is only barely a Climber, and which might well have been included among the bush varieties. On a wall it may be expected to achieve perhaps 6ft. When well grown it can produce rather small, perfectly scrolled flowers of a deep coppery-pink which hang elegantly from their stems. Under poor conditions it does not have such beautiful buds, as the petals remain short and open quickly into informal rosettes. It can be particularly fine when grown under glass. Bred by Nabonnand (France), introduced 1878.

LADY HILLINGDON, CLIMBING. One of the best Tea Roses still in existence. Indeed, I would place it high in any list of Climbing Roses. It is remarkably hardy for this class, so much so that it is hard to believe it is the result of a cross between the Tea Roses 'Papa Gontier' and 'Madame Hoste'. It would be easy to believe a Hybrid Tea comes into its breeding somewhere, but the records say otherwise. Nonetheless, I would still give it the protection of a wall. The flowers are made up of large petals which result in long, elegant buds of deep apricot-yellow. These hang gracefully from the branch and emit a strong and delicious tea fragrance. Although not shapely when they open, this does not matter so much with a Climbing Rose whose flowers are usually seen from a distance. 'Lady Hillingdon' has lush growth, with large dark green leaves tinted with red when young, and it continues to flower with admirable regularity. It may be expected to grow to 15ft. The bush variety was bred by the English firm of Lowe & Shawyer in 1910, making it one of the latest of the Tea Roses to be introduced. The sport was discovered by Hicks (U.K.), 1917.

MADAME JULES GRAVEREAUX. Large, very full flowers of soft flesh-pink, shaded with peach and yellow. I am not fully acquainted with this rose, but understand it will reach 12ft. on a wall. The foliage is dark and glossy, the scent only slight. It is not a pure Tea Rose, being a cross between 'Rêve d'Or' and the Hybrid Tea 'Viscountess Folkestone'. It would appear to be well worthy of preservation. Bred by Soupert & Notting (Luxemburg), 1901.

MRS. HERBERT STEVENS, CLIMBING. The result of a cross between 'Frau Karl Druschki' (which in the companion to this volume, *Old Roses and English Roses,* in the section on Hybrid Perpetuals, I have described as being very close to a Hybrid Tea) and the old Tea Rose 'Niphetos'. It could, therefore, more accurately be described as a Hybrid Tea, but it is so close to a Tea Rose in appearance that we have to place it here. The flowers are white with long pointed buds tinged with green towards the centre, and have a strong, typically Tea Rose fragrance. They are produced freely and repeat well. The foliage is light green. This rose will grow strongly on a wall, often reaching 18ft. Unfortunately the flowers are easily damaged by rain, more particularly if planted away from a wall, where it is otherwise usually quite hardy. The original rose was bred by McGredy (U.K.), and the climbing sport was discovered by Pernet-Ducher (France) in 1922. See page 59.

NIPHETOS, CLIMBING. Not a rose for the outdoors in Great Britain, for if it survives the frost, the flowers are likely to be spoiled by rain. These are large and hang their heads slightly, with perfect creamy buds opening to pure white. They have a light Tea Rose fragrance. It would be worth growing this rose under glass — in fact its bush parent was once widely used for this purpose. Discovered by Keynes, Williams & Co. (U.K.), 1889.

PAUL LÉDÉ. A sport discovered by Lowe in 1913 on the Bush Rose bred by Pernet-Ducher in 1902. Its hardiness perhaps belies its Tea Rose ancestry, but however this may be it is a rose of great beauty and has a

SOMBREUIL, *Climbing Tea Rose. A hardy rose with perfectly formed blooms.*

delicious tea fragrance. The flowers are large, semi-double, with exposed stamens, and of a rather loose formation. They have a lovely buff-yellow colouring and are flushed with carmine at the centre. The growth is strong, to about 12ft., and it flowers well later in the year. All in all, a most pleasing and reliable Climbing Rose.

SOMBREUIL, CLIMBING. A rose bred by Robert of France in 1850, little is known of its parentage other than that it was a seedling from a Hybrid Perpetual called 'Gigantesque'. However, the refinement of its flowers would make it almost certain the other parent was either a Tea Rose or a Noisette. It is, therefore, really a Hybrid Tea, but to place it in that section would be most misleading. In fact, it is a variety that stands on its own. The flowers have numerous petals, and open to form flat rosettes that can only be described as the most perfect Old Roses. They are creamy-white with the slightest flush tint at the centre, have a delicious

PAUL LÉDÉ, *a continuous and free-flowering Climbing Tea Rose with buff-yellow blooms and a delicious scent. Quite hardy. Gallica 'Duc de Guiche' can be seen in the background.*

and in quality and refinement compare with the very best of the Old Roses. 'Sombreuil' is completely hardy and may be grown on a pillar or other support, though is perhaps best on a wall where it will reach 12ft. I know of no other old variety that produces better flowers in autumn.

SOUVENIR DE MADAME LÉONIE VIENNOT. Not one of the finest Tea Roses, but worth a place in our list. The flowers are of loose Tea Rose shape, pale yellow shaded with coppery-pink. Although not very free flowering it is recurrent and hardy. The growth is strong and quite hardy, to about 12ft. in height. Fragrant. Bred by Bernaix (France), 1898.

Climbing China and Bourbon Roses

The Chinas and the Bourbons have produced only a few climbing varieties, but I think they are sufficiently different to warrant gathering them into a section on their own. The Bourbons 'Blairi No. 2' and 'Souvenir de la Malmaison' have the advantage of producing truly 'old' blooms, while at the same time being good Climbers. 'Zéphirine Drouhin' and 'Kathleen Harrop' are both remarkably free and continuous flowering. Climbing 'Pompon de Paris' is a short, twiggy Climber that would be difficult to compare with any other rose. Some of the taller Bourbons listed as Shrub Roses may also be treated as Climbers, particularly 'Madame Isaac Pereire' and 'Madame Ernst Calvat'.

BLAIRI NO. 2. Were it not for the fact that this Bourbon Rose does not repeat flower and has a tendency to mildew, I would be inclined to regard it as my favourite Climber. The flowers are indeed the very personification of an Old Rose at its best. They are cupped in shape, full of petals, pale pink at the edges, and deepening towards the centre. The growth is rather lax, perhaps 12 or 15ft. in height, with the blooms borne elegantly on the branch. The young shoots are mahogany coloured, and the mature leaves rough textured and matt green. The whole plant makes a most charming picture. Raised by a Mr. Blair of Stamford Hill in 1845, it is said that the parents are *Rosa chinensis* x 'Tuscany'. There is also a 'Blairi No. 1', which is very similar, but the flowers are less fine, and I think there is little point in growing them both, although the colour of the latter is a more even pink. I have only seen 'Blairi No.1' growing at Hidcote Manor in Gloucestershire. See page 67.

CRAMOISI SUPÉRIEUR, CLIMBING. This is a climbing form of the bush China Rose described in *Old Roses and English Roses*. I find it grows to a height of 7ft., although I understand it will reach very much further with the protection of a sunny wall. It produces small, cupped, crimson flowers in clusters. The growth is twiggy and bushy with small, dark green leaves. It repeat flowers quite well, but hardly so well as we would expect from a China Rose. Climbing sport discovered by Couturier (France), 1885.

FELLEMBERG ('La Belle Marseillaise'). A rose of doubtful origin, sometimes regarded as a Noisette, but perhaps better classified as a China Rose. It bears small, semi-double cupped flowers in rather close clusters, their colour being cerise-crimson with yellow stamens. This rose flowers freely and repeats well, while the growth tends to be bushy, to 8 or 10ft., indeed it will form a good broad shrub or may even be pruned for bedding. Good, dark green, disease-free foliage. A useful and reliable if somewhat dull rose. Bred by Fellemberg (Germany), introduced 1857. See page 66.

GRUSS AN AACHEN, CLIMBING. I have never seen the climbing form of this rose, although I can imagine its pearly-pink, full-cupped flowers looking particularly beautiful on a Climber, and would like to obtain stock of it. It was discovered at Sangerhausen, and distributed by Kordes (Germany), 1937. See *Old Roses and English Roses*.

GRUSS AN TEPLITZ ('Virginia R. Coxe'). A rose of no particular persuasion, but rather a mixture of Bourbon, China and Tea Rose, the breeding being ('Sir Joseph Paxton' x 'Fellemberg') x ('Papa Gontier' x 'Gloire des Rosomanes'). The flowers are dark crimson and have retained the quality of a China Rose, in that the colour intensifies rather than fades in hot sunshine. They are medium sized, loosely and informally double, and have a rich, spicy fragrance. The foliage is purplish at first, becoming green later. This rose is frequently grown as a rather straggly shrub of some 6ft. in height, but is perhaps more satisfactory as a Climbing Rose when it will grow to a height of 12ft. Bred by Geschwind (Hungary), introduced by P. Lambert (Germany), 1897.

KATHLEEN HARROP. A soft pink sport from 'Zéphirine Drouhin' with a deeper pink on the reverse of the petals, but otherwise entirely similar, except that it may be a little less vigorous. It has perhaps the more pleasing colour of the two. Discovered by Dickson (U.K.), 1919. See 'Zéphirine Drouhin' below.

MARTHA. Like 'Kathleen Harrop' a sport from 'Zéphirine Drouhin', having paler pink flowers with a creamy tinge at the centre. Discovered by Zeiner (France), 1912.

Left: FELLEMBERG, *a Climbing China Rose of bushy growth.*

Right: ZÉPHIRINE DROUHIN, *a most reliable and continuous-flowering Bourbon Climber. Good for a north wall.*

POMPON DE PARIS, CLIMBING ('Climbing Rouletii'). A sport of the Miniature Rose, it makes dense, twiggy growth up to 6ft. in height, providing a good display of small rose-pink, pompon flowers in June, but rather surprisingly has very little bloom later. The foliage is small, to match the flowers, and of a greyish-green. It enjoys considerable popularity, perhaps more than it deserves, although no doubt is useful for very small gardens and certain positions in larger gardens. Maximum height about 7ft.

SOUVENIR DE LA MALMAISON, CLIMBING. The climbing form of this famous old Bourbon Rose has strong growth and will achieve a spread of 12ft. It is possible that its beautiful, delicate, flesh-pink flowers will not be quite so fine as the bush variety. Nonetheless, they take on an added charm when seen on a Climber rather than on the somewhat squat growth of the bush. Unfortunately the Climber does not repeat quite so well. Climbing sport discovered by Bennett (U.K.), 1893.

ZÉPHIRINE DROUHIN. A Bourbon Rose. Although this variety was introduced as early as 1868 it is still one of the most popular and widely distributed of all Climbing Roses and is to be found in most catalogues and even on supermarket shelves. The reason is not far to seek, as no

BLAIRI NO. 2, *an old Bourbon Climber of great beauty and true old-fashioned formation.*

Modern Rose has been able to excel it for sheer performance and continuity of flowering. The blooms are of a bright cerise-carmine, semi-double, of no very definite form and with a wonderful fragrance. It is very free-flowering and seen in the mass the effect is quite outstanding. Its one defect is that it is subject to mildew, but this can be overcome by planting it against a north-facing wall; indeed, no other rose that I know thrives quite so well in such a position. For this reason, if for nothing else, it is a valuable acquisition. It will achieve anything up to 15ft., maybe more on a north wall. Although sometimes recommended as a shrub, I have never found it to be very satisfactory when so grown, the growth often appearing too open and straggly, but perhaps if closely planted in a large group the appearance would be quite different. It is said that it will form a good hedge. Parentage unknown. Bred by Bizot (France), 1868.

Climbing Hybrid Tea Roses

Very few Climbing Hybrid Teas have been bred, perhaps because it is not an easy thing to do, or because it was thought to be much less profitable than the breeding of bush roses. In spite of this there are, in fact, innumerable Climbing Hybrid Teas to choose from. The explanation for this apparent anomaly lies in the fact that bush Hybrid Teas have proved very prolific in the production of climbing sports, and this is what most Climbing Hybrid Teas are. They form an important contribution to our stock of Climbing Roses, not least because they extend the colour range considerably.

Anyone whose preferences among roses lie with the Old Rose, or perhaps have some prejudice against Modern Roses, should think again in the case of the Climbing Hybrid Teas, for even those bearing flowers which may look rather ordinary on a squat bush often have greater appeal when seen from the branches of their climbing form. This perhaps illustrates better than anything else the advantages a shrub rose has over a bush rose, or, likewise, a Climbing Rose over a bush. That is to say the advantages of scale — the balance between the size of the flower, and the growth of the plant.

There can be little doubt that, in general, the older Hybrid Teas make better climbing sports than those of more recent introduction. The early Hybrid Teas were rather weak in growth, but it is an odd fact that such roses often produce strong climbing forms. They also have the advantage that they often inherit a more lax and elegant growth from their parent (a sport only has one parent), so that the flowers, instead of looking up towards the sky, look down on us for our appreciation. They have a further advantage in that they are often more gentle in colour, substance and general appearance. Fortunately it is the early Hybrid Teas that have produced the most Climbers. This may be because they were the result of rather distant crosses and had not settled down genetically. The contemporary Hybrid Tea bushes are of much stronger growth, but sometimes their climbing sports make growth and foliage at the expense of bloom and, more often than not, their flowers stand up like ramrods. It may be possible to overcome this by training the branches horizontally and not too high up.

The climbing forms of early Hybrid Teas may then be said to be good Climbers growing strongly and often repeating well. In fact, if the early varieties are to be preserved, it is perhaps as Climbers that this is best done. Having said this, modern varieties do from time to time produce good sports, and it is important we do not ignore them.

ALLEN CHANDLER. A vigorous Climbing Rose bearing very large, semi-double flowers of brilliant crimson, opening to show contrasting yellow stamens. It blooms very freely early in the season and regularly thereafter. Good red Climbing Roses are rather scarce and this is one of the best of them. It will grow to about 15ft., sometimes much more, is fragrant and has ample large foliage. A cross between 'Hugh Dickson' and an unnamed seedling. Bred by Chandler (U.S.A.).

ALTISSIMO. Large, single flowers of unfading blood-red, each some 5ins. across, opening flat and neatly rounded, with a large boss of deep gold stamens. They have no scent but are produced freely, both in early summer and quite regularly later. The growth is strong, to at least 10ft., with large, deep matt-green leaves. A very good Climber, but perhaps a little artificial in appearance. Such a colour is best kept away from red brick and is better against a light green background or perhaps clambering over shrubs. It can also be grown as a large shrub if kept in check by pruning. Bred by Delbard-Chabert (France), introduced 1966.

BETTINA, CLIMBING. A rose which bears some of the most perfectly formed Hybrid Tea flowers, with tightly scrolled buds of orange shading to gold at the base and attractive heavy veining of red and bronze. Unfortunately, the flower shoots are of the stiff and upright type. The glossy foliage is dark green tinted with bronze. It should grow to 10 or 12ft. on a wall. Sport discovered by Meilland (France), 1958, who was also the original raiser.

Left: EASLEA'S GOLDEN RAMBLER, *a strong Climbing Hybrid Tea Rose with large flowers.*

Right: CUPID, *Climbing Hybrid Tea Rose. The large shapely blooms are summer flowering only.*

CAPTAIN CHRISTY, CLIMBING. A sport of an early Hybrid Tea, bearing large, very full, globular flowers of a pale flesh-pink that deepens towards the centre. A lovely Old Rose, but with only a slight fragrance. The growth is strong, to a height of 10 or 12ft. It flowers in early summer and provides occasional blooms later. Discovered by Ducher (France), 1881.

CHÂTEAU DE CLOS VOUGEOT, CLIMBING. One of the darkest of dark red roses: rich, velvety crimson overlaid with garnet, unfading and pure. It is not a typical Hybrid Tea flower, having numerous rather short petals and opening wide, with a particularly strong and rich fragrance. The growth is suitably lax, holding its flowers well. I have not found it to be very strong, although the growth is quite adequate with good cultivation. It should reach 15ft. on a wall. Sport found by Morse (U.K.), 1920, from the original Hybrid Tea bred by Pernet-Ducher (France).

CHRISTINE, CLIMBING. A Climbing Hybrid Tea of considerable beauty. Its flowers are fragrant and quite small, with long elegantly scrolled buds of pure golden-yellow. A good first crop is followed by intermittent

70

bloom later. Good, glossy foliage. Height 15ft. Discovered by Willink, from the bush variety bred by McGredy (U.K.), 1918.

COMTESSE VANDAL, CLIMBING. The climbing sport of a beautiful and shapely Hybrid Tea. Coppery-orange buds open to salmon-pink with a coppery-pink reverse. These are held on rather upright stems and have a slight fragrance. Good healthy foliage and growth, to a height of perhaps 10 to 12ft. Found by Jackson & Perkins (U.S.A.), from the bush bred by Leenders (Holland), 1932.

CRIMSON GLORY, CLIMBING. A particularly fine rose in its climbing form. The flowers start as typical Hybrid Tea buds of deepest velvety crimson, eventually becoming an attractive informal cup of a pleasing purplish shade. They are richly fragrant and tend to be evenly placed along the branch, holding themselves admirably. In summer the whole plant is studded with flowers, to be followed by occasional blooms later. Height 10 to 12ft. We have found it to be very successful on a tall pillar. Bush bred by Kordes (Germany), 1935; sport discovered by Jackson & Perkins (U.S.A.), 1946.

CUPID. Very large, single, delicate flesh-pink flowers shaded with apricot; these may be 5ins. across with attractively waved and crinkled petals and ample stamens. Although summer flowering only, this variety has large orange-red hips in the autumn. It will grow to 15ft. or more. Graham Thomas suggests it might be allowed to trail over shrubs, and I can imagine it being very effective when so grown. Fragrant. Bred by Cant (U.K.), 1915. See page 71.

DAINTY BESS, CLIMBING. The climbing sport of an early, single Hybrid Tea. Its pink flowers, with their fringed edges, darker reverse, and red and brown stamens are, if anything, more dainty when grown as a Climber. The growth is slight and rather thin, but fits the flower well. It requires rich soil if it is to reach its height of 8ft. Discovered by van Bernaveld (U.S.A.), 1935; the original bush bred by Archer (U.K.), 1925.

EASLEA'S GOLDEN RAMBLER. Although this rose bears the name Rambler, it is, in effect, a Climber. The buds are tipped with red and open to large loosely-filled deep yellow flowers, with a strong fragrance. They are held either singly or in small clusters. The growth is heavy and robust with thick, olive-green, shiny leaves. A reliable rose that will reach 15ft. Bred by Easlea (U.K.), 1932. See page 70.

ELEGANCE. In spite of the strong mixture of *Rosa wichuraiana* in this Climber, it has much of the appearance of a Climbing Hybrid Tea. It does, as the name suggests, have truly elegant blooms, which start as long shapely buds of clear yellow, opening to very large, very full blooms of pale lemon. The foliage is a dark glossy green. There is one profuse blooming, with only occasional flowers later. A beautiful rose that will grow to a considerable height — 15 to 18ft. Its parentage is 'Glenn Dale' x ('Mary Wallace' x 'Miss Lolita Armour').

ENA HARKNESS, CLIMBING. This is a good climbing sport of the Bush Hybrid Tea, with pointed buds of bright crimson-scarlet. The bush form, popular in the 1940s and 1950s, had a weakness in that it tended to hang its head. In the climbing form this becomes a virtue, enabling us to view the bloom from below. Vigorous growth of at least 18ft.

ÉTOILE DE HOLLANDE, CLIMBING. A climbing sport of the once popular bush Hybrid Tea, and still one of the best and most reliable crimson Climbers. It has long buds of deepest crimson and the rich heavy fragrance we expect of such a rose. The buds open to a rather shapeless flower, but this is made up for in quantity, both early and late in the season. It has been said climbing 'Étoile de Hollande' does not like cold, but this has not been my experience. It will grow to 18ft. Discovered by Leenders (Holland), 1931, on the bush by Verschuren, also of Holland. See page 81.

GENERAL MACARTHUR, CLIMBING. A rose with loosely-formed flowers that vary in colour from crimson-scarlet to deep rosy-red. They are nicely poised on the branch and open flat, with a rich fragrance. It is both free-flowering and recurrent, growing strongly to about 12ft. Discovered by Dickson (U.K.), 1923, on the bush bred by Hill (U.S.A.), 1905.

GOLDEN DAWN, CLIMBING. The bush form of this variety was sometimes classified as a Tea Rose. Its breeding, 'Élégante' x 'Ethel Somerset', would make it a Hybrid Tea, but there is, in fact, something of the Tea Rose about it. It has a delicious Tea Rose perfume and rather lax stems that make it particularly suitable as a Climber. The buds are large, well formed, full and heavy, pale lemon-yellow in colour with just a tint of rose on the reverse of the petals. Occasionally the buds may split instead of opening properly. There is a smaller crop in autumn, when the flowers are often of the highest perfection. 'Golden Dawn' has large, deep green leaves and will grow to 12ft. This climbing sport was discovered by Le Grice (U.K.), 1947, and by others at various times; bush bred by Grant (Australia), 1929.

GUINÉE. The result of a cross between 'Souvenir de Claudius Denoyel' x 'Ami Quinard', the first of which has 'Château de Clos Vougeot' as one of its parents, and the exceptionally deep colouring of that rose has been passed down with equal intensity. 'Guinée' has pointed buds opening to attractive, flat, neatly formed blooms. They are so dark that in the shade they can appear almost black; indeed, they become barely visible against its dark green foliage. For this reason it is best grown against a light background. A few contrasting stamens are visible, and there is a very rich fragrance. Although perhaps just a little lacking in strength, with generous treatment it will grow well to about 15ft. The problem may be that it is not altogether hardy and would be better grown on a warm wall. Bred by Mallerin (France), introduced 1938.

HOME SWEET HOME, CLIMBING. I am not well acquainted with this early Hybrid Tea Rose as a Climber, but as a bush the flowers are so charming that I think it is worthy of inclusion here. Its flowers are held rather too erectly to be of much use high up, but if it is trained at a low level it might prove most effective. Fragrant, purest pink, cupped flowers. Height 10ft. Bush bred by Wood & Ingram (U.K.); we do not know who discovered the climbing form.

IRISH FIREFLAME, CLIMBING. The climbing form of the dainty, single Hybrid Tea. Its colour is a mixture of orange and gold, the petals being veined crimson, with a bunch of fawn-coloured anthers. Slender growth, but quite healthy and reliable. Height about 10ft. Discovered by A. Dickson (U.K.), 1916, on the bush by the same breeder.

JOSEPHINE BRUCE, CLIMBING. As a bush, this variety produces shapely flowers of a particularly rich and pure crimson. They are very fragrant. It is perhaps even better as a Climber, growing to 15ft. and flowering well, with another crop of flowers in late summer. Discovered by Bees (U.K.), 1954, on the bush form bred by the same firm.

LADY FORTEVIOT, CLIMBING. Large, high-centred blooms of golden-yellow and apricot, with a rich fragrance. The growth is strong, if a little stiff, with bronzy, glossy foliage. Spread 12ft. One good flowering, with occasional blooms later in the year. Discovered by the Howard Rose Company (U.S.A.), 1935, on the bush by B.R. Cant (U.K.).

LADY SYLVIA, CLIMBING. I discuss 'Ophelia' and its two sports, 'Lady Sylvia' and 'Madame Butterfly', under the early Hybrid Teas in Chapter 4. Climbing 'Lady Sylvia' has all the qualities of the bush form with exquisitely shaped buds of flesh-pink tinged yellow at the base. As a Climber 'Lady Sylvia', is first rate, growing to about 20ft. and repeating well. This rose, 'Ophelia' and 'Madame Butterfly' are all particularly fine in the greenhouse, where they will produce flowers of the utmost

LADY SYLVIA, *a climbing sport of an early Hybrid Tea Rose with shapely blooms of soft colouring.*

perfection. Outside, they are among the best of the Climbing Hybrid Teas, although they are a little upright in habit. Discovered by Stevens (U.K.), 1933.

LADY WATERLOW. Large blooms opening to loosely formed, almost semi-double flowers of salmon-pink edged with carmine and with attractive veining. It produces strong growth to about 12ft., and is often recommended as a pillar rose, although it is equally suitable for a wall. Delicious tea scent. 'La France de '89' x 'Madame Marie Lavalley'. Bred by Nabonnand (France), 1903. See page 78.

LA FRANCE, CLIMBING. This early Hybrid Tea is rare as a Climber and I have not seen a mature plant in this form, though I should expect it to be attractive when so grown, particularly on a wall, where it would have some protection from the damp. It has silvery-pink cupped Old Rose flowers with a strong fragrance. Growth about 12ft. Discovered by Henderson (U.K.), 1893, on the bush by Guillot Fils (France).

MADAME ABEL CHATENAY, CLIMBING. I have already said that the bush form of this rose is one of the most exquisitely beautiful of all Hybrid Tea Roses. The Climbing form is no less desirable, although with me it has not proved too reliable. When well grown it will achieve 15ft., with attractive, not too stiff growth, and slightly nodding flowers. These are pale pink, deepening towards the centre with a darker reverse and lovely fragrance. Discovered by Page (U.K.), introduced 1917; bush form bred by Pernet-Ducher (France), 1895.

MADAME BUTTERFLY, CLIMBING. The Climbing form of the beautiful bush rose described among the early Hybrid Teas in Chapter 4, having the same perfect buds and blush-pink colouring. An excellent rose of up to 20ft., with good repeat-flowering qualities, the later blooms being finer than those in early summer. Very fragrant. Discovered by E.P. Smith (U.K.), 1926. See also 'Lady Sylvia' above.

MADAME CAROLINE TESTOUT, CLIMBING. The bush form of 'Madame Caroline Testout' was, in its day, almost as popular as 'Peace' in our time. Like 'Peace' it was extremely tough, and the climbing form is no less so. We have on our house an interesting example: photographs taken in 1919 show it as a mature Climber even then, and it is still there today, growing strongly and flowering well. This is in spite of the fact that it was cut to the ground in the winter of 1981/2 when, in Shropshire, we suffered the lowest temperatures ever recorded in England. It is interesting to note that this plant was budded on a Rugosa stock, which is usually regarded as short lived. The flowers are large and globular, of an even silvery-pink colour, not particularly full, with the petals rolled back at the edges. The growth is strong and rather stiff with the flowers held upright, though this does not seem to matter with a bloom of this form. It will achieve at least 20ft. Only a slight scent. Discovered by Chauvry (France), 1901, on the rose bred by Pernet-Ducher (France), 1890.

MADAME EDOUARD HERRIOT ('Daily Mail Rose'). A rose of unique and mixed colouring, so much so that the descriptions we read are as various as they are numerous. *Modern Roses* says: 'Coral-red, shaded yellow and light rosy-scarlet, passing to prawn-red', but in fact the overall effect is an almost terracotta shade. However we put it, it is beautiful and ever changing in appearance. The individual flowers are not outstanding, being loosely double, but they provide a sheet of bloom in early summer, and are followed by occasional blooms later on. The foliage is glossy green and there are very few thorns. It will grow to about 15ft. Fragrant. Breeding 'Madame Caroline Testout' x unnamed Hybrid Tea. Bush bred by Pernet-Ducher (France); climbing sport discovered by Ketten (Luxemburg), 1921.

MADAME GRÉGOIRE STAECHELIN. A fine Climbing Rose bred by Pedro Dot of Spain, who also gave us the Shrub Rose 'Nevada'. Known in some countries as 'Spanish Beauty', this is perhaps a more suitable name, for indeed it is one of the best of all the Climbing Roses. The flowers start as slender buds of deep pink, but soon open wide and flat to form very large semi-double blooms of fresh, glowing pink, with a deeper shade on the reverse. The stamens are visible, and there is a delicious fragrance. This Climber produces one magnificent flush of flowers in early summer, but nothing thereafter. Perhaps this would be too much to expect. It has strong growth, usually to about 15ft., but often more on a wall. The foliage is dark, glossy and luxuriant. If it has a fault, it is that the lower part of the plant becomes bare as it ages, the flowers appearing mainly on its upper branches. To avoid this it is necessary to train it horizontally so far as possible. A good rose for growing on a north wall. The result of a cross between 'Frau Karl Druschki' and 'Château de Clos Vougeot', an almost pure white and one of the darkest of dark red roses, it was introduced in 1927. See page 79.

MADAME HENRI GUILLOT, CLIMBING. It is interesting to note that the original bush form of this climbing sport is given as a cross between the Hybrid Tea 'Rochefort' and a *Rosa foetida bicolor* seedling — presumably itself a hybrid. It produces long, pointed buds which open to form flat, rounded, almost camellia-like flowers of a deep salmon-pink flushed with orange. There is a slight fragrance. The growth is vigorous, to 12ft., with

MADAME GRÉGOIRE STAECHELIN, *one of the finest Climbing Hybrid Tea Roses, with large flowers and very tall.*

glossy, green foliage. Discovered by Meilland (France), 1942, on the bush bred by Mallerin (France), 1938.

MEG. This Climbing Rose is thought to be the result of a cross between 'Paul's Lemon Pillar' and 'Madame Butterfly', and its general appearance would suggest that this is, in fact, true. It bears very large, single or semi-double flowers of pale apricot-pink, with a large boss of quite dark stamens. The flowers are fragrant and held in small clusters. This is a beautiful rose that may be grown on a pillar or wall, but is perhaps best of all when encouraged to clamber over bushes or hedges. Here its large and elegantly waved blooms display themselves with the most pleasing

LADY WATERLOW, *Climbing Hybrid Tea Rose with beautiful mingling colours.*

effect. There is only occasional repeat flowering after the first flush. Height 9ft. Bred by Dr. A.C.V. Gosset (U.K.), 1954.

MICHÉLE MEILLAND, CLIMBING. I write in Chapter 4 with some enthusiasm of this Modern Hybrid Tea in its bush form, and it is also beautiful as a Climber, with the same perfectly formed, soft pink flowers. It will grow to 12ft. Fragrant. Discovered by Meilland (France), 1951, on the bush by the same breeder.

MRS. AARON WARD, CLIMBING. The climbing sport of an early Hybrid Tea bred by Pernet-Ducher in 1907. It produces fine, high-centred blooms of bright yellow washed with salmon, the colour varying considerably according to the season and paling with age. Strong fragrance. Growth about 12ft. Discovered by Dickson (U.K.), introduced 1922.

MRS. G.A. VAN ROSSEM, CLIMBING. A Climbing Hybrid Tea of unusual and beautiful colouring, its large flowers a mixture of dark golden-yellow and orange attractively veined with bronze. These are held on long, rather too rigid stems and have a strong fragrance. Vigorous growth to about 12ft., and deep bronzy-green foliage. Bush bred by Van Rossem (Holland); the climbing sport discovered by Gaujard (France), 1937.

MRS. SAM MCGREDY, CLIMBING. A good example of an early Hybrid Tea that is much better in its climbing form. The bush is not strong, but the Climber has no such trouble and will easily achieve 15ft. Its flowers are coppery-orange flushed with scarlet, with crisp buds, and associate well with the glossy, dark, bronzy foliage. The growth is not too rigid and the flower stems suitably lax. It repeats well. Bush bred by McGredy (U.K.); climbing sports have been discovered by various people, the first being Buisman (Holland), 1937. See Chapter 4.

OPHELIA, CLIMBING. A good Climber that will achieve anything up to 20ft., with beautifully formed blush-pink flowers repeating well and a rich fragrance. Discovered by A. Dickson (U.K.), 1920. See Chapter 4.

PAUL'S LEMON PILLAR. A cross between 'Frau Karl Druschki' and 'Maréchal Niel', two roses of classic bud formation and, as we might expect, this rose too has flowers of similar perfection. Their colour is a creamy-yellow with a tint of green at the base of the petals. They are very large, hanging slightly with their weight, the petals being neatly scrolled at the edges as the buds unfold. It will grow to a considerable height, at least 20ft. on a warm wall. However, it is surprising it should

ÉTOILE DE HOLLANDE. *The climbing form of this old Hybrid Tea Rose is very reliable.*

bear the name 'Pillar', for which it is not particularly well suited. There is no repeat flowering. A majestic flower with a wonderful fragrance. Bred by William Paul (U.K.), introduced 1915.

PAUL'S SCARLET CLIMBER. A once-popular Climbing Rose bearing small clusters of semi-double, scarlet-crimson flowers in late June. It is, perhaps, not so worthwhile today, as it does not repeat and the flowers are not of outstanding quality — equally good Climbers can be found amongst the 'Moderns' which do repeat. Nonetheless, it flowers freely and is hardy and reliable. Slightly fragrant. A good pillar rose; height about 10ft. The parents were probably 'Paul's Carmine Pillar' x 'Rêve d'Or'. Bred by William Paul, introduced 1916.

PICTURE, CLIMBING. This Hybrid Tea Rose is described in its bush form in Chapter 4. The climbing sport has the same charming, pink, buttonhole buds on a plant that will grow to 15ft. It flowers both in summer and autumn. Discovered by Swim (U.S.A.), introduced 1942.

REINE MARIE HENRIETTE. A cross between the Tea Rose 'Madame Berard' (which has 'Gloire de Dijon' as one parent) and the Hybrid Perpetual 'Général Jacqueminot'. Large, fully double cherry-red flowers, opening wide like those of an Old Rose. The growth is vigorous, flowering freely and recurrently. It is fragrant and will achieve 12ft. Bred by Levet (France), 1878.

RÉVEIL DIJONNAIS. The result of a cross between the Hybrid Perpetual 'Eugène Fürst' and the Hybrid Tea 'Constance', this rose is, therefore, not too distantly related to *Rosa foetida,* and this fact is evident in its appearance. It is a short growing Climber with glossy, deep green leaves. The buds are of Hybrid Tea type, opening to large, semi-double flowers of bright scarlet-crimson with a yellow centre, and yellow tints on the reverse of the petals, giving a distinct bicolour effect. It flowers in late June and, to a limited extent, later. Slightly fragrant. Growth 10ft. Somewhat subject to blackspot. Bred by Buatois (France), 1931.

RICHMOND, CLIMBING. 'Richmond' was a popular bush Hybrid Tea in the first half of this century, and this is its climbing form. It bears long, slim buds of bright scarlet turning to carmine with age and varying considerably according to the season. The open flowers are inclined to burn in the hot sun, and for this reason it is perhaps better not to plant it on a south wall. Growth 10ft. Bush bred by Hill from 'Lady Battersea' x 'Liberty', 1905; Climber discovered by A. Dickson (U.K.), 1912.

SHOT SILK, CLIMBING. A good climbing sport of the well-known early

Hybrid Tea, with vigorous growth, fine, glossy green foliage and a good crop of flowers both in early and late summer. These are cerise-pink shot with orange-scarlet and shaded with yellow at the base of the petals. Fragrant. 18ft. Discovered by Knight (Australia), 1931.

SOUVENIR DE CLAUDIUS DENOYEL. The breeding of this rose is 'Château de Clos Vougeot' x 'Commander Jules Gravereaux', and it has the rare unfading crimson of the first parent, though in a brighter shade. The flowers are large, opening to a rather informal, semi-double cup shape, with a strong, rich fragrance. It is laden with bloom hanging nicely from the branches in early summer, and has a rather smaller crop later on. It may achieve at least 12ft. One of the best of our rather limited selection of crimson climbing roses. Bred by Chambard (France), introduced 1920.

SUPER STAR, CLIMBING. In spite of the excessive popularity of this rose as a bush, I do not recollect having seen the Climber growing in a garden — I myself have not grown the climbing form to maturity. I understand it is quite vigorous, reaching 8ft., and can can well imagine it might be a more pleasing rose in its climbing form given a suitable background. Its bright vermilion colouring is unique among Climbing Roses. Discovered by Blaby Rose Gardens (U.K.), 1965, and found in Europe and the U.S.A. in the same year.

SUTTER'S GOLD, CLIMBING. The climbing form of one of the most beautiful Hybrid Teas. It has the same shapely buds of orange-yellow colouring, flushed with pink and veined with red, and a delicious fragrance. Growth about 12ft. Discovered by Armstrong Nurseries (U.S.A.), 1950.

VICOMTESSE PIERRE DU FOU. It is difficult to know where to place this variety as it is the result of crossing the Noisette 'L'Idéal' with the Hybrid Tea 'Joseph Hill'. However, I think it leans towards the latter parent. The flowers are of a coppery-pink colour, deeper at first, paling a little later on. They open to a quartered formation hanging nicely from the branch. The growth is vigorous, spreading to 20ft., the foliage large and bronzy-green. Tea Rose fragrance. Bred by Sauvageot (France), introduced 1923.

Modern Climbers

If we look back over this chapter, it will be seen there has been very little in the way of the deliberate breeding of Climbing Roses. With the exception of the Noisettes, most Climbing Roses have been either sports

SCHOOLGIRL.

SWAN LAKE.

GOLDEN SHOWERS.

Three Modern Climbers, all reliable and of fairly short growth,
which will flower repeatedly.

84

BREATH OF LIFE, *a reliable Modern Climber.*

or chance offsprings from the breeding of bush roses. It was only after the Rambler Rose 'Dr. W. Van Fleet' sported to produce 'New Dawn' in 1930, that any definite move was made towards breeding Climbing Roses, and even then nothing happened until the 1950s. 'New Dawn' had many of the characteristics of a repeat-flowering Climber having flowers of almost Hybrid Tea size and form like its parent. It was eventually crossed with various Hybrid Teas to produce a number of useful repeat-flowering Climbing Roses. Along with these, other crosses were made between bush roses and Ramblers, and sometimes between strong growing Hybrid Teas to produce further Climbers. It is a combination of all these roses that we gather together under the heading 'Modern Climbers'.

To obtain recurrent flowering in a Climbing Rose is no easy matter, and many of these roses do not grow to a great height, indeed some of them are little more than shrubs. On a pillar or more open structure they will often remain rather short, but given the benefit of a wall this will draw them up to a considerable height. Here they can achieve 10ft. or more. There are, of course, times when a short Climber is required, as on a low wall, or fence, and here Modern Climbers come into their own. Most of them are in the modern mould, often with strong colours and with very much of the appearance of a Hybrid Tea. One thing is certain — they can be relied on to give continuity of colour over a long period

ALOHA. I have recommended that this should be regarded as a shrub but it also makes a useful low climber. See pages 27-28.

BREATH OF LIFE. A low growing Climber of 7ft., bearing large, full, well-formed Hybrid Tea flowers of a lovely apricot colouring which turns to apricot-pink. Fragrant. Bred by Harkness (U.K.), 1982. See page 85.

CASINO. Clusters of large, globular, soft-yellow flowers, with dark, glossy, light green foliage. A cross between 'Coral Dawn' and the tall Hybrid Tea 'Buccaneer'. Height 10ft. Bred by McGredy (U.K.), 1963.

COMPASSION. Well-shaped Hybrid Tea flowers with a sweet fragrance, their colour being salmon-pink tinted with apricot-orange. The growth is rather stiff and bushy and there is plentiful dark green foliage. One of the best and most popular roses in this group, as well as being one of the most fragrant. Height 10ft. It may also be grown as a shrub. Breeding: 'White Cockade' x 'Prima Ballerina'. Harkness (U.K.), 1973.

COPENHAGEN. Medium-sized flowers of good Hybrid Tea shape and dark scarlet colouring. The growth tends to be upright, to about 7ft. Quite fragrant. Breeding seedling x 'Ena Harkness'. Bred by Poulsen (Denmark), 1964.

CORAL DAWN. Quite large, full blooms of coral-pink colouring, against plentiful, healthy, dark green foliage. Fragrant. Growth 10 to 12ft. ('New Dawn' x a yellow Hybrid Tea) x an orange-red Polyantha. Bred by Boerner (U.S.A.), 1952. See page 89.

DANSE DU FEU. Bright orange-scarlet flowers of medium size, the colour deepening with age. The buds are quite short but well formed and the flowers open flat. They are produced very freely and continuously against plentiful foliage. Little scent. Growth 8ft. Breeding 'Paul's Scarlet' x unnamed Multiflora seedling. Mallerin (France), 1953.

GALWAY BAY. Large, double, Hybrid Tea flowers of salmon-pink colouring. A vigorous plant with plentiful, glossy, dark green foliage. Height 10ft. 'Heidelberg' x 'Queen Elizabeth'. McGredy (U.K.), 1966.

GOLDEN SHOWERS. A short growing Climber of many virtues. Large, open golden-yellow flowers, fading to light yellow. The individual blooms may be of no exceptional beauty, but they are produced very freely and continuously throughout the summer, providing a good splash of colour. The plant grows well and it is unusually happy on a north wall, perhaps more so than any other rose except 'Zéphirine Drouhin'. Also good as a shrub. 'Charlotte Armstrong' x 'Captain Thomas'. Lammerts (U.S.A.), 1956. See page 84.

HANDEL. Quite small semi-double flowers that are closer to a Floribunda than a Hybrid Tea in character. The colouring is unusual, being creamy-blush and edged with pink. The growth is tall, perhaps 12ft. and it repeats well. There is some tendency to blackspot. 'Columbine' x 'Heidelberg'. McGredy (U.K.), 1956.

HIGHFIELD. A sport from 'Compassion', see above, with all the virtues of that rose. Here we have light yellow flowers with occasional peachy tints. Fragrant. Harkness (U.K.), 1981.

NEW DAWN. As I said in the introduction to this section, this is a recurrent-flowering sport from the summer flowering Rambler 'Dr. W. Van Fleet', and an important influence in this group. With its conversion to repeat-flowering, the growth reduced from 20ft. in its parent to about 10ft. in this rose. It has pretty, rather pointed buds, opening to medium-sized, pearly-blush coloured flowers held in large clusters and with a sweet fragrance. The growth is vigorous with plentiful foliage. It may be pruned to form a shrub, or grown as a hedge. 'New Dawn' is one of the most disease-free of roses, and was the first rose ever to receive a patent. Discovered by Somerset Rose Nursery (U.S.A.), introduced 1930. See page 88.

NORWICH GOLD. There are three 'Norwich' varieties, all good strong-growing and very reliable Climbers. This one has clusters of full-petalled flowers of yellow shaded with orange and opening flat. Little repeat flowering. Growth 10ft. Kordes (Germany), 1962.

NORWICH PINK. Large, semi-double flowers of bright cerise-pink. Strong fragrance. Good, dark, glossy foliage. 10ft. Kordes (Germany), 1962.

NORWICH SALMON. Fully double, soft salmon-pink flowers in large clusters. Vigorous, bushy growth, with dark green, glossy foliage. Growth 10ft. Kordes (Germany), 1962.

PARADE. Here we have a rose that deserves more attention. Like 'Aloha' the growth is short, with large, deep cerise-pink flowers that are fully double and of almost 'Old Rose' persuasion. They have a strong fragrance. It is exceptionally free and continuous in flower. The growth is very vigorous and healthy, and will achieve 7 or 8ft., though it can also make a good lax growing shrub. Bred from a seedling from 'New Dawn' x 'World's Fair'. Boerner (U.S.A.), 1953.

NEW DAWN, *a Modern Climber growing on a roof — a pleasing way to train a Climbing Rose.*

PINK PERPÉTUE. A variety that will grow a little taller than most of the others, perhaps to 12ft. In colour it is a rather harsh pink with a carmine reverse, the flowers being medium sized, double, slightly cupped and held in trusses. The growth is vigorous and reliable and it repeats well. There is some fragrance. 'Danse du Feu' x 'New Dawn'. Gregory (U.K.), 1965.

ROYAL GOLD. Not one of the most reliable Climbers, but with flowers of the deepest yellow colouring, a characteristic it gains from its parent 'Lydia', its other parent being the Floribunda 'Goldilocks'. The blooms are large and of good Hybrid Tea formation; the foliage is dark green and glossy. Height about 8ft. Bred by Morey (U.S.A.), 1957.

SCHOOLGIRL. This has been a popular Climber for some time, and although a beautiful rose at its best, having shapely buds in a pleasing coppery-orange shade, it is not reliable. The foliage is not good and is rather subject to blackspot, often resulting in poor growth. Fragrant. 10ft. 'Coral Dawn' x 'Belle Blonde'. McGredy (U.K.), 1964. See page 84.

CORAL DAWN, *Modern Climber.*

PINK PERPÉTUE, *Modern Climber.*

SWAN LAKE. One of the most beautiful Modern Climbers, with large well-shaped, white Hybrid Tea blooms delicately flushed with pale pink at the centre. Good, dark green foliage. Slight fragrance. 8ft. 'Memoriam' x 'Heidelberg'. McGredy (U.K.), 1968. See page 84.

SYMPATHIE. Shapely, high-centred blooms of bright blood-red. Vigorous growth, with large, glossy foliage. It will achieve 10 or 12ft. A good reliable variety, flowering intermittently throughout the summer. Kordes (Germany), 1964.

WARM WELCOME (Chewizz). A superb miniature Climbing Rose, bearing masses of small orange coloured flowers from top to bottom of its growth. Few, if any, Climbing Roses flower so continually. One of an entirely new group of roses, developed by Chris Warner. An excellent pillar rose — with a little support it should also make a good shrub. Height 7ft. Breeding, Warner (U.K.), 1991.

WHITE COCKADE. A rose which produces some of the most beautiful and shapely flowers in this group. They are pure white and most attractive against its large, dark green leaves. Unfortunately it does not grow very quickly, nor to a great height, so would perhaps be better grown as a shrub. A good cut flower. Fragrant. 'New Dawn' x 'Circus'. Cocker (U.K.), 1969.

Other Climbing Roses

Having covered the various classifications of Climbing Roses, we are inevitably left with a number of varieties that do not fit comfortably into any of these groups. Such roses are usually the result of crossing one or other of the garden climbers with a Climbing Species Rose.

BELLE PORTUGAISE ('Belle of Portugal'). A cross between *Rosa gigantea* and the early Climbing Hybrid Tea 'Reine Marie Henriette'. *R. gigantea* is the largest-flowered of all Climbing Species and, as we have seen, is one of the main ancestors of our modern roses. It was, therefore, obviously a good idea to back-cross some of our modern roses to this species. Unfortunately such hybrids are not hardy in this country, though this variety, and one or two others, will survive most winters in warmer areas of the U.K. if given a protected position, when it may be expected to grow to 20ft. It has long, silky, pointed buds that hang their heads in the most elegant and pleasing manner. Their colour is a pale salmon-pink and their petals beautifully scrolled, eventually opening to rather loose flowers which appear in mid-June only, but in some abundance. It has fine, long, pointed, grey-green, drooping foliage. Strong Tea Rose fragrance. Raised at the Botanic Gardens, Lisbon, 1903.

CÉCILE BRUNNER, CLIMBING. A description of the bush form of this variety is to be found in Chapter 5. This rose has miniature, blush-pink, Hybrid Tea Rose blooms, with scrolled buds of the utmost perfection. It may, therefore, come as something of a surprise to find that its climbing form is of exceptional vigour, with fine luxuriant foliage. It can, in fact, achieve 25ft. of rampant growth. The flowers are exactly similar to those of the bush, except that they can be a shade larger, as are the leaves. Unlike the bush, however, there is little or no repeat flowering. It is a most charming and reliable Climbing Rose, and free of disease. A good variety for growing into trees. Discovered by Hosp (U.S.A.), 1894.

DORTMUND. In the early 1940s the rose 'Max Graf', a hybrid between *Rosa rugosa* and *R. wichuraiana,* produced a chance seedling which Herr Wilhelm Kordes named *R. x kordesii.* This turned out to be tetraploid, and may have been a chance hybrid with another rose. It was a very hardy Climber, and Kordes hybridized it with other garden roses to produce a race of hardy Climbers, most of which are repeat flowering. I include here 'Dortmund', 'Leverkusen' and 'Parkdirektor Riggers'.

'Dortmund' is a vigorous Climber, with very dark, glossy green leaves. It bears large, single, crimson flowers, with a white eye at the centre and yellow stamens, and will bloom recurrently if dead headed, otherwise there will be numerous hips. A very reliable, disease-free, hardy rose, but perhaps a little coarse. Height 8 to 10ft. Breeding seedling x *R.* x *kordesii.* Kordes (Germany), 1955.

DREAMGIRL. A cross between the Wichuraiana Rambler 'Dr. W. Van Fleet' and a Hybrid Tea called 'Senora Gari', though it does not really fit in with the Wichuraiana Hybrids. The flowers are of a lovely soft coral-pink and of typical Old Rose rosette formation with numerous small petals. The growth and foliage is rather similar to 'Dr. W. Van Fleet', but it will achieve no more than 10ft. in height. There is a strong spicy fragrance. 'Dreamgirl' flowers very late, continuing for a long time, but cannot be said to be repeat flowering. A charming rose, ideal for a pillar. Bred by Bobbink (U.S.A.), 1944.

ICEBERG, CLIMBING. Floribundas, unlike the Hybrid Teas, have not been fruitful in the production of climbing sports and I am aware of only two worthwhile varieties, this and climbing 'Masquerade'. Climbing 'Iceberg' lives up to the high expectations we would have of its parent, and even takes on a new elegance with its longer growth. Its only drawback is a tendency to revert to the bush form when first planted. When this occurs it is worth trying again with another plant. Growth 10ft. Discovered by Cant (U.K.), 1968. See page 92.

LA FOLLETTE. Like 'Belle Portugaise', this is a *Rosa gigantea* hybrid, and is in many ways similar to the former rose, with long, pointed buds and loosely-formed, open flowers. The colour is rose-pink, with coppery-salmon on the outside of the petals. A most beautiful rose, it is only for the warmest areas and sheltered walls in this country where it will grow to 20ft., although it may be massive in countries with warmer climates. Strong fragrance. One season of flowering only. Its other parent is not known. Raised by Busby, gardener to Lord Brougham, at Cannes, France.

LAWRENCE JOHNSTON (originally known as 'Hidcote Yellow'). A hybrid between the Hybrid Perpetual Rose 'Madame Eugène Verdier' and *Rosa foetida* 'Persiana', it is strange this cross should produce such a vigorous Climber which can be relied upon to reach 20ft., and often as much as 30ft. As is usually the case with *R. foetida* crosses, it is this species that dominates. The flowers are large, of loosely-cupped shape, and of a bright

ICEBERG, *a Floribunda Rose looking even better in its climbing form.*

LAWRENCE JOHNSTON, *a very tall Climber. Few Climbing Roses make a better show.*

clear yellow that shows up well against the excellent, glossy, dark green foliage. They have a strong fragrance and are produced in one magnificent crop early in the season, with the chance of an occasional bloom later. If it has a weakness, it is a susceptibility to blackspot, a not surprising fact in a *R. foetida* hybrid, but please do not let this deter you from growing it, as it is one of our finest Climbers. Raised by Pernet-Ducher of France, in 1923, who rather surprisingly rejected it. Lawrence Johnston, of Hidcote Manor fame, rescued it when visiting the French nursery, and it was eventually made available to the public by Graham Thomas. See page 93.

LE RÊVE. A sister seedling to 'Lawrence Johnston', from 'Madame Eugène Verdier' and *Rosa foetida* 'Persiana', it was selected by Pernet-Ducher in preference to 'Lawrence Johnston', although it has, in fact, turned out to be inferior. We should not be too surprised at this, for it is difficult even to be sure of a new Shrub Rose until it has been grown in gardens for some years. With Climbers, which may take many years to reach their full potential, the task becomes even more difficult. Nonetheless, the virtues of this variety should not be totally obscured by its more illustrious sister, for 'Le Rêve' does have a certain grace that is its own. It is similar to 'Lawrence Johnston', but a little less robust, with almost single flowers of a paler yellow which are deliciously fragrant. Fine, glossy-green foliage. Growth 20ft. Introduced in 1923.

LEVERKUSEN. Perhaps the most attractive of the Kordesii hybrids, the result of a cross between *Rosa* x *kordesii* and the climbing Hybrid Tea 'Golden Glow'. It bears quite large, double rosette-shaped flowers of rather Old Rose appearance and of a creamy-yellow colouring, deepening towards the centre. There is a pleasing, fruit-like fragrance. The growth is strong and rather bushy, to a height of 10ft., and the foliage is a deep glossy green, with rather small leaflets. This rose flowers freely in summer and, to a lesser extent, later on. Kordes (Germany), 1954.

MAIGOLD. A cross between 'Poulsen's Pink' and 'Frühlingstag', which makes it three generations removed from *Rosa pimpinellifolia hispida,* and it still carries many of the qualities of that rose, particularly in that it is extremely tough and hardy and will thrive under the most difficult conditions. Indeed, it would be hard to think of any Climbing Rose of moderate height that is more suitable for such conditions. It has short, reddish buds which open to quite large, strongly-fragrant, semi-double flowers of bronzy-yellow with golden stamens. There is one very free-flowering period, early in the season, with occasional flowers later. The growth is extremely vigorous, producing strong, very thorny stems to a height of 12ft., with plentiful, glossy-green foliage. Although often recommended as a shrub, I find the growth rather too untidy for this. Little or no disease. Raised by Kordes (Germany), 1953. See page 96.

MASQUERADE, CLIMBING. The climbing sport of the Floribunda of the same name. It will grow to 18ft. and flower freely, but only in the summer. Its unusual mixture of yellow, pink and deep red has its uses in the garden scheme. Discovered by Gregory (U.K.), 1958.

MERMAID. A true classic — one of the most beautiful of all Climbing Roses, bearing large, single, soft canary-yellow flowers of 5ins. and more across, with a boss of long, sulphur-yellow stamens that remain attractive for some time after the petals have fallen. Its flowers are delicately scented and of a soft sheeny texture, the slightly waved petals giving an elegantly sculptured effect. 'Mermaid' blooms with remarkable regularity throughout the summer; in fact few Climbers can rival it in this respect. The result of a cross between *Rosa bracteata* and an unspecified yellow Tea Rose, one cannot but wonder what this Tea Rose might have been to provide such a lovely shade of yellow. The foliage is similar to that of *R. bracteata,* but larger, and almost evergreen, with a smooth, shiny surface. It is no doubt due to *R. bracteata* that 'Mermaid' is almost completely resistant to disease. Inevitably there is one snag: it is not completely hardy, but it is certainly worth growing in all but the coldest areas, and deserves the best wall you have — if this is out of the morning sun to avoid too quick a thaw after a night of frost so much the better. 'Mermaid' has, rather surprisingly, proved successful on a north-facing wall where it is protected from cold winds. It is frequently slow in the early stages, making little progress in the first two or three years, but once it starts it can grow very quickly, easily achieving 25ft. Little pruning is necessary or desirable — no more than is required to keep it within bounds. It may also be grown as a sprawling shrub, but will require a warm corner if it is not to stay short and appear impoverished. The credit for this fine rose goes to William Paul (U.K.), who introduced it in 1918, and it must be regarded as the crowning glory of that famous rose breeder. See page 97.

PARKDIREKTOR RIGGERS. A rose similar to 'Dortmund', but with large clusters of semi-double flowers of deep velvety crimson. It has similar glossy, dark green foliage. Recurrent flowering. Slight fragrance. Height 12ft. *Rosa* x *kordesii* x 'Our Princess'. Bred by Kordes (Germany), 1957.

MAIGOLD, *a hardy and reliable Climbing Rose, ideal for an exposed position.*

SÉNATEUR AMIC. Another *Rosa gigantea* hybrid, along with 'Belle Portugaise' and 'La Follette'. This rose is, perhaps, a little hardier than the other two, but is still only suitable for warm walls. The flowers are borne singly or in twos and threes, and have a strong scent. They are rich pink in colour, with long buds opening to large, semi-double flowers with prominent stamens. The growth is strong, with fine foliage. It may be expected to achieve about 20ft. It is a cross with the Hybrid Tea 'General MacArthur'. Bred by Nabonnand (France), introduced 1924.

MERMAID, *Climbing Rose. An aristocrat among roses, with large flowers from early summer until autumn.*

CHAPTER 3

Rambling Roses

The typical Rambling Rose has long, lax growth and bears large sprays of often small flowers in abundance which provide a massed bower-like effect of great beauty. They flower only in the summer, although certain varieties frequently provide a few blooms later on. Many people tend to associate them with the past, and indeed their popularity was at its height in Edwardian times and soon after. They do not, however, belong to the more distant past, as most of them were introduced in the first quarter of this century. Prior to this time there was no more than a very limited selection available, bred mainly from *Rosa arvensis* (the Field Rose), *R. sempervirens* (the Evergreen Rose) and *R. moschata* (the Musk Rose). It was only with the introduction of certain species Ramblers from the Far East, notably *R. multiflora* and *R. wichuraiana,* that the majority of the varieties we now enjoy came into being. These two species were crossed with the garden roses of the day — the Tea Roses, the Hybrid Perpetuals and the Hybrid Teas, thus providing a much wider variety of colour and form of flower.

Since the Second World War the popularity of Ramblers in the average garden has given way to the more continuous flowering Modern Climbers, and there are only a few varieties to be found in the average nursery catalogue or garden centre. This could not be more unfortunate, for Rambling Roses have a place in the garden that no other rose can fill, and are capable of a beauty that is hard to equal. They have a natural grace — often exceeding that of the Climbing Roses, their branches and large sprays hanging gracefully from their support. Not only this, but they are frequently very vigorous and can grow to a great height.

The variety of different uses for Ramblers is perhaps more extensive than for any other class. While they are not always suitable for growing on walls, since they may be difficult to manage, and some of them are inclined to suffer from mildew, they are ideal for many other purposes: for trellises, arches, pergolas, pillars, tripods, the covering of small unsightly buildings and other objects as well as for growing into trees and over shrubs and hedges.

In fact the possibilities are almost endless, providing great scope for ingenuity. Rather surprisingly, some varieties can be grown successfully without support, as large shrubs, and where space can be spared they will grow into great arching mounds. There are also a number of very lax growing varieties that will creep along the ground, forming excellent ground cover.

Ramblers are usually fragrant and, since they arise from many different species, many different fragrances can be found among them. Often this fragrance carries freely — a quality that is most desirable in any rose. Some have the fresh, sharp, fruit-like fragrance of *R. wichuraiana*, others have a Musk Rose fragrance, but it is possible to detect among Ramblers most of the fragrances of the rose, and indeed the scents of other flowers. The scent of the double white Banksian Rose (*R. banksiae banksiae*) is, for example, said to be similar to that of violets. I have not made a sufficiently close study of rose fragrances to classify them properly (the sense of smell is so personal that I do not dare to do so), but Graham Thomas, in his book *Climbing Roses Old and New*, does go into the subject in some detail, and such knowledge adds to our pleasure in any rose.

The pruning and maintenance of Ramblers need not give us much trouble. Although there are exceptions in the case of the Multifloras, Ramblers are often best left to take their own course. Pruning is better kept to a minimum so that the plants can create their own natural effect, with no more than an occasional tidying and removal of old growth. Tying will, of course, be necessary, as will the careful and artful guidance of growth, but as time goes on new growth will often intertwine with the old and become, to some degree, self-supporting. Ramblers are in general the most disease free and trouble free of roses; the worst that we can say of them is that a few varieties suffer from mildew. This in fact does not matter so much as with other roses, since we view Ramblers from a greater distance.

Ayrshire Hybrids

Rosa arvensis is the wild trailing rose of our hedgerows that flowers a little later than the Dog Rose. The Ayrshire Hybrids are a descendant of this species, and it seems that the Sempervirens Hybrids may also have had some part in their development. Unfortunately there are no precise records, but the Ayrshire Hybrids appear to have originated in Scotland. They cannot be said to be in the front rank of Ramblers, but all of them are very hardy, and have the advantage that they will grow under the partial shade of trees better than any other climbing rose. They are useful if only for this reason and, like nearly all older roses, do have their own modest beauty. Of those that remain, the following four varieties are worth consideration.

BENNETT'S SEEDLING ('Thoresbyana'). This was raised or discovered by Bennett, gardener to Lord Manners at Thoresby, in 1840. It appears to be a double form of *Rosa arvensis* with fragrant white flowers. It is very hardy and particularly suitable for growing in partial shade. Growth 20ft.

DUNDEE RAMBLER. Small, very double, white flowers, tinted with pink at the edges. Spread 20ft. It has been suggested it is *Rosa arvensis* x a Noisette Hybrid. Raised by Martin (Scotland), about 1850.

RUGA. A hybrid of *Rosa chinensis,* it has pale pink, semi-double flowers in large, loosely-formed clusters. The growth is vigorous, often more than 20ft. Raised in Italy, prior to 1830.

SPLENDENS (the 'Myrrh-scented Rose'). One of the more worthwhile of the Ayrshire Hybrids. Its flowers are blush-white, tinted with cream and cupped at first, opening to a semi-double flower. They have a pleasing myrrh scent that was at one time almost unique amongst roses, although we do find it in the Sempervirens Hybrids, and again in the English Roses. It will grow vigorously to over 20ft. The breeding is not known, nor do we know who raised it.

Sempervirens Hybrids

Rosa sempervirens, the Evergreen Rose, is a native of Southern Europe and North Africa. It is a climbing or trailing species which, as its name suggests, has the ability to hold its foliage well into the winter, and has passed something of this quality on to its hybrids. Early in the nineteenth century the French breeder Jacques, gardener to the Duke d'Orléans, (later King Louis-Philippe), used *R. sempervirens* to create the small but very beautiful group which we call Sempervirens Hybrids. They were almost exclusively the result of his work, and since his time little has been done with them. This is unfortunate, for few Ramblers bred since have been able to rival them for their grace of growth or for the charm of their flowers. These are small, typically Rambler, and held in graceful sprays.

ADÉLAIDE D'ORLÉANS, *Sempervirens Hybrid. A Rambler with dainty, elegant hanging blooms.*

Although *R. sempervirens* is not completely hardy, its hybrids seem to be almost entirely so. They have long, lax growth that is excellent for almost any purpose required of a Rambler, including growing on pillars or as weeping standards. They may also be grown as low, sprawling shrubs. Their foliage is small and neat and the flowers are usually fragrant. They flower only once in the summer.

ADÉLAIDE D'ORLÉANS. One of the most beautiful of Rambling Roses, not only for its creamy-white, semi-double flowers, but for the elegance with which they hang down, like the flowers of a Japanese cherry. Each flower is held a little apart from the next, in small dainty sprays, and the whole effect is charming. All this makes it an ideal rose for an arch or pergola. The growth can be slight by comparison with others in this robust group, but under reasonable conditions can be relied on to reach 15ft. It has a pleasant myrrh fragrance. Jacques (France), 1826.

FÉLICITÉ ET PERPÉTUE. A very beautiful rose which must be regarded as one of the most reliable and generally useful of the Ramblers. It flowers with great abundance, the individual white blooms being small, of neat full-petalled pompon formation, and held in large, slightly hanging sprays. They have a light fragrance. The foliage is dark, small and neat, holding well into the winter. The whole plant has a look of 'rightness' and balance. It is hardy, and often to be seen in old gardens, where it may have been for a long time. This rose should not be pruned more than is necessary to keep it within bounds, as this will lead to more growth and less bloom. It flowers late in the season and is quite happy on a north wall. Growth 15ft. The name refers to two Christian martyrs who died in A.D. 203, although I am told by Professor Fineschi of Italy that these were also the names of the breeder's daughters. Bred by Jacques (France), 1827.

FLORA. A free-flowering Rambler with attractively cupped blooms opening flat and filled with petals. The colour is lilac-pink with deep pink at the centre, and there is a delicate perfume. Strong but graceful growth to about 12ft. Raised by Jacques (France), 1829.

PRINCESSE LOUISE. A very similar rose to 'Félicité et Perpétue', described above, and much of what I have said about that rose can equally well be applied to this one. It differs in the soft pink colouring of its buds which soon turns to a creamy-blush fading almost to white. The flowers are held in large clusters with typical Sempervirens elegance and are in every way delightful, while the growth is long and pliable with small, dark green foliage. Growth 12ft. Jacques (France), 1828.

SPECTABILIS. An altogether shorter rose than the other Sempervirens Hybrids, growing to about 7ft. in height. The flowers open from pretty rounded cupped buds into the most perfect delicate pink rosettes with closely packed petals, and have a sweet fragrance. It flowers late with occasional blooms in the autumn and is a charming little rose worthy of extra encouragement. This rose has also been known as 'Noisette Ayez', and there is little doubt that it is a Noisette Hybrid. Breeder unknown, introduced 1848.

Multiflora Hybrids

The majority of the Ramblers we enjoy in our gardens today are hybrids of either *Rosa multiflora* or *R. wichuraiana*. Here we have the first of these two important groups, the Multiflora Hybrids.

R. multiflora is a native of Korea and Japan, and was introduced to Britain in 1862. It is a rather stiff-growing Climber or shrub that is both robust and hardy, and is frequently used as a root stock in continental Europe, producing large plants with few suckers. Before the introduction of the species, a garden variety known as *R. multiflora* 'Carnea' had been brought to England from Japan by Thomas Evans of The East India

Company in 1804. This had clusters of small double pink flowers. In 1817 the 'Seven Sisters' Rose' arrived from Japan, and later, in 1878, another Rambler known as 'Crimson Rambler'. It was these three roses from Japan, hybridized with various other garden varieties, that gave us the basis for the Multiflora Hybrids.

It is usually not difficult to differentiate between the Multiflora Hybrids and the Wichuraiana Hybrids. The former have rather stiff growth like the original species, with many strong shoots arising from the base of the plant. Their leaves are usually of a duller, more opaque green. The Wichuraianas, on the other hand, are inclined to be more flexible in growth, with long thin stems and frequently have more polished, darker green leaves.

Multiflora Hybrids nearly always have small flowers in large, tightly packed clusters and have the advantage in that many of them flower earlier than the Wichuraianas, thus lengthening the season of bloom. *R. multiflora* has a pleasing fragrance which carries well, and this quality is often to be found in the garden varieties. Generally, the flowers of the Multiflora Hybrids have the appearance of what most people would consider to be typical Rambler Roses, whereas the flowers of the Wichuraianas tend a little more towards the Climbing Roses. They flower only once in the summer.

By the nature of their growth many varieties of this class make excellent large shrubs, as do a number of other Ramblers. Indeed it is surprising that they are not more often seen growing in this form in the wilder areas of large gardens. They are also ideal for municipal planting, roadside sites, public places, or anywhere where a large space has to be covered. I cannot think of a less expensive or more satisfactory way to do this.

It is not possible to be too dogmatic about pruning Ramblers in general, but in so far as the Multifloras are concerned we can say that much of the old growth should be removed at the base in order to encourage the remaining young growth. This is because the Multifloras tend to make so much growth from the base of the plant that they easily become choked. However, the gardener should use his discretion in this matter, paying due attention to the result that he may wish to attain and the general state of the plant. Pruning is best done immediately after flowering.

BLEU MAGENTA. The Multifloras are notable, amongst other things, for the fact that they have produced the only truly purple flowers among the Climbers and Ramblers. Later, through the Polyantha Pompon Roses, they were responsible for such purple shades as we find in the Polyantha 'Baby Faurax'. That they should have this capacity is somewhat surprising, but such are the mysteries of genetics. Other rather similar Multifloras of purplish colouring include 'Rose Marie Viaud', 'Veilchenblau' and 'Violette'. All are beautiful in their own way, valuable for the rarity of their colouring, and particularly desirable for mingling with roses of other colours, especially the pink shades. 'Bleu Magenta' is the last of the four to flower. It is of a violet-cerise shade fading to pale violet. The flowers are small, double and held in closely packed clusters. Growth of about 15ft. may be expected. There is little scent. It was brought to England by Graham Thomas from Roseraie de l'Hay. Nothing is known of its breeding.

BLUSH RAMBLER. Once one of the most popular Ramblers, this rose was bred by B.R. Cant, in 1903, from a cross between 'Crimson Rambler' and 'The Garland'. It is, therefore, one quarter Musk Rose, although in fact

BLUSH RAMBLER, *a strong growing and fragrant Multiflora Hybrid.*

Opposite: BOBBIE JAMES, *a very robust Multiflora Hybrid Rambler.*

it is of very typical Multiflora appearance. The flowers are blush-pink, small and cupped, opening to show golden stamens. They are held in quite large, closely-packed, rather conical clusters. It flowers very freely and the growth is vigorous, with ample light green foliage. Deliciously fragrant. A good Rambler worthy of more attention.

BOBBIE JAMES. The parents of this rose are not known, but its overall appearance indicates it has at least some connection with the Multifloras, so it seems reasonable to place it here. It is a Rambler of exceptional vigour, growing far taller than other Multiflora Hybrids. Indeed, it is one of the five or six varieties that we, as nurserymen, tend to recommend when asked for a rose to cover large areas such as an unsightly building, or to grow into a tree. It produces long, thick stems with glossy, pale green leaves. The flowers are small, semi-double, cupped in shape, pearly-white in colour, with yellow stamens, and are held in enormous clusters which, with their weight, tend to hang down from the branch. In fact each large cluster provides what I can only describe as a glistening, pearly effect. This is a very heavy rose that produces a mass of bloom, and it will require a strong structure to support it. It has an exceptional fragrance. Small oval hips. Growth to at least 25ft. Introduced by Sunningdale Nurseries (U.K.), 1961, and named in honour of the Hon. Robert James, at Richmond, Yorkshire. See page 105.

CRIMSON RAMBLER ('Turner's Crimson Rambler', the 'Engineer's Rose'). This is one of the original Ramblers brought to England from Japan in 1878. In China it was known as 'Shi Tz-mei' or 'Ten Sisters', and in Japan as 'Soukara-Ibara'. Sent to a Mr. Jenner in England from Japan, by Professor R. Smith, an engineer, Jenner named it in Smith's honour. Charles Turner, a nurseryman of Slough, purchased the entire stock of this rose and introduced it in 1893 as 'Turner's Crimson Rambler'. It soon became a popular rose, and although there are not many crimson Ramblers, we do not value it very highly today. The flowers are small, crimson, soon fading to an unattractive bluish-crimson. It is particularly subject to mildew. There is little or no scent. Height 15ft.

GOLDFINCH. A vigorous Rambler of typical Multiflora growth and character, bearing close bunches of small button-like flowers of a buff-apricot colour, fading almost to white, with yellow stamens and a strong fruit-like fragrance. There are not many yellow Multifloras and this must be regarded as one of the most satisfactory examples. It makes dense growth with many stems coming from the base and so may require quite a lot of thinning. It will also form an unusually fine, arching shrub of 7ft. in height and, eventually, considerably more across. There are almost no thorns. A hybrid between 'Hélène' and an unknown variety. Bred by George Paul (U.K.), introduced 1907. See page 108.

HIAWATHA. Small, single, crimson flowers with a white centre. The growth is vigorous, to 15ft., with light green foliage. Not perhaps one of the most beautiful Ramblers. No scent. The result of a cross between 'Crimson Rambler' and 'Paul's Carmine Pillar'. Bred by Walsh (U.S.A.), introduced 1904.

PHYLLIS BIDE. A unique rose in that it is of truly Rambler-like character, with typical small flowers in clusters, while at the same time being reliably repeat flowering. Its colour is pale yellow flushed with pink, and it has a pleasant fragrance. A dainty rose of modest beauty, which should be used in such a way as to display itself to full effect, without being lost amongst more robust neighbours. Growth about 10ft. Bred by S. Bide of Farnham, Surrey, in 1923, who gave the parentage as 'Perle d'Or' x 'Gloire de Dijon', though there is some doubt about this statement.

RAMBLING RECTOR. Rose names are not expected to amuse, but here we have an exception, evoking all sorts of images. The rose itself bears large heads of bloom which are small, semi-double, cream at first, later fading to white, with yellow stamens and a good fragrance. These are produced in great abundance on strong, unusually dense and bushy growth of 20ft. or more. Such growth makes it ideal for growing as a shrub, but it is also well suited for scrambling over trees and bushes. A magnificent sight in full bloom with numerous small hips in autumn. Origins unknown. See page 109.

ROSE MARIE VIAUD. This is the second of our purplish Ramblers, its colour being a rich violet at first, fading by degrees to a pale lilac, providing a pleasing mixture of shades. The flowers are small, of neat rosette shape, borne in large clusters, and appear late in the season. The growth is vigorous, to about 15ft. It has little or no scent. Like 'Veilchenblau', from which it is a seedling, it has some tendency to mildew, but this need not worry us too much in a Rambler. Bred by Igoult (France), introduced 1924.

RUSSELLIANA. This rose is probably a Multiflora/Rugosa cross, with predictably coarse results, but with equally predictable toughness and hardiness, giving it a certain value for demanding conditions. It has small semi-double crimson-purple flowers with the Old Rose fragrance. They are held in small clusters. The foliage is dark green, the growth robust and thorny. It flowers freely, providing a pleasing colour effect

GOLDFINCH, *a Multiflora Hybrid Rambler, seen here growing as a shrub.*

RAMBLING RECTOR, *Multiflora Hybrid.* A very free-flowering Rambler with bushy growth bearing a mass of bloom with good fragrance.

from a distance. The shrub rose 'Gipsy Boy' is a seedling from this variety. First introduced in 1840, and from time to time variously known as 'Russell's Old Cottage Rose', 'Scarlet Grevillea' and 'Old Spanish Rose'.

SEAGULL. A vigorous Rambler of some 15ft., bearing large clusters of small semi-double white flowers with the greatest freedom. Close to *Rosa multiflora* in appearance, it has a particularly strong fragrance. An excellent rose for smaller trees, producing a magnificent display of billowing white. Breeding not recorded. Raised by Pritchard, 1907. See page 112.

SEVEN SISTERS' ROSE (*Rosa multiflora* 'Platyphylla', 'Grevillei'). This rose was brought to Britain from Japan by Sir Charles Greville in 1817. Very popular in Victorian times, it is still worthy of a place in the garden. It gained its name from the varying shades of colour to be found in its flowers as they pass on to maturity — the idea being that there were seven different colours to be seen at one time. The flowers are double, quite large for a Multiflora, and held in big clusters, while the colour ranges from cerise to pale mauve, and eventually almost to white. It is free flowering and strong growing, to a height of about 18ft. Fresh, fruit-like fragrance.

THALIA ('White Rambler'). A hybrid between *Rosa multiflora* and 'Paquerette', which was one of the two original Dwarf Polyantha Roses and itself a seedling from a Multiflora Hybrid. 'Thalia' bears large clusters of small, double, white flowers. Strong fragrance. The growth is vigorous, to about 12ft. Bred by Schmitt (France), introduced 1895.

THE GARLAND ('Wood's Garland'). An early Rambler believed to be the result of a cross between *Rosa moschata* and *R. multiflora*. The flowers are small and semi-double, with quilled petals giving the blooms an unusual daisy-like appearance, while the buds are cream tinged with blush, opening to white, with yellow stamens. The clusters are of small to medium size and are held upright on the branch. Vigorous and bushy in growth to about 15ft., with quite small, dark green leaves, it will also form a good shrub. There is a strong fragrance that carries well, and small, oval hips. Bred, or perhaps discovered, by a man called Wells, 1835.

VEILCHENBLAU ('Violet Blue'). The third of the purplish Multifloras, this is a vigorous Rambler of 12 to 15ft. and typical Multiflora character, with large, closely-packed clusters of small, cupped, purple-violet flowers. These are white at the centre with yellow stamens, and have an occasional streak of white. The colour becomes dark violet later, and finally turns to lilac-grey, presenting an attractive range of colour; better colours are achieved in a shady position, where there may also be less likelihood of mildew, to which it is subject. There is a fresh fragrance. The foliage is light green, the growth almost thornless. A cross between 'Crimson Rambler' and 'Erinnerung an Brod'. Bred by Schmidt (Germany), 1909.

VIOLETTE. The fourth of our purplish-coloured varieties, bearing large sprays of small, cupped, crimson-purple flowers turning to maroon-purple, with an occasional white streak and contrasting yellow stamens. Light, fruit-like fragrance. The growth is vigorous, attaining about 15ft., with few thorns and dark green foliage. Breeding unknown. Bred by Turbat (France), introduced 1921.

Wichuraiana Hybrids

The Wichuraianas are the largest and most important group of Rambler Roses. The species, *Rosa wichuraiana,* comes from Japan, East China, Korea and Taiwan. Unlike *R. multiflora,* it is a naturally prostrate, trailing or scrambling rose, which is equally capable of being grown as a Climber, and no doubt frequently does so in its natural state. It has large clusters of quite small flowers (although bigger than those of Multiflora) of about 1½ to 2ins. across. Brought to Britain in 1891, the breeders wasted no time in making use of it in the development of new Ramblers. While *R. multiflora* is rather stiffly upright in growth — perhaps too much of a shrub to be quite what we require for a Rambler — no such complaint can be levied against *R. wichuraiana.* Its long, trailing growth, great vigour and glossy disease-free foliage have made it an ideal parent.

Whereas the Multifloras usually have small, typical Rambler flowers, the flowers of the Wichuraiana Hybrids vary considerably between varieties, having a wider range of colour and form than the Multifloras, often with flowers that are more like those of the Climbing Roses. These frequently differ from the Old Rose colouring and come closer to those of the Modern Roses, but they are never crude or garish. They are nearly always fragrant, often with the delicious fruit-like scent of fresh apples. It is interesting to note that many Wichuraiana Hybrids were hybrids of the Tea Roses, others were hybrids of China Roses, while still others were crosses with the early Hybrid Teas, which were themselves frequently close to the Tea Roses. In this Wichuraianas were fortunate, for it enabled them to perpetuate something of the delicacy of those roses. Where we have Wichuraianas crossed with Hybrid Perpetuals or with

SEAGULL, *a Multiflora Hybrid Rambler with large sprays of small flowers and wonderful fragrance.*

Multiflora Hybrids, we have a rose much closer in appearance to that of a Multiflora Hybrid and such varieties are often less beautiful. The Wichuraianas often grow to a greater height than the Multifloras, frequently to 20 or 25ft., and tend to be of a more branching and attractive habit of growth. All Wichuraianas have one season of flowering, although a few of them, like 'Albéric Barbier' and 'Paul Transon', frequently have a small crop of flowers in the autumn.

These hybrids can usually be left to their own devices for a long time without much pruning, making them ideal for a great many uses, such as growing into trees, over arches and pergolas, or perhaps over a wall. They also include some of the best roses for weeping standards, while others, like 'Albéric Barbier', easily take on the trailing habit of the species, making them suitable for ground cover.

When pruning Wichuraianas, we can allow a great deal of latitude, according to the position in which they are grown and the tastes of the grower. I myself prefer to see them run riot so that the growth builds up into a twiggy mass. We can afford to leave them for some years although, of course, the time will come when we have to start removing old growth.

ALBÉRIC BARBIER. A very vigorous Rambler that will easily reach 25ft. under suitable conditions. Its parents were *Rosa wichuraiana* x 'Shirley Hibberd', the latter being a yellow Tea Rose. Its pretty, yellow buds open into quite large, fully-double, quartered flowers of a creamy-white shade with a strong fruit-like fragrance. These are held in small clusters and produced with great freedom. The long, thin, flexible stems have excellent glossy, dark green foliage that will last well into the winter. I had a particularly fine specimen which grew on the wall of an old granary; gradually, without any assistance, it clambered on to the roof covering it completely and providing a most magnificent effect. Unfortunately it was killed by the exceptionally severe winter of 1981/2. In spite of this, 'Albéric Barbier' should not be regarded as tender in our climate, and hopefully we are unlikely to encounter such a winter again for a long time. This Rambler has some capacity to provide flowers later in the year, no doubt due to the influence of its Tea Rose parent. One of the best and most reliable in this class. Bred by Barbier (France), introduced 1900.

ALBERTINE. One of the most popular of Ramblers available from most garden centres and not without good reason, for it is a most reliable rose that blooms very freely. It was the result of a cross between *Rosa wichuraiana* and the Hybrid Tea 'Mrs. Arthur Robert Waddell', and its flowers, though of loose, open formation, have something of the stamp of

113

a Hybrid Tea. Starting as salmon-red buds, they open into large, coppery-pink flowers with a rich fragrance. The growth tends to be branching and bushy, making it an excellent subject with which to cover a fence. The leaves are small, thick, deep green, and have something of the Hybrid Tea about them. It will grow to 25ft. as a Climber, and will, if desired, form a dense shrub of 5ft. in height, spreading broadly. Bred by Barbier (France), introduced 1921.

ALEXANDER GIRAULT. A useful Rambler, providing strength of colour in a class rather lacking in strong shades. The flowers are tinted red in the bud, turning to a deep coppery-carmine on opening, and have numerous slightly quilled petals. There is a green eye and yellow stamens. The growth is vigorous, to 20ft., with dark, glossy foliage and few thorns. 'Alexander Girault' will provide a magnificent and unusual massed colour effect. Parentage *Rosa wichuraiana* x the Tea Rose 'Papa Gontier'. Barbier (France), introduced 1909. See page 122.

A MAGNIFICENT *group of Ramblers on pillars at Roseraie de l'Hay, Paris.*

CRIMSON SHOWER, *Wichuraiana Hybrid. Best of the crimson Ramblers.*

ALIDA LOVETT. Large, double blooms of soft shell-pink, shaded yellow at the base and opening to flat flowers with a good fragrance. The growth is quite vigorous and the foliage is dark, glossy green. Height 12ft. Breeding 'Souvenir du Président Carnot' x *Rosa wichuraiana.* Van Fleet (U.S.A.), 1905.

AMERICAN PILLAR. After many years of popularity this rose has now become one of the least loved of Ramblers due, I think, to its harsh colouring and rather stiff character — both in flower and growth. Nonetheless, we still receive some demand for it. The single flowers are produced in large clusters and are bright carmine-pink with a distinct white centre. It is extremely tough and robust, but may have some mildew. There is no scent. Breeding (*Rosa wichuraiana* x *R. setigera*) x a red Hybrid Perpetual. Bred by Dr. W. Van Fleet (U.S.A.), 1902.

AUGUSTE GERVAIS. For me one of the most beautiful of the Wichuraiana Ramblers. It does not produce flowers with the abundance that we might expect of a first class Rambler, but they have a Tea Rose delicacy and are beautifully poised on elegant growth, providing the most pleasing effect. The flowers are semi-double, with large petals arranged in nicely sculptured informality, their colouring being a delicate mixture of cream-apricot and pale yellow, with copper flame-pink on the reverse. They are deliciously fragrant, and are produced over an extended period, with an occasional bloom later. Height 18ft. Good on a pillar. The breeding was *Rosa wichuraiana* x the yellow Hybrid Tea Rose 'Le Progrès'. Barbier (France), 1918.

AVIATEUR BLÉRIOT. A vigorous Rambler of rather upright growth, bearing large trusses of double apricot-yellow flowers that fade to a creamy shade later. Dark green foliage. Fragrant. Height 12ft. Breeding *Rosa wichuraiana* x 'William Allen Richardson'. Fauque (France), 1910.

BLUSHING LUCY. This variety was recently sent to me by Graham Thomas and as yet I do not know very much about it. It has the rare distinction amongst Rambler Roses that it is reliably repeat-flowering – a characteristic that it shares with only Phyllis Bide and New Dawn – the latter usually being classified as a Climbing Rose. I understand that it has particularly pretty blush-pink flowers.

BREEZE HILL. Large, very full, cupped flowers of flesh-pink tinted with apricot and held in small clusters. The growth is tall, heavy and bushy, to about 20ft. Fragrant. *Rosa wichuraiana* x Hybrid Perpetual 'Beauté de Lyon'. Bred by Van Fleet (U.S.A.), introduced 1926.

CRIMSON SHOWER. A comparatively new variety with two particularly useful qualities: it is a richer crimson than any other Rambler, and it does not begin to flower until midsummer, continuing into September. The flowers are small and rosette shaped and held in large clusters. There is little scent. 'Crimson Shower' will grow to about 12ft. in height, and has small, very glossy foliage. Its long, flexible growth makes it ideal for a weeping standard. A seedling from 'Excelsa', it was bred by the successful amateur breeder A. Norman (U.K.), introduced 1951. See page 115.

DÉBUTANTE. This excellent and charming rose bears small, cupped flowers of a fresh rose-pink colouring, the petals gradually reflexing and paling to blush-pink. They are held in quite small, dainty sprays and have a delicate and pleasing fragrance. The growth is healthy and strong, to about 15ft., with dark green foliage, the whole adding up to a most delightful picture. Rather surprisingly, there are not many soft pink Ramblers, and this is one of the most beautiful. It was the result of a cross between *Rosa wichuraiana* and the Hybrid Perpetual 'Baroness Rothschild'. It has recently provided us with an equally fine though rather different seedling called 'Weetwood'. Bred by Walsh (U.S.A.), introduced 1902.

DOROTHY PERKINS. In its day the most popular Rambler, but it has fallen from grace in more recent times. This is not surprising, as it is by no means one of the best and suffers badly from mildew. We should not be too hard on it, however, as it does have a certain appeal with its large sprays of small, double or semi-double flowers and flexible growth. The colour is a strong, almost matt pink, and unlike that of any other Rambler. It seems to require a good moist soil, and does not like to be in a baked, sunny position — certainly not against a wall where it is sure to have mildew. Fragrant. Growth about 12ft. The breeding was *Rosa wichuraiana* x Hybrid Perpetual 'Madame Gabriel Luizet'. Bred in 1901 by Jackson & Perkins (U.S.A.), who are still leading American rose specialists.

DR. W. VAN FLEET. This rose has, to a large extent, been succeeded by its own sport 'New Dawn', a repeat-flowering form that has been influential in the production of many of the Modern Climbers of the present day. The two are, in fact, identical, except that 'New Dawn' is considerably shorter in growth, due, no doubt, to the fact that more energy is taken up by the latter's long season of flowering. For this reason it is worth retaining the parent variety which will grow to at least 20ft. Its flowers are double, medium sized, with pointed buds and of a soft, even, pearly blush-pink. These are produced with great freedom, making an excellent effect in the mass. Breeding (*Rosa wichuraiana* x Tea Rose 'Safrano') x Hybrid Tea 'Souvenir du Président Carnot'. Bred by Dr. W. Van Fleet (U.S.A.), introduced 1910.

EMILY GRAY. Medium-sized clusters of semi-double buff-yellow flowers are shown off to advantage by glossy, dark green foliage, which is richly tinted with brown when young. The growth, unfortunately, is somewhat variable, and not entirely hardy, probably due to the fact that this rose is three-quarters China and Tea Rose, its breeding being 'Jersey Beauty' x 'Comtesse du Cayla'. In a warm position it will grow to 20ft., but in less favourable places it can languish at 8 or 10ft. It is, at its best, an attractive rose. Bred by Williams (U.K.), introduced 1918.

EVANGELINE. Clusters of small, single, pale pink flowers, make a dainty effect against dark green foliage. They are fragrant and appear late in

Left: WEETWOOD, *Wichuraiana Hybrid. This Rambler has medium-small almost Old Rose flowers.*

Right: MAY QUEEN, *Wichuraiana Hybrid. A Rambler with flowers similar to an Old Rose.*

the season. It is good to have a single flowered Rambler. Growth about 18ft. Breeding *Rosa wichuraiana* x 'Crimson Rambler'. Bred by Walsh (U.S.A.), introduced 1906.

EXCELSA ('Red Dorothy Perkins'). Large clusters of small, double, crimson flowers of globular formation, with white at the centre. It is vigorous, growing to 18ft., with glossy, light green leaves. Its flexible branches make it suitable for a weeping standard, or for growing in prostrate form. Somewhat inclined to mildew. Bred by Walsh (U.S.A.), introduced 1909.

FRANÇOIS JURANVILLE. An excellent, tall and vigorous Rambler of 25ft., with flowers of a rich coral-pink that deepens towards the centre, and with a touch of yellow at the base, eventually fading with age. They are of medium size, opening flat and double, with slightly quilled petals, and have a fresh, fruit-like fragrance. They are held in small clusters on graceful lax growth with purple-red stems. The foliage is glossy green,

FRANÇOIS JURANVILLE, *Wichuraiana Hybrid. A graceful and charming Rambler of 25ft.*

118

tinted with bronze at first. A useful rose for pergolas or growing into small trees, but not suitable for a wall, where it may develop mildew. A cross between *Rosa wichuraiana* and the China Rose 'Madame Laurette Messimy'. Bred by Barbier (France), introduced 1906.

GARDENIA. Small sprays of prettily pointed buds, opening to creamy-white flowers that deepen to yellow at the centre and eventually fade almost to white. These are of medium size, very full, slightly quartered, and have a fresh apple scent. The growth is vigorous, with graceful, flexible stems and small, dark, glossy green leaves. Height 20ft. A cross between *Rosa wichuraiana* and Tea Rose 'Perle des Jardins'. Bred by Manda (U.S.A.), introduced 1899.

GERBE ROSE. Large, cupped, quartered flowers of a soft pink, with a lovely fragrance. The growth, though robust, is not typical of a Wichuraiana Hybrid, being short and rather stiff with large, glossy, dark green leaves. This is no doubt due to its Hybrid Perpetual background — it is a *Rosa wichuraiana* x 'Baroness Rothschild' cross, and it appears that the latter parent has been influential. It is, however, a good pillar rose, and has some ability to flower again after its main crop. Growth 12ft. Bred by Fauque (France), introduced 1904.

JERSEY BEAUTY. This variety is the result of crossing *Rosa wichuraiana* with the Tea Rose 'Perle des Jardins'. It has sprays of quite large single flowers of creamy-yellow colouring and deep yellow stamens. The growth is strong, to about 16ft., its magnificent dark, glossy foliage forming an excellent background for its bloom. There is a strong fragrance. Bred by Manda (U.S.A.), introduced 1899.

LADY GAY. A cross between *Rosa wichuraiana* and the Hybrid Perpetual 'Bardou Job' has resulted in a rose that is not dissimilar to 'Dorothy Perkins', though with the advantage that it is less subject to mildew. The small flowers are of a richer pink than 'Dorothy Perkins' and are held in nice sprays. The growth is vigorous, to about 15ft. Bred by Walsh (U.S.A.), 1905.

LADY GODIVA. A sport from Dorothy Perkins to which it is similar, except for the colouring of its small flowers which are blush-white, turning to almost pure white, and in this shade the effect is perhaps more distinct and pleasing. Fragrant. Growth 12ft. Discovered by G. Paul (U.K.), introduced 1908.

LA PERLE. A tall and vigorous Rambler with a spread of up to 30ft., the result of a cross between *Rosa wichuraiana* and the pale yellow Tea Rose

'Madame Hoste'. It seems that the Tea Roses, with their close relationship to *R. gigantea*, often produce tall Ramblers, and frequently combine this with flowers of exquisite delicacy. In this case they are creamy-white, deepening to yellow at the centre. They are cupped at first, opening flat with quilled petals, and have a strong, fresh fragrance. The young leaves are tinted with brown, becoming a glossy green as they develop. 'La Perle' was bred by Fauque (France), introduced 1905.

LÉONTINE GERVAIS. I regard this as one of the most attractive of the Wichuraiana Ramblers. It is the result of a cross between *Rosa wichuraiana* and the dainty Tea Rose 'Souvenir de Catherine Guillot'. The flowers are a delicate mixture of pink, copper and orange; they have large, gracefully sculptured petals, and are held nicely poised on rather branching growth, providing a beautiful airy effect. Fragrant. It will grow to about 25ft., but can successfully be confined to a pillar. Bred by Barbier (France), introduced 1903. See page 123.

MARY WALLACE. A cross between *Rosa wichuraiana* and an unnamed Hybrid Tea, showing the influence of the latter parent, the flowers being large, loosely-formed, semi-double and of a warm rose-pink colouring. It has a good fragrance. The growth is strong and rather upright, spreading to about 25ft., with rather sparse foliage. Bred by Van Fleet (U.S.A.), introduced 1924.

MAY QUEEN. Graham Thomas tells us there were two Ramblers of this name, both from the U.S.A., and introduced in the same year, 1898. One was bred by Manda from *Rosa wichuraiana* x 'Champion of the World'; the other by Dr. Van Fleet, from *R. wichuraiana* x 'Madame de Graw'; the pollen parents in each case being Bourbons. It may be that neither breeder was willing to step down and change the name; it is more likely that the distributor confused two roses and sent them out under the same name. Such a confusion is by no means unheard of. The variety we have shows distinct signs of Old Rose parentage, the blooms starting as rounded shallow cups, well filled with petals, later becoming flat and eventually reflexing. They are of medium size, and, in fact, not dissimilar to those of the Bourbon 'Louise Odier'. The colour is a clear rose-pink, and there is a fresh, fruit-like fragrance. Individually the flowers are of considerable beauty, and this is equalled by the massed effect, the plant producing numerous long shoots that intertwine to form a mat of growth. It will grow to about 15ft. in height and will also form an excellent large shrub. See page 118.

ALEXANDER GIRAULT, *Wichuraiana Hybrid. A Rambler useful for its dark colouring.*

PAUL TRANSON, *Wichuraiana Hybrid. A good Rambler which usually produces a small second crop in autumn.*

122

LÉONTINE GERVAIS, *Wichuraiana Hybrid. One of the most beautiful of the large-flowered Ramblers.*

MINNEHAHA. Large clusters of small, double, pink flowers, fading almost to white, on a strong Rambler. Once a very popular rose, perhaps more so than it deserved, although it will make a good weeping standard. Height 15ft. *Rosa wichuraiana* x 'Paul Neyron'. Bred by Walsh (U.S.A.), 1905.

PAUL TRANSON. Small coppery-orange buds in small sprays opening flat to form medium-sized double flowers of coppery-buff paling with age. The growth is strong and bushy with dark, glossy green foliage, the young stems and leaves being tinted with bronze. An excellent free-flowering Rambler, useful for its strong colouring. It almost invariably provides further flowers in late summer, and few Ramblers can compare with it in this respect. There is a strong, fruit-like fragrance. Growth 15ft. Breeding *Rosa wichuraiana* x the dusky red-pink Tea Rose 'L'Idéal'. Breeder Barbier (France), introduced 1900.

RÉNÉ ANDRÉ. Gracefully hanging sprays of small, semi-double flowers of a soft apricot-yellow which later becomes flushed with pink. The growth is vigorous with long, slender, flexible stems and plentiful dark, glossy

123

green foliage. Fresh, fruit-like scent. Occasional repeat flowering. Growth about 15ft. *Rosa wichuraiana* x 'L'Idéal'. Bred by Barbier (France), introduced 1901.

SANDERS' WHITE ('Sanders' White Rambler'). A very good white Rambler, bearing large clusters of small, semi-double flowers with golden stamens and a wonderful fragrance — more powerful than any other member of this class. The growth is vigorous, long and flexible, to 18 or 20ft., with glossy foliage. An altogether beautiful rose, it flowers with great freedom, and is useful in that it does so when most other Ramblers have nearly finished. It will also make excellent ground cover. Bred by Sanders & Sons (U.K.), introduced 1912.

THELMA. Small to medium-sized clusters of quite large semi-double flowers in a delicate mixture of coral-pink and carmine, with a hint of yellow at the centre. This variety is not always very vigorous, but it will flower freely when well grown. Height 12ft. *Rosa wichuraiana* x 'Paul's Scarlet Climber'. Bred by Easlea (U.K.), 1927.

WEETWOOD. We were asked to introduce this rose by Mrs. H.E. Bawden of Offwell, Honiton, Devon. It was a self-sown seedling found in her garden, and arose from the beautiful Rambler 'Débutante', which was itself a cross between *Rosa wichuraiana* and the Hybrid Perpetual 'Baroness Rothschild'. 'Weetwood' represents a further distillation of that cross, with slightly larger, but still small flowers, of shapely, flat, rosette formation, each one a perfect miniature Old Rose. They are a lovely soft rose-pink colour and hang from the branch in small clusters. The growth is exceptionally vigorous, and I understand that the original seedling grows to a great height in a tree. Its only weakness is a tendency towards mildew, but this need not be taken too seriously in a non-repeating Rambler. Growth possibly 20 to 25ft. See page 118.

Other Rambling Roses

As with the Climbing Roses, there are a number of Ramblers, some of them particularly beautiful, that do not belong to any of the previous four groups. Some belong to small groups like the Banksian and the Boursault Roses; others are one-off hybrids between various species.

BALTIMORE BELLE. A hybrid between *Rosa setigera* and a Gallica Rose bred by an American nurseryman called Feast in 1843, this rose bears hanging sprays of very double cupped flowers of pale pink fading to ivory-white. They have an attractive formality which gives some hint of the Gallica parent, and are freely produced on a strong but graceful plant, with good, medium green foliage. Flowering occurs late in the season, after most other Ramblers. It will grow to 12ft.

PINK BOUQUET. Hybrids of *Rosa filipes* 'Kiftsgate' are proliferating apace, which is good news, for I can think of few better Species than *R. filipes* as a parent for extra-strong Ramblers. This would appear to be one of the most promising. It bears massive airy sprays of small, shell-pink flowers with a deeper reverse and fades with age to white. The blooms are of pronounced cup shape and fully double with a strong fragrance. It is very vigorous and the foliage is disease resistant. I would expect it to grow to at least 20ft. and probably a great deal more. Breeding, *R. filipes* 'Kiftsgate' x a China Rose. Treasure (U.K.).

BANKSIAN ROSES

The Banksian Roses form a small group of Ramblers that stand very much on their own. The wild species is a native of West China, growing at 5,000 ft. in Hunan, Shensi and Hupeh, and both this and its garden forms have an individuality and character that places them among the most desirable of all climbing roses. Small flowers, with a strong fragrance, are borne in hanging sprays and appear in late May or early June, long before most other Ramblers. The branches are almost thornless, the foliage pale green with long, glossy pointed leaflets of polished appearance. Unfortunately these roses are not completely hardy in this country, but they are so special that it is worth retaining your best and warmest wall for at least one of them, for their wood requires the warmth of the sun to enable it to ripen properly and resist frost. The flowers are produced on the second and third year's growth, and for this reason it is necessary to confine pruning to the removal of old wood and generally keeping the rose tidy and within bounds. In a favourable position Banksian Roses may be expected to reach the roof, or at least 25ft. Propagation is best done from cuttings or by grafting, for the Banksian Roses will not bud successfully on to the usual root stocks.

ROSA BANKSIAE BANKSIAE. This variety, frequently known as *R. banksiae* 'Alba-Plena', was brought to England by William Kerr on behalf of the Royal Society in 1807. He discovered it in a Canton garden. It was named after Lady Banks, the wife of the famous Director of Kew Gardens at that time, thus giving its name to the species. The flowers are white, small (no more than 1in. across), full petalled and form a near button-like rosette with a fragrance that is similar to violets, and more powerful than any other in the group.

ROSA BANKSIAE LUTEA, *Banksian Rose. One of the most beautiful of Ramblers, seen growing in Italy. In Britain it would require the protection of a warm wall.*

ROSA BANKSIAE LUTEA. The most widely grown of the Banksian Roses, this is rather more free-flowering than the white form, and probably a little hardier, although it does not grow quite so strongly. The flowers are small, cupped and double, of a lovely deep yellow colour, but have only a light scent. Introduced from China by J.D. Park for the Horticultural Society of London, it first flowered in this country in 1824. One of the great classic roses.

ROSA BANKSIAE LUTESCENS. This form has small, single canary-yellow flowers in sprays. It is believed to have been brought to England in 1870 from La Mortola, the famous garden on the Italian Riviera. It has a strong fragrance.

ROSA BANKSIAE NORMALIS. The wild species from Western China, bearing sprays of single white flowers with a strong fragrance. Probably introduced to England in 1877.

BELVEDERE. Until recently this variety has been known as 'Princesse Marie' and placed with the Sempervirens Roses. It may well have connections with that class, but these are slender at best; indeed it is

ROSA BANKSIAE
LUTESCENS, *Banksian Rose.*
A single-flowered form in
this beautiful group of
Ramblers.

difficult to say what are its origins. Graham Thomas has suggested it should be named 'Belvedere' after the house in Ireland, whence it was procured by Lady Ross. It is a very robust Rambler of 20ft., and frequently much more under favourable conditions. It bears large trusses of small flowers that are distinctly cupped and remain so to the end. Their colour is a strong clear pink which fades a little with age, and they have a pleasant fragrance. This is a most charming Rambler, but unfortunately it has one bad fault — it tends to become shabby in the rain. It appears to require a rich soil and a cool climate. In drier areas the flowers are often a dirty white. In the richer soil at Nymans it is beautiful, growing into trees. If you can provide suitable conditions, I would certainly recommend this rose. It is also ideal as a large shrub.

BOURSAULT ROSES

These form a small group of almost thornless Ramblers which were once thought to be the result of crossing *Rosa pendulina* with *R. chinensis*, but it has since been discovered that the chromosome count excludes this possibility. We are thus left with a mystery. They have never become a major class, but they do have an Old Rose character that still appeals.

AMADIS ('Crimson Boursault'). Small semi-double, cup-shaped flowers of deep crimson-purple with an occasional white streak. These are held in both small and large clusters and produced freely on strong, rather bushy growth of about 15ft. The foliage is dark, and there are no thorns. An attractive Rambler in the mass, providing a splash of rich colouring. There is no fragrance. Bred by Laffay (France), 1829.

BLUSH BOURSAULT ('Calypso', 'Rose de l'Ile', 'Florida'). Double flowers of pale blush-pink, opening flat and with a rather ragged appearance. Long, arching, thornless growth, with plentiful dark green foliage. 15ft. 1848. See page 130.

MADAME SANCY DE PARABÉRE. A unique rose, and the most beautiful of the group, with large, double, soft pink blooms of up to 5ins. across, opening flat. These are unusual in that the small inner petals are frequently, but not always, surrounded by distinctly larger outer petals, creating the attractive effect of a rosette within a single flower. They have a slight scent, and are produced early in the season. It will grow to about 15ft. and has good dark green foliage and no thorns. Its large flowers and general habit would make it more suitable for inclusion amongst the Climbers, but as it is a Boursault Rose I place it here for convenience. Bred by Bonnet (France), introduced 1874.

FRANCIS E. LESTER. One of the surest and most reliable of Rambler Roses. A seedling from the Hybrid Musk Rose 'Kathleen', this rose is thus of rather mixed origin. The flowers are single, delicate blush-pink at the edges, soon becoming almost white, and giving something of the impression of apple blossom. They are held nicely spaced in large trusses and have a particularly strong and pleasing fragrance. This rose blooms in exceptional abundance and in autumn there are plentiful small, oval, orange-red hips. The growth is strong and bushy, to about 15ft., and it will, if desired, make a first class large shrub. The foliage is elegant, a glossy dark green, with pointed, widely spaced leaflets. Bred by Francis E. Lester, founder of the Californian nursery now known as 'Roses of Yesterday and Today', introduced 1946.

KEW RAMBLER. A cross between *Rosa soulieana* and 'Hiawatha', this rose might have been included amongst the Multiflora Hybrids, but *R. soulieana* has placed a very definite stamp upon it, providing us with quite a different rose. The foliage is an attractive grey-green colour, similar to that of *R. soulieana,* the growth vigorous, bushy, and rather stiff. The flowers have a wild rose charm, being single, of soft pink colouring, with a white centre and yellow stamens. They are held in close but not over-packed trusses. The fragrance is strong and typically Multiflora, and there are small orange-red hips in autumn. It will achieve about 18ft. Raised at Kew, introduced 1912. See page 130.

LYKKEFUND. A seedling from *Rosa helenae,* thought to have 'Zéphirine Drouhin' as its pollen parent. If, in fact, this is true, it is a rather interesting cross, for I know of no other rose that has the excellent 'Zéphirine' in its make up. The two roses have this much in common — they are both entirely thornless. The flowers are of medium size, semi-double, pale creamy-yellow, deeper at the centre, and tinged with pink. They are held in medium-sized clusters and soon fade to white in the hot sun. The growth is strong and bushy, probably to 10 or 15ft., the foliage a deep glossy green, with rather small leaflets. 'Lykkefund' is suitable for growing in trees, and may also be used as a large shrub. Strong fragrance. Bred by Olsen (Denmark), introduced 1930.

MOUNTAIN SNOW. Although this rose was bred at our nursery, I am ashamed to say I have no idea of its parentage. It was one of those little mysteries that are apt to occur from time to time in rose breeding, but I feel it is worth preserving. The growth is particularly robust, with plentiful dark green foliage. The flowers, which are semi-double and of medium size, are borne in large, shapely sprays, providing a cascade of pure white. It makes a good Rambler or may be used as an elegantly arching shrub. As a Climber it may be expected to reach 12 to 15ft. and 5 by 8ft. as a shrub. Introduced 1985.

PAUL'S HIMALAYAN MUSK. This is the attractive, if somewhat fanciful name for a very beautiful Rambler; indeed, to me, one of the most beautiful of all the Ramblers. It will grow to 30ft. over a pergola or into trees, making long, thin, flexible branches, trailing gracefully and hanging down from their support. Its small, dainty, fully-double, soft pink, rosette-like flowers are held in large open sprays, with each bloom held separately from the next on long, thin stems, giving a delicate, airy effect; the whole plant being garlanded with beauty in season. The light greyish-green foliage is long and pointed. Small, oval hips. First distributed by W. Paul (U.K.), date and parents unknown. See page 131.

SILVER MOON. The breeding of this rose is thought to be (*Rosa wichuraiana* x 'Devoniensis') x *R. laevigata*. It is a particularly vigorous climber, capable of 30ft., and has abundant dark, glossy foliage, inherited from *R. laevigata*. The buds are yellow, opening to form large, single or semi-double flowers of creamy-white, with a bunch of yellow stamens. These are borne in clusters, and have a strong fruit-like fragrance. It flowers in mid-June but does not repeat. Raised by Dr. W. Van Fleet (U.S.A.), introduced 1910.

TREASURE TROVE. This aptly named, self-sown seedling, was discovered in the garden of Mr. John Treasure of Burford House, Tenbury Wells, Hereford, growing beneath a plant of *Rosa filipes* 'Kiftsgate', and was

PAUL'S HIMALAYAN MUSK, *a tall and strong-growing Rambler of cherry blossom beauty.*

Above left: KEW RAMBLER, *a Boursault Rambler growing over a wall.*

Left: BLUSH BOURSAULT, *Boursault Rose. An early flowering Rambler with attractive Old Rose flowers.*

introduced in 1979. The other parent is believed to have been the Hybrid Musk Rose 'Buff Beauty', and indeed if we had been planning a yellow hybrid it would have been hard to have found a better pollen parent. 'Treasure Trove' has the vigour of 'Kiftsgate', and promises to grow to a similar size (35ft.), or at least 30ft., although it may not be quite so hardy. It flowers profusely in summer, bearing sprays of about twenty blooms which are loosely double, cupped, about 2ins. across, and have a delicious fragrance. Its colour, a warm apricot, is particularly valuable in a rose of such growth. No doubt we shall hear much more of this rose in the years to come.

UNA. The pollen parent of this rose is *Rosa canina,* the seed parent is thought to be a Tea Rose, or perhaps 'Gloire de Dijon'. The flowers are almost single, about 3ins. across, creamy-buff in the bud, opening to creamy-white, with a pleasing fragrance. They are followed by large, round hips, which have difficulty in ripening in our climate. The growth is strong, with good foliage that bears some resemblance to *R. canina.* Height 15ft. or more. Bred by George Paul (U.K.), introduced 1900.

WEDDING DAY. A seedling of *Rosa sinowilsonii,* raised by Sir Frederick Stern in 1950. The other parent is not recorded. Like *R. sinowilsonii,* 'Wedding Day' has fine, glossy foliage, although the individual leaves are smaller, but unlike *R. sinowilsonii* it is completely hardy. The growth is very strong, to at least 25ft. The flowers are single and held in large clusters which mingle with the dark foliage. They are yellow in the bud, opening to creamy-yellow, but almost immediately becoming white; the massed effect being white dotted with yellow. The petals are wedge shaped, narrow at the base, broadening to the outer edges. Its only fault is that the petals become spotted in wet weather. An ideal rose for growing in trees or to cover some unsightly object. Exceptionally fragrant.

CHAPTER 4
Hybrid Tea Roses and Floribunda Roses

Hybrid Tea Roses

The Hybrid Teas are far too well known to require any introduction here. They are to be seen in almost every garden in the land and are grown, to a greater or lesser extent, in almost every country in the world.

Although we refer to them as Modern Roses to differentiate them from the Old Roses, the Hybrid Teas have now been with us for a long time, and as early as the middle of the last century the stage was set for their arrival on the scene. There were two main classes of roses in the latter half of the nineteenth century — Hybrid Perpetuals and Tea Roses. It was the cross fertilization of these two breeds that gave us what we now call Hybrid Teas. This was in many ways a happy combination of talents. The Hybrid Perpetuals provided the hardiness, vigour, size of flower, fragrance and stronger shades of colour; while the Tea Roses brought recurrent flowering qualities together with those characteristics that they had themselves drawn from *Rosa gigantea* — the large, thick, sheeny petals which provide us with the long pointed buds that are so popular today. The Tea Roses also brought something of their own fragrance.

For a long time it was supposed that 'La France' was the first Hybrid Tea and that with its arrival a new class was born, but this was not, in fact, true. The first reliably documented rose that could be classified as a Hybrid Tea was 'Victor Verdier'. Bred by Lacharme of Lyons and introduced in 1859, it was a cross between the Hybrid Perpetual 'Jules Margottin' and the Tea Rose 'Safrano'. It is by no means impossible that there were other unrecorded crosses before this, but it was only when Guillot crossed a Hybrid Perpetual named 'Madame Victor Verdier' (not to be confused with 'Victor Verdier') with the Tea Rose 'Madame Bravy', to produce 'La France' in 1867, that people began to realise a new class of rose had arrived. Even then it was a long time before the Hybrid Teas were officially recognised in countries other than France, where they were classified under the heading *R. odorata indica*.

In Britain it was Henry Bennett who first bred Hybrid Teas. He was a farmer and cattle breeder of Stapleford, Wiltshire, and later of

Shepperton, Middlesex, who turned his attention to the rose, and I must admit to a certain fellow feeling for this man, as I myself started life as a farmer. Bennett quickly saw the possibilities of the Hybrid Teas and in a very short time bred a number of important varieties — no doubt he used his experience with livestock to good effect. He was the first to use the term Hybrid Tea or, as he put it, Pedigree Hybrids of the Tea Rose. It was Bennett and a French breeder called Jean Sisley who first applied systematic cross breeding to roses. Before this, rose breeding had been a much more haphazard affair, but Bennett and Sisley made deliberate crosses with certain objectives in view and may thus be said to be the first modern rose breeders. Unfortunately Bennett's career in this field only lasted from 1879 until his death in 1890. Even so, he is usually regarded as the father of the Hybrid Tea Rose.

The Hybrid Tea was quite different from all the roses that had preceded it. In the first place it is a bush rose, whereas previous roses had usually been true shrubs. It was designed for planting in rose beds, being about 3 to 3½ft. in height and of upright growth. With such growth, together with hard pruning, there came a remarkable ability to flower repeatedly throughout the summer — something that is hard to equal in roses of taller, more shrubby growth. No comparable garden flower can come close to it in this respect, and it is to this, more than anything else, that it owes its great popularity.

The second important difference is the formation of its flower. Interest in the Hybrid Perpetuals, which were bred primarily for the show bench, had for some time tended towards the bud-shaped flower and some, but not all, Tea Roses had flowers with pointed buds. In the Hybrid Teas the process was complete, and we have the bud-shaped flower only. The whole nature of the flower had been completely changed — a happening that must be almost unique in horticulture. Its arrival heralded what was, to all intents and purposes, a new flower. So popular was this flower, that all other types were pushed almost into oblivion.

We have had Hybrid Tea Roses now for over 120 years, although they did not fully come into their own until the turn of the century. Many thousands of varieties have been introduced in that time — far more than any other type of rose. Most of them have gone the way of all flesh and disappeared from the scene, for obviously they could not all survive and most are not worth preserving. The question is, what should we do with those earlier varieties that are still with us? Would it not be better to let them go? For the average garden, I would say 'yes'. But for those with a rather deeper interest in roses there is much to be said for retaining at least the best from the past. Certainly my experience as a commercial

A SUPERB *formal layout of Hybrid Tea and Floribunda Roses at the Royal National Rose Society's Gardens at St. Albans, U.K.*

rose grower suggests the demand is there.

In the first place, they are always of interest to the collector and those who like the antique with all its associations. More importantly, there are a number of old Hybrid Teas that earn a place in the garden on pure merit — for the beauty of their flowers and their value as garden plants. The majority of the earlier Hybrid Teas, however, do not come up to the standard of present day varieties for sheer performance. What they do have is a character of flower that is different from later introductions. Some of the first Hybrid Teas had flowers that were closer to the Old Rose formation, but it was not long before these were superseded by roses with the bud formation of the present day. Even then they were different to present day Hybrid Teas, being less heavy in all their parts and usually with lighter, more pastel shades of colour. They were, in short, often close to the Tea Rose. As the rose proceeds on its way through history it is always evolving: new species and strains are brought into its breeding, and every time this happens the rose changes. The roses of the last twenty years are different from those of the 1920s and 1930s. It is for this reason that we should retain and grow them.

On the other side of the scales, it is important to remember that these earlier varieties do not always have the vigour of their descendants. Whether they have lost it, or never had it, is a moot point. Certainly deterioration does take place. Why this should be is a matter of some speculation — it would be easy to write a chapter on this subject alone. It may be the result of a virus entering the stock, or it may be due to some form of genetic breakdown. What is rather odd is that the truly Old Roses, like the Gallicas or Albas, which may be hundreds of years old, do not seem to suffer in this way.

The selection of Hybrid Tea Roses described here represents only a small fraction of those that still survive. I cannot be sure that they are necessarily the best. They are simply those that appeal to me. I have tried to include such varieties that seem to have something to offer which is not to be found in Modern Hybrid Teas. I have also included a few single-flowered varieties, of which there were a number in the early days. They have their own particular charm and are sufficiently different from other singles to be worthy of inclusion.

Three further important developments in these roses should also be mentioned. The first was due to the work of the French breeder, Joseph Pernet-Ducher. He spent many years in the latter part of the nineteenth century in an effort to bring the uniquely brilliant yellow of R. foetida into the flowers of the Hybrid Tea Roses. His first successful variety was 'Soleil d'Or', a seedling from a rose that was itself the result of a cross between the Hybrid Perpetual 'Antoine Ducher' and *R. foetida* 'Persiana'. 'Soleil d'Or' was one of those roses that was due to make a shift in the general character of the rose. Through it came not only the first of the truly intense yellows, but a whole range of associated shades. The successors to 'Soleil d'Or' were first known as Pernetiana Roses, but gradually they were absorbed into the family of Hybrid Teas. Some of the colours produced have not been very desirable, but this development has increased the colour range of all types of roses that came after 'Soleil d'Or' and will no doubt continue to do so indefinitely.

A second development was the appearance of the colour vermilion in Hybrid Teas. This was a unique happening among roses. It was due to the occurrence in the plant of a chemical called pelargonidin, instead of the normal cyanidin. These are two of the chemicals that control the colour of the flowers.

The first Hybrid Tea to carry pelargonidin in its make up was the popular 'Super Star'. It had occurred earlier among Floribundas in a little known rose called 'Independence' in the year 1951. Before this it had appeared in two Polyantha Pompon Roses, 'Golden Salmon' and 'Gloria Mundi', both of which were sports from 'Superb'. It is extremely rare to find a chemical change of this kind and we know of no similar case in roses. The new colour, like the yellow of *R. foetida*, has had a profound effect on the character of modern roses. It has resulted in many new shades and mixtures of colour. Pure vermilion is a beautiful colour, but perhaps a little foreign to the rose, and roses of this shade should be planted with restraint. Used with care it can have value in the garden scheme.

With the arrival of the Floribundas, which we shall be discussing in the latter half of this chapter, another important shift was to take place. The Floribundas have many sterling qualities. They are, on the whole, tough, hardy and very free flowering. For this reason, breeders have mixed their genes with those of the Hybrid Teas, and this has led to an improvement in their hardiness and ability to flower freely. Unfortunately, with these improvements there has frequently been some loss of beauty in the flowers, for the Floribundas lack the character we find in the Hybrid Teas.

The present day Hybrid Teas, then, are much stronger in growth and are altogether better and more reliable performers than those of earlier days. They have better disease resistance and flower more continuously and freely than earlier varieties. Moreover their colour range has been continually extended. Unfortunately, these new colours have too often tended towards the gaudy, while the tone of colour is frequently too harsh. Such colours tend to swamp the more gentle shades and even clash with each other. Although a certain amount of nonsense is sometimes talked about the arrangement of colour in the garden, when it comes to the Modern Roses it is necessary to be very careful indeed and avoid the temptation to use the more brilliant shades too freely. A greater choice of colour makes more demands on our skill, but fortunately good colours are to be found and, if we select with care, pleasing effects can be achieved. Indeed I have recently detected a tendency towards better colours and more refined flowers. The more brilliant shades should, in my opinion, be used sparingly to highlight the others, rather than fill the garden with a continual blaze of colour which, in the end, can only become tiresome.

To achieve their full potential the Hybrid Teas require generous treatment. A mulch of farmyard manure or compost will work wonders and should be combined with the application of a balanced fertilizer in spring, and again after the first flush of flowers; if this too is organic-based, so much the better. Spraying against mildew and blackspot is desirable. Good proprietary brands of spray are available at all garden centres.

Pruning is, of course, quite different from that of Shrub Roses. In the first year, when the rose has just been planted, it is best to prune back severely to 4 to 6ins. from the soil. This will help to form the basis of a good bush. In subsequent years, prune away all weak, ageing and dead wood, and then cut back the remaining growth to perhaps 10 to 12ins. Stronger growers can be left longer. On the whole, hard pruning produces fewer but finer flowers; lighter pruning a greater quantity of flowers.

Some Older Hybrid Tea Roses

ANGÈLE PERNET. Large loosely-formed flowers of pale orange-red shaded with chrome-yellow. Shiny, bronzy-green foliage. Fragrant. Height 2ft. 'Bénédicte Seguin' x a Hybrid Tea. Bred by Pernet-Ducher (France), 1924.

ANTOINE RIVOIRE. Cupped flowers of rosy-blush colouring shaded cream, with yellow at the base of the bloom. Fragrant. A hybrid between the Tea Rose 'Dr. Grill' and the famous early Hybrid Tea 'Lady Mary Fitzwilliam'. Pernet-Ducher (France), 1895.

AUGUSTINE GUINOISSEAU ('White La France'). This is thought to be a sport from 'La France' to which it is very similar, the difference being that the flowers are white, tinted with flesh-pink. Like its parent it has globular Old Rose flower formation. Introduced by Guinoisseau (France), 1889.

BARBARA RICHARDS. Buff-yellow, the reverse of the petals being flushed

DAINTY BESS, *a fine Hybrid Tea Rose.*

with pink. Free flowering and sweetly scented. Inclined to hang its head. A. Dickson (U.K.), 1930.

BETTY UPRICHARD. Long, elegant buds opening to semi-double flowers of salmon-pink with carmine reverse. Vigorous and free-flowering, with light green foliage. Very fragrant. A. Dickson (U.K.), 1922.

COMTESSE VANDAL. A perfect bloom, with high pointed buds and delicate colouring. Salmon-pink at first, veined with gold, becoming buff-pink with yellow-flame on the outside. Slight scent. Some mildew. ('Ophelia' x 'Mrs. Aaron Ward') x 'Souvenir de Claudius Pernet'. M. Leenders (Holland), 1932.

CRIMSON GLORY. The leading crimson rose of the period immediately preceding the Second World War. The colour is deep and velvety, later becoming a pleasing purple, particularly in hot weather. It opens to a rather cupped flower with a rich fragrance. It is not very vigorous and has a spreading habit of growth. Particularly fine in its climbing form which has ample vigour. A 'Cathrine Kordes' seedling x 'W.E. Chaplin'. W. Kordes (Germany), 1935.

DAINTY BESS. A single-flowered rose and one of the finest of its class. It has large rose-pink flowers with a deeper pink on the outside and contrasting red-brown stamens. The petals are slightly fringed or cut at the edges. Light refreshing fragrance. 'Ophelia' x 'K. of K'. W.E.B. Archer (U.K.), 1925.

DAME EDITH HELEN. Large and shapely, slightly globular, very double flowers of pure glowing pink, with a rich fragrance. Bred by A. Dickson (U.K.), 1926.

DIAMOND JUBILEE. This rose, although introduced in 1947, has much in common with the earlier Hybrid Teas, for it was the result of a cross between the famous old Tea-Noisette Rose 'Maréchal Niel' and 'Feu Pernet-Ducher'. The flowers are very fine, of a lovely corn-yellow colouring, with petals of great substance and perfect formation. It has the Tea Rose fragrance of its Tea-Noisette parent. The growth is strong and hardy, but unfortunately the flowers rot in damp weather. Bred by Boerner (U.S.A.), 1947.

ELLEN WILLMOTT. A single flowered rose rather similar to 'Dainty Bess' from which it was a seedling, the result of a cross with 'Lady Hillingdon'. It has creamy flowers which are tinged with pink at the edges, with golden anthers and red filaments. The petals are attractively waved. Dark purple-tinted foliage. It does not perform quite so well as 'Dainty Bess'. Bred by Archer (U.K.), 1936.

EMMA WRIGHT. A charming little button-hole rose. It has small, perfectly formed nearly single orange-salmon buds on a dwarf plant. Glossy green foliage. McGredy (U.K.), 1918.

GEORGE DICKSON. Very large though not very full flowers of deep scarlet-crimson. The stems are rather weak, so that it tends to hang its head. Growth, strong and tall. Fragrant. A. Dickson (U.K.), 1912.

GOLDEN OPHELIA. Not a sport from 'Ophelia', as the name would suggest, but a seedling from that rose. It has perfectly formed creamy-yellow buds which deepen to yellow at the centre. B.R. Cant (U.K.), 1918.

GUSTAV GRÜNERWALD. An early Hybrid Tea with large, cupped, deep pink flowers. The growth is vigorous and reliable, with glossy, deep green foliage. It is a cross between the Tea Rose 'Safrano' and 'Madame Caroline Testout'. Bred by Lambert (Germany), 1903.

HOME SWEET HOME. Perhaps the most remarkable thing about this rose is the fact that it was ever introduced in the first place. The flowers are not large, being globular in shape and opening to a cup like an Old Rose — something quite out of line with the accepted standards of its time. It is of a particularly clear and rich rose-pink, with no trace of any other colour. The petals are short, thick and velvety and there is a rich fragrance. A small but healthy bush. Bred by Wood & Ingram (U.K.), introduced 1941.

IRISH BRIGHTNESS. Single flowers of cerise-crimson with a pleasing fragrance. Date and breeding not known. Bred by A. Dickson (U.K.).

IRISH ELEGANCE. This is one of a number of single roses from A. Dickson of Northern Ireland, most of which bear the prefix 'Irish'. It has long, slim buds opening to quite substantial deep pink flowers shaded with gold. Bronze-green foliage. Slightly fragrant. Introduced 1905.

IRISH FIREFLAME. Single orange and gold flowers veined with crimson, and with attractive light fawn-coloured anthers. Fragrant. A. Dickson (U.K.), 1914.

ISOBEL. Slightly cupped single flowers of delicate rose-pink flushed with yellow at the centre. Vigorous growth. Slight fragrance. McGredy (U.K.), 1916.

JOSEPHINE BRUCE. Although this rose has its weaknesses it is still planted quite widely. The reason is to be found in the purity of its deep rich crimson colouring — a purity which has been largely lost in the crimson roses of today. It has fair vigour, the growth being broad rather than upright with the branches coming out at an angle. This makes it an ideal rose for a standard. Rich fragrance. Somewhat susceptible to mildew. 'Crimson Glory' x 'Madge Whipp'. Bred by Bees (U.K.), 1949.

K. OF K. Named after Kitchener of Khartoum. Bright crimson-scarlet flowers opening semi-double with about ten petals. A strong bush that blooms with exceptional continuity, providing a brilliant effect. A. Dickson (U.K.), 1917.

LADY ALICE STANLEY. Large open flowers with many petals of silvery-pink, deeper pink reverse. Free, branching growth and leathery green foliage. Fragrant. McGredy (U.K.), 1909.

LADY BARNBY. Shapely, highly-scented buds of clear glowing pink shaded with red. Bushy growth. Fragrant. Bred by A. Dickson (U.K.), 1930.

LADY BELPER. Large, rather globular flowers opening to a cup shape. Bronze-orange shaded with light orange. Fragrant. Dark, glossy foliage. 'Mrs. G.A. Van Rossem' x a seedling. Bred by Verschuren (Holland), 1948.

LADY FORTEVIOT. Large high-centred buds varying from golden-yellow to deep apricot. Glossy bronzy-green foliage. Fragrant. B.R. Cant (U.K.), 1928.

Left: LA FRANCE, *one of the older Hybrid Tea Roses.*

Right: MRS. OAKLEY FISHER, *a good single-flowered Hybrid Tea Rose.*

LADY SYLVIA. A sport from 'Madame Butterfly'. Discovered by Stevens (U.K.), 1926. See 'Ophelia' below.

LA FRANCE. This famous rose is one of the earliest Hybrid Teas. Its origins are not known for certain but Guillot, who bred it in 1867, was of the opinion that it was probably a hybrid of the Tea Rose 'Madame Falcot'. It is still a worthwhile rose, although it is said to have lost some of its vigour. The blooms are full petalled and of globular Old Rose formation, remaining so until the petals fall. The colour is a silvery-pink with a rose-pink reverse. The flowers are richly fragrant. A climbing sport is also available.

MADAME ABEL CHATENAY. Another historic Hybrid Tea and, to me, still one of the most beautiful, retaining much of the charm of a Tea Rose at its best. Raised by Pernet-Ducher and introduced in 1895, it is the result of a cross between the Tea Rose 'Dr. Grill' and the Hybrid Tea 'Victor Verdier'. The flowers are of a charming scrolled bud formation, pale pink in colour, deepening towards the centre, the reverse side of the petals being a deeper pink. An exquisite rose that seems to retain its vigour. Delicious fragrance. There is a climbing sport but, rather unusually amongst early Hybrid Teas, this is not particularly vigorous.

LADY SYLVIA, *a Hybrid Tea Rose which is a colour sport of 'Ophelia'.'*

MADAME BUTTERFLY. Discovered by Hill (U.S.A.), 1918. See 'Ophelia' below.

MRS. OAKLEY FISHER. One of the most beautiful of the single-flowered Hybrid Tea Roses, with neatly outlined deep orange-yellow flowers. These are delicately poised in small clusters on a branching bush of reasonable vigour. The foliage is bronzy-green and there is a light, pleasing fragrance. B.R. Cant (U.K.), 1921. See page 142.

MRS. SAM MCGREDY. A popular rose of the 1930s and 1940s. Its modern but pleasing colouring is coppery-orange flushed with scarlet that tones in nicely with its glossy, coppery-red foliage. The flowers are not large and have shapely, high centred, clean-cut buds that last well. The growth is branching and of moderate vigour. This rose is perhaps better grown in its more vigorous climbing form. Fragrant. ('Donald Macdonald' x 'Golden Emblem') x (seedling x 'The Queen Alexandra Rose'). McGredy (U.K.), 1929.

OPHELIA, (including 'Madame Butterfly', 'Lady Sylvia' and 'Westfield Star'). It is convenient to discuss these four varieties together, as the last three are all colour sports of the first. More than others, these roses set the ideal for perfect Hybrid Tea buds. These are not large but are of exquisitely scrolled formation; indeed, for perfection of Hybrid Tea form, they have few rivals even today. They differ only in the colour of the flowers: 'Ophelia' is blush pink, 'Madame Butterfly' is a slightly deeper shade and 'Lady Sylvia' is blush suffused with apricot. In all three the colour deepens a little towards the centre to give the most delicate effect. 'Westfield Star' is creamy-white. Although they do not form large bushes — they are rather slender and grow to about 2½ft. in height — all are reliable growers. The foliage is neat and of a greyish-green colour. All four have a delicious fragrance and are first-class as cut flowers. With the exception of 'Westfield Star' each has excellent climbing sports and, as is so often the case with old Hybrid Teas, this may be the best way to grow them. See Chapter 2.

The origin of 'Ophelia' is a mystery. It was introduced by Arthur Paul of Waltham Cross in 1912. Paul was unable to say where it came from, though thought it arrived with a consignment of 'Antoine Rivoire' he had bought from Pernet-Ducher in 1909. It was probably a seedling that had been included by mistake. The French firm should, therefore, share the credit, even though it must have failed to realise the true worth of the variety. It attracted little attention at the time but, eventually, both it and its sports became some of the most popular roses ever introduced and they are still in demand. It is interesting to note that 'Ophelia' was responsible for no less than thirty-six sports in all; this must be some kind of record. See page 146.

PICTURE. A dainty and much loved button-hole rose, with small perfectly formed buds of a clear velvety rose-pink with reflexing petals. These are produced on a short, free flowering bush. Height 2½ ft. Slight fragrance. McGredy (U.K.), 1932. See page 147.

POLLY. Long, elegantly formed buds of cream with gold at the base, paling with age. Fragrant. 'Ophelia' x 'Madame Colette Martinet'. Beckwith (U.K.), 1927.

SHOT SILK. Once much prized for its colour effect: cerise-pink shot with orange, shading to lemon deep in the centre. Glossy green foliage. Fragrant. A. Dickson (U.K.), 1924.

SOLEIL D'OR. This is one of the most important varieties in the history of garden roses, and I have already given a few details on its origins in the introduction to this class. The rose itself has considerable beauty, being in the Old Rose style, cupped, opening rather flat and of an attractive orange-yellow shade with a hint of red. The growth is upright and has some of the appearance of the 'Persian Yellow'. Unfortunately, it is so subject to blackspot that it is doubtful whether it should be grown. If it is, it will require continual spraying. Bred by Pernet-Ducher (France), introduced 1900.

SOUVENIR DE MADAME BOULLET. Long, pointed buds of deep yellow. Spreading habit of growth. 'Sunburst' x unnamed variety. Bred by Pernet-Ducher (France), introduced 1921.

SOUVENIR DU PRÉSIDENT CARNOT. Exquisite buds of delicate flesh-pink shading to shell-pink at the centre. Fragrant. Unnamed seedling x 'Lady Mary Fitzwilliam'. Pernet-Ducher (France), 1894.

THE DOCTOR. This rose has exceptionally long narrow petals resulting in long, pointed buds of unusual character and large satiny-pink blooms. Rather short growth for such a large flower. It has a particularly strong and unusual fragrance. 'Mrs. J.D. Eisele' x 'Los Angeles'. Bred by F.H. Howard (U.S.A.), 1936.

VESUVIUS. A large single rose with long pointed buds opening to velvety-crimson flowers. McGredy (U.K.), 1923.

OPHELIA, *Hybrid Tea Rose.*　　　　WHITE WINGS, *Hybrid Tea Rose.*

VIOLINISTA COSTA. A typically modern flower, opening carmine-red and becoming strawberry-pink shaded with orange. This is a reliable rose by any standards, with vigorous, branching growth and glossy green foliage. It retains its place among Modern Roses for its ability to produce an unfailing mass of bloom 'Sensation' x 'Shot Silk'. Camprubi, 1936.

WESTFIELD STAR. A sport from 'Ophelia', with perfectly formed creamy-white flowers. Still one of the better white Hybrid Teas. Discovered by Morse (U.K.), 1922. See 'Ophelia' above.

WHITE WINGS. One of the most beautiful of the single Hybrid Teas. Long buds opening to large pure white flowers with conspicuous chocolate-coloured anthers. Dark green foliage. A healthy bush, but it may require a little time to establish itself. Height 4ft. A cross between 'Dainty Bess' and an unnamed seedling. Bred by Krebs (U.S.A.), introduced 1947.

PICTURE, *a dainty Hybrid Tea Rose with perfectly formed buds.*

Modern Hybrid Tea Roses

ADOLF HORSTMANN. Very large full flowers of a yellow that tends a little towards bronze. The growth is tall, robust and healthy. Little scent. Height 3½ft. 'Königin der Rosen' x 'Dr. A.J. Verhage'. R. Kordes (Germany), 1971.

ALEC'S RED. One of the most reliable red roses. It is vigorous, free flowering and repeats well. The flowers are large and tend towards a globular shape. Their colour is cherry-red but with a rather purplish tinge, making them perhaps a little dull. It has a powerful fragrance for which it was awarded the Edland Medal of the Royal National Rose Society. The growth is upright, with healthy, medium green, slightly glossy foliage. Height 3ft. 'Fragrant Cloud' x 'Dame de Coeur'. Cocker (U.K.), 1970.

ALEXANDER ('Alexandra'). Similar to its parent 'Super Star', but of an even brighter shade of vermilion, and taller and stronger, being about 4ft. in height. It must have one of the most brilliant and luminous colours to be found in roses. Slight fragrance. 'Super Star' x ('Anne Elizabeth' x 'Allgold'). Harkness (U.K.), 1972. See page 151.

ALPINE SUNSET. Exceptionally large, very full flowers of cream, flushed peach-pink on the inside of the petals. Glossy foliage. Very fragrant. Healthy, vigorous, upright growth. 'Grandpa Dickson' x 'Dr. A.J. Verhage'. Bred by Roberts (U.K.), introduced 1973.

APRICOT SILK. This is not the most robust of roses, being more subject to blackspot than some, but it is one of the most beautiful of its colour. It has elegant buds in an attractive shade of apricot and the petals have a silky texture. Glossy, bronze-tinted foliage. Height 4ft. A seedling from 'Souvenir de Jacques Verschuren' x unnamed variety. Bred by Gregory (U.K.), 1965.

BEAUTÉ. Particularly fine, long slender buds of apricot-yellow, opening to a rather loosely formed flower. The growth is bushy, not very strong, but free flowering. There is only a slight fragrance. Glossy, dark green foliage. Height 2½ft. 'Madame Joseph Perraud' x unnamed seedling. Bred by Mallerin (France), 1953.

BETTINA. Nicely shaped orange-coloured flowers, the petals being attractively veined with copper and shading to gold at the base. This is an attractive rose but of only moderate vigour. It may require protection from blackspot. Little scent. Glossy, bronze-tinted foliage. Height 2½ft.

The breeding is 'Peace' x '(Madame Joseph Perraud' x 'Demain'). Bred by Meilland (France), 1953.

BLACK BEAUTY. Popular for its exceptionally deep garnet-red colouring which, unlike most dark roses, seems to survive well in the sun. It is free flowering and bushy, but only slightly fragrant. Height 3ft. ('Gloire de Rome' x 'Impeccable') x 'Papa Meilland'. Delbard (France), 1973.

BLESSINGS. A reliable, prolific and continuous flowering variety of soft pink colouring. The blooms are not large, rather loosely formed, with only a slight scent. It is an ideal bedding rose, with strong, upright, branching growth. Healthy, medium green foliage. Height 3ft. The result of a cross between 'Queen Elizabeth' and an unnamed seedling. Bred and introduced by Gregory (U.K.), 1967. See page 162.

BLUE MOON. The Old Roses, particularly the Gallicas, have provided us with flowers in beautiful shades of purple, lilac and mauve. The Hybrid Tea has never been able to do this. 'Blue Moon' is, of course, not blue, its flowers being of a silvery-lilac or perhaps lilac-pink shade. This colour cannot be said to be pleasing for it is altogether too dead and metallic. Nonetheless, it is certainly the best Hybrid Tea of this colour group. It has medium sized flowers of shapely, high centred form with a strong lemony fragrance. Its growth and disease resistance are satisfactory. Foliage medium green and glossy. Height 3ft. It is said that one of its parents was 'Sterling Silver', but we do not know the other. Bred by Tantau (Germany), 1964. See page 150.

BLUE PARFUM. Another rose that, like 'Blue Moon', is far from being blue. Blush-mauve would be nearer to the correct shade. The flowers are large and very fragrant with ovoid shaped buds. The foliage is dark green and glossy. Height 3ft. Bred by Tantau (Germany), 1978.

BONSOIR. Large, full, shapely peach-pink flowers with deeper shading. The growth is quite vigorous and upright, with large, glossy, deep green leaves. Moderate fragrance. The blooms can be damaged by rain. Height 3ft. Bred by A. Dickson (U.K.), 1968.

BUCCANEER. This rose is now dropping out of catalogues, but we retain it for its long, narrow, slightly arching, almost shrub-like growth, which makes it suitable for positions farther back in the border. The flowers are medium sized, of a bright, clear and unfading yellow, pointed at first and opening to an urn shape. Height 4ft. Good, healthy, medium green, matt foliage. Fragrant. Breeding 'Golden Rapture' x ('Max Krause' x 'Captain Thomas'). Bred by Swim (U.S.A.), 1952.

Left: BLUE MOON, *the most reliable of the lilac Hybrid Tea Roses.*

Right: CHAMPION, *a large-flowered Hybrid Tea Rose.*

CHAMPION. As the name suggests, this variety has exceptionally large flowers, their colour being cream and gold heavily flushed with pink. They are borne on a strong and healthy bush. It may be it could be used to a good effect by the flower arranger, where one or two really big' blooms are required. Strong fragrance. Height 2½ft. 'Grandpa Dickson' x 'Whisky Mac'. Bred by Fryer (U.K.), introduced 1976.

CHESHIRE LIFE. Large, well formed flowers of vermilion-orange. Strong, bushy growth of medium height, with ample, dark, leathery foliage. One of the best of its colour, but with little fragrance. A good bedding rose. Height 2½ft. 'Prima Ballerina' x 'Princess Michiko'. Fryer (U.K.), 1972.

CHICAGO PEACE. A colour sport from 'Peace', see page 161, to which it is similar in every way except for the fact that the flowers are phlox-pink shading to canary-yellow at the base. Otherwise it has all the virtues of its parent. Large, glossy foliage. Healthy, vigorous growth. Slight fragrance. Height 3½ to 5ft. Discovered by Johnston (U.S.A.), 1962.

CHRYSLER IMPERIAL. Large, well formed flowers of velvety-scarlet with a paler reverse, but with little scent. The growth is tall, about 4ft. in

ALEXANDER, *a brilliantly coloured Hybrid Tea Rose.*

height, with medium green foliage. Some mildew. 'Charlotte Armstrong' x 'Mirandy'. Bred by Dr. W.E. Lammerts (U.S.A.).

DIORAMA. Large, apricot-yellow flowers that become flushed with pink as they open. The growth is vigorous and branching, making it a good bedding rose. It flowers particularly well in the autumn. Height 3ft. Fragrant. 'Peace' x 'Beauté'. Bred by de Ruiter (Holland), 1965.

DORIS TYSTERMAN. Shapely, medium-sized flowers of coppery-orange, freely produced on a vigorous, bushy, upright plant with glossy bronze-tinted foliage. A good bedding rose. Little fragrance. Height 3ft. 'Peer Gynt' x unnamed seedling. Wisbech Plant Co. (U.K.), 1975. See page 159.

DUTCH GOLD. Large, unfading golden-yellow flowers with a strong fragrance. The growth is vigorous and upright, with good healthy medium green foliage. Height about 3ft. 'Peer Gynt' x 'Whisky Mac'. Wisbech Plant Co. (U.K.), 1978.

ELIZABETH HARKNESS. For me one of the most beautiful of the more recent Hybrid Teas. It has large flowers of shapely spiral formation, and its colour is ivory-white delicately touched with pink and amber. It can be affected by damp weather but, at its best, it produces buds of pristine perfection. The growth is upright, bushy, of medium height and strength, with medium green foliage. Light fragrance. It is particularly fine when grown under glass. Height 2½ft. The breeding rather surprisingly is 'Red Dandy' x 'Piccadilly'. Raised by Harkness (U.K.), introduced 1969.

ERNEST H. MORSE. An extremely strong and healthy red rose with large, dark green foliage. It is in fact one of the most reliable of all red Hybrid Teas – its only fault being that its colour soon becomes rather dull. It has a strong fragrance. Height 3ft. Kordes (Germany), 1965.

EVENING STAR. Large flowers of pure white which seem to resist the damp better than most white roses. Good fragrance. The growth is vigorous and upright, with healthy, dark green foliage. 'White Masterpiece' x 'Saratoga'. Bred by Warriner (U.S.A.), 1974.

FANTAN. Not a typical Hybrid Tea, nor is it very widely grown but I include it for its cupped flowers and unusual burnt-orange colouring. It is of moderate vigour. Slight fragrance. Height 2½ft. ('Pigalle' x 'Prélude'), self fertilized. Meilland (France), 1959.

FRAGRANT CLOUD ('Duftwolke'). Large flowers, coral-scarlet at first, taking on smoky overtones as they develop, and becoming a purplish-red as they fade, particularly in hot weather. The growth is strong and bushy, about 3½ ft. in height, with plenty of large leaves. Free flowering and continuous. It lives up to its name with its strong fragrance. Occasional mildew. Unnamed seedling x 'Prima Ballerina'. Tantau (Germany), 1963.

GAIL BORDEN. Large flowers tending towards a globular shape, the colour being rose-pink on the inside of the petals and pale gold on the reverse. Ample large, leathery foliage. This is a reliable rose — prolific in flower and vigorous in growth. Height 3ft. Slight fragrance. 'Mevrouw H.A. Verschuren' x 'Viktoria Adelheid'. Bred by Kordes (Germany), 1956.

GRACE DE MONACO. This rose is now rarely listed in catalogues, but we continue to grow it for its large, warm, rose-pink blooms. These are full and rather globular in shape, and have a very strong fragrance. The growth is tall and angular. 'Peace' x 'Michéle Meilland'. Meilland (France), 1956.

GRANDPA DICKSON ('Irish Gold'). Large and perfectly formed flowers of pale yellow colouring, though the growth is rather short and the foliage too sparse for their size. However, it is a good bedding rose and repeats very well. It requires good soil and cultivation if it is to give of its best. Slight fragrance. Height 3ft. ('Perfecta' x 'Governador Braga da Cruz') x 'Piccadilly'. Dickson (U.K.), 1966. See page 167.

GREAT NEWS. Large blooms of rich plum-purple, the petals being silver on the reverse side — a pleasing colour effect, and one that is entirely new to the Hybrid Tea. The growth is of medium strength, but it flowers freely and has a strong perfume. Height 2½ ft. Breeding 'Rose Gaujard' x 'City of Hereford'. Le Grice (U.K.), 1973.

HARRY WHEATCROFT. This rose was named after one of the great characters of the rose world who, up to the time of his death, was as well known to the public as a pop star. He also brought some of the best foreign Hybrid Teas and Floribundas to this country. It is a good choice to bear his name as it is unlikely to be superseded for a very long time. A sport from 'Piccadilly', see page 164, it has most of the qualities of that rose. The difference is that the outside of the petals is yellow, while the inside is red striped with yellow. Such colour effects are uncommon among Old Roses, but very rare indeed among Hybrid Teas. Slight fragrance. Height 2½ ft. Introduced by Harry Wheatcroft & Sons (U.K.), 1972.

HONEY FAVORITE. A sport of 'Pink Favorite', see page 164, with all the excellent practical qualities of that rose, but with flowers of pale saffron

PINK FAVORITE, *one of the most reliable of all Hybrid Tea Roses.*

SAVOY HOTEL, *a charming Hybrid Tea Rose with perfectly formed flowers.*

ROYAL WILLIAM, *a really good red Hybrid Tea Rose.*

yellow lightly suffused with pink. It is surprising that although 'Pink Favorite' has always been widely grown, this rose is seldom seen, in spite of the fact that reliable yellow roses are more difficult to come by. Height 2½ to 3ft. Excellent disease resistance. Discovered by Von Abrams (U.S.A.), 1962.

JOHN WATERER. Large, well formed flowers of a deep, rich, unfading crimson. Here, as so often happens, we have a red Hybrid Tea with little fragrance. This apart, it is one of the best of its colour. Its growth is strong and upright with dark green, disease-resistant foliage. Height 2½ft. 'King of Hearts' x 'Hanne'. McGredy (U.K.), 1970.

JULIA'S ROSE. A rose of unique colouring. This is usually described as a mixture of copper and parchment, but I find it hard to give an exact impression; perhaps it is more parchment than copper. Its nicely shaped buds open to rounded flowers. The growth is not very strong. Slight scent. Height 2½ to 3ft. Named for Miss Julia Clements. 'Blue Moon' x 'Dr. A.J. Verhage'. Raised by Wisbech Plant Co. (U.K.), 1976.

JUST JOEY. Elegant pointed buds of a coppery-fawn colour, with attractively waved petals which pale a little towards the edges, the flowers remaining pleasing to the end. The growth is spreading and of medium strength, with dark green matt foliage. Quite healthy. Height 2½ft. Fragrant. 'Fragrant Cloud' x 'Dr. A.J. Verhage'. Raised by Cants (U.K.), 1972. See page 167.

KING'S RANSOM. For a long time this variety was the most popular deep yellow Hybrid Tea. There may be better varieties coming along, but it is still a good rose and is easily obtainable. It has well formed, high-centred flowers of medium size, whose colour does not fade and which are freely produced. Light fragrance. The foliage is dark green, glossy and abundant. It is not really happy on light or poor soil, where it requires careful cultivation. Height 3ft. 'Golden Masterpiece' x 'Lydia'. Bred by Morey (U.S.A.), 1961.

KRONENBOURG ('Flaming Peace'). A sport from 'Peace' which occurred at McGredy's Nurseries, then in Northern Ireland. 'Peace' is yellow, but in this variety the colour has become a rich crimson on the inside of the petals, the outside remaining the same yellow as its parent. The overall effect is predominantly a rich crimson which quickly turns to purple, varying considerably according to weather conditions: in cool weather it can be magnificently rich; in hot weather it becomes a not unpleasing dusky purple. It is interesting to note how a change of colour can alter the whole character of a rose — the heavy blooms of this rose being perhaps better suited to the crimson colouring. In all other respects it is similar to its redoubtable parent. Height 4ft. 1965.

LAKELAND. Very large full-petalled, shapely blooms of soft shell-pink, with a slight fragrance. It is fairly vigorous, with branching growth and medium green foliage. Healthy. Height 2½ft. 'Fragrant Cloud' x 'Queen Elizabeth'. Bred by Fryer (U.K.), 1976.

L'OREAL TROPHY. An orange-salmon coloured sport from 'Alexander', with all the health and strength of that variety — useful attributes in roses of this colour, which are not notable for these virtues. Height 4ft. When used for flower arrangements, it is suggested this rose and its parent 'Alexander' are best cut when quite young and before the outer petals separate. Discovered by Harkness (U.K.), 1980.

MADAME LOUIS LAPERRIÈRE. I would place this variety very high on any list of deep red Hybrid Teas. It is particularly good as a bedding rose; its growth is short and bushy, sending up numerous base shoots; it flowers very freely and continuously — well into autumn. The individual blooms are quite short in the petal which means that the buds are rather globular, though still attractive. The flowers are of medium size and have a rich fragrance. Medium green foliage. Good disease resistance. Height 2½ft. 'Crimson Glory' x unnamed seedling. Laperrière (France), 1951.

MAESTRO. For some time Sam McGredy has been producing what he has called 'hand-painted' roses. These are bicoloured, with one colour splashed upon another, and are usually Floribundas. This is the first of his Hybrid Teas of this kind. The background is crimson which is delicately flecked and edged with white, giving very much the same effect we find in Old Roses. It has good bushy growth of about 2½ft. in height. Introduced in 1981.

MESSAGE ('White Knight'). A beautiful rose, with shapely flowers of pure white, the buds being tinted with green at first. Unfortunately it is not a strong grower and is subject to mildew. Slightly fragrant. Height 2½ft. Its breeding is ('Virgo' x 'Peace') x 'Virgo'. Meilland (France), 1956.

MICHÉLE MEILLAND. Although this rose is now seldom found in catalogues, I regard it as one of the most pleasing of modern Hybrid Teas. It has quite small flowers with exquisitely shaped buds of soft pink, flushed with salmon and amber as they open, deepening towards the centre. They are borne on a branching bush of about 2½ft. in height, with light green matt foliage and hardly any thorns. Slightly fragrant. Good disease resistance. Cross between 'Joanna Hill' and 'Peace'. Bred by F. Meilland (France), 1945. See page 158.

MICHÉLE MEILLAND, *a most pleasing modern Hybrid Tea.*

DORIS TYSTERMAN, *a reliable Hybrid Tea Rose with shapely flowers of attractive modern colouring.*

159

MISCHIEF. Medium-sized flowers of pointed formation, their colour being pink tinted with coral. This is a vigorous medium-sized, compact bush with ample light green foliage. Ideal for bedding. Slight fragrance. Height 2½ft. 'Peace' x 'Spartan'. McGredy (U.K.), 1961.

MISTER LINCOLN. A deep velvety crimson rose of strong fragrance, the result of a cross between 'Chrysler Imperial' and 'Charles Mallerin'. Its growth leaves something to be desired, being rather straggly with poor foliage, but its fragrance and colour make it very worth while. The buds are nicely formed, opening to rather cup-shaped flowers exposing their golden stamens. Height 3½ft. Swim & Weeks (U.S.A.), 1964.

MOJAVE. A beautiful and unusual rose, with very tightly scrolled buds. The flowers are not large, orange-pink in colour, attractively veined with orange-red. It forms an upright bush of medium vigour, with medium green glossy foliage. Slight scent. Height 3ft. 'Charlotte Armstrong' x 'Signora'. Bred by W.C. Swim (U.S.A.), 1954.

MULLARD JUBILEE. Very large, full, deep pink blooms on a vigorous bushy plant of medium height. Dark green foliage. Fragrant. Height 2½ft. 'Paddy McGredy' x 'Prima Ballerina'. McGredy (U.K.), 1970.

NATIONAL TRUST. It is interesting to compare this rose with 'Mister Lincoln' or 'Papa Meilland'. It has all the virtues required of a Hybrid Tea: stiff, upright growth, ample dark green disease-resistant foliage and good repeat flowering. The flowers are of the required spiral formation and of a bright unfading crimson, but lack fragrance, and there is something almost mechanical in the general appearance of this variety, both in flower and growth. The secret lies perhaps in its parentage, which is 'Evelyn Fison' x 'King of Hearts'. It is thus a cross between a Floribunda and a Hybrid Tea, and that cannot but affect the whole character of the rose. What we gain in productivity and efficiency, we can lose in character. This rose illustrates very well the remarks I made in the introduction to this class. Height 2½ft. McGredy (U.K.), 1970.

PAPA MEILLAND. Here we have one of the most perfect crimson Hybrid Tea Roses: the colour is rich and of remarkable purity, the flowers well formed, and there is a delicious perfume. Up to this point it is everything a red rose should be. Unfortunately there is a snag — it has very poor growth. We have to make the choice between a perfect flower and reliable constitution. If you decide to grow this variety, it is essential you treat it generously. Very fragrant. Height 2½ft. 'Chrysler Imperial' x 'Charles Mallerin'. A. Meilland (France), 1963.

PASCALI. This variety has for some time been regarded as being the best white Hybrid Tea. It is a cross between 'Queen Elizabeth' and 'White Butterfly', the former having passed on some of her strong growth as well as disease resistance, and in this respect it is unusual among white roses of this class. Although 'Queen Elizabeth' does not have flowers of classic bud shape, many of its progeny do and, as this rose's other parent was a hybrid of 'Madame Butterfly', it is not altogether surprising that 'Pascali' is a beautifully formed rose. The flowers are not very large and have an appearance of delicate refinement. Although they give the impression of being pure white, there is a barely noticeable tinge of pink in their make up. It is free flowering, but has only a moderate fragrance. Height 2½ ft. Bred by Lens (Belgium), introduced 1963. See page 163.

PAUL SHIRVILLE. A beautiful rose of elegant bud formation, with delicate apricot and peach-pink colouring. Good spreading growth with plenty of foliage, making it suitable for the mixed border. It has a strong fragrance, for which it was awarded the Edland Medal. Height 3ft. A cross between the Climbing Rose 'Compassion', which probably gives it its excellent habit of growth, and 'Mischief'. Harkness (U.K.), 1983. See page 162.

PEACE ('Gloria Dei', 'Madame A. Meilland'). This is probably the most popular and widely grown rose ever bred. It is, in fact, the only rose to have had a book written about it — For the Love of a Rose by Antonia Ridge. Its influence on the development of the Hybrid Tea Rose has been enormous, not only as a parent, but also as a standard set for roses that came after it. To my way of thinking this influence has not always been for the best, and has led to a much coarser bloom. One thing is certain: it is a rose of exceptional vigour, being both tall and branching. In fact, it will form an excellent specimen shrub growing to about 4ft. in height, taller with light pruning. The foliage is large, healthy, glossy, of deep green colouring and seldom affected by disease. The flowers are very large and full, yellow flushed with pink, paling with age. They are produced freely both in early summer and autumn, with frequent flowers in between, and are not without beauty, being heavy and rather globular. 'Peace' was bred by Meilland in France and first budded in 1936. By the time it was ready for distribution the Second World War had started, though buds had already been sent to the United States. After the War it was distributed in the States under the very appropriate name by which we now know it and was an instant success. In France it is known as 'Madame A. Meilland'. Its rather complicated parentage is as follows: ('George Dickson' x 'Souvenir de Claudius Pernet') x ('Joanna Hill' x 'Charles P. Kilhan') x 'Margaret McGredy'. Meilland (France), 1945.

PAUL SHIRVILLE, *Hybrid Tea Rose.*   PRISTINE, *Hybrid Tea Rose.*

BLESSINGS, *a reliable and prolific Modern Hybrid Tea.*

PASCALI, *the best white Hybrid Tea Rose.*

PEAUDOUCE. A beautiful and refined rose in the best Hybrid Tea tradition, with perfect bud formation, the colour being ivory-white itensifying to lemon at the centre. The growth is bushy, about 3ft. in height, with plentiful foliage of mid- to dark green. Breeding 'Nana Mouskouri' x 'Lolita'. Dicksons (Northern Ireland), introduced 1985. See page 166.

PEER GYNT. A strong growing, bushy rose of medium height. The flowers are of large size, bright yellow, lightly flushed with pink towards the edges, and of a rather globular shape, opening to form an attractive cupped bloom. The flowers are produced with unusual continuity, usually in clusters. Healthy, glossy, dark green foliage. Only slight fragrance. 'Colour Wonder' x 'Golden Giant'. Bred by Kordes (Germany), 1968.

PICCADILLY. A scarlet and yellow bicolour; scarlet on the inside of the petals and yellow on the reverse, becoming suffused with orange as the flower ages. The blooms are medium sized and fairly full, with a slight scent. The growth is strong and branching, with glossy, bronze-tinted foliage. Height 2½ft. 'McGredy's Yellow' x 'Karl Herbst'. McGredy (U.K.), 1959.

PINK FAVORITE. The result of a cross between the Hybrid Tea Rose 'Juno' and a seedling that was itself a cross between the Hybrid Perpetual 'Georg Arends' and the repeat-flowering climber 'New Dawn'. This most unusual combination has resulted in one of the strongest, most reliable and disease free of all the Hybrid Teas. Unfortunately the flowers, although large and well formed, are lacking in character, and its rose-pink colouring rather lifeless. The foliage is glossy and dark green, the growth branching. This said, there can be few Hybrid Teas better suited for use in a difficult site. Little scent. Height 2½ to 3ft. Bred by Von Abrams (U.S.A.), 1956. See page 154.

PINK PEACE. Not a sport from 'Peace' as the name seems to suggest, and it has little resemblance to that rose. It does, however, have something of the same robust and reliable constitution. The flowers are a deep rose-pink in colour, large and full and of cupped formation, with a good scent. It has healthy, bronze-tinted foliage and vigorous, upright growth of 3½ft. in height. It is interesting to note that the breeder, Meilland, has returned to the Old Hybrid Perpetual 'Mrs. John Laing' for part of its parentage, the breeding being ('Peace' x 'Monique') x ('Peace' x 'Mrs. John Laing'). Introduced 1957.

POLAR STAR. A comparatively new white rose that promises to become popular. The flowers are quite large and of perfect high-centred form but with little fragrance. The foliage is dark green and the growth vigorous, to about 3 or 3½ft. in height. Bred by Tantau (Germany), introduced 1982.

POT OF GOLD. Fragrant, well formed, small to medium-size flowers of clear yellow colouring. It is very free flowering, usually in large sprays, with strong bushy growth and plentiful glossy foliage. The height is about 2½ft. which makes it an ideal bedding rose. 'Eurorose' x 'Whisky Mac'. Raised by Dickson (U.K.), 1980.

PRECIOUS PLATINUM ('Red Star', 'Opa Potschke'). The outstanding characteristic of this rose is the sheer brilliance of its crimson colouring. The flowers are of medium size, the foliage plentiful and glossy, and its vigorous and bushy growth makes it a first class bedding rose. Fragrant. Height 3ft. 'Red Planet' x 'Franklin Engelmann'. Dickson (U.K.), 1974.

PRIMA BALLERINA ('Première Ballerine'). For a long time this was considered to be the best pink Hybrid Tea, and it is still high on the list. The blooms are of medium size, beautifully shaped in the early stages, with a strong fragrance. The growth is vigorous, upright and about 3ft. in height. It has healthy, dark, glossy foliage. Bred by Tantau (Germany) from a seedling by 'Peace', 1958. See page 170.

PRISTINE. Large shapely blooms of ivory-white, delicately flushed with pink and held upon a tall bush against contrasting large dark green leaves which set them off beautifully. It has good, robust leafy growth of 3ft. in height. Strongly fragrant. A cross between 'White Masterpiece' and 'First Prize'. Bred by Warren (U.S.A.), 1978. See page 162.

RED DEVIL ('Coeur d'Amour'). Exceptionally large blooms of rosy-scarlet, the reverse of the petals being a lighter shade. These are of a perfect high-centred formation, and are much valued by exhibitors, though unfortunately they are easily damaged by rain. Strong, bushy growth, with healthy, dark green, glossy foliage. Powerful fragrance. Height 3½ft. 'Silver Lining' x 'Prima Ballerina'. Dickson (U.K.), 1967.

ROSE GAUJARD. A reliable and easily grown rose with strong, spreading growth and dark green, glossy foliage. The flowers are large, carmine-pink on the inside of the petals and a contrasting silvery-white on the outside. They are of globular shape, produced freely, but have little fragrance. A cross between 'Peace' and a seedling from 'Opera'. Bred by Gaujard (France), 1957.

ROYAL WILLIAM (Korzaun). There is always a shortage of really good red varieties and this is true of whatever class we consider. It seems that they either have good colour and scent and are weak in growth, or that the reverse is true. Among the Hybrid Teas, 'Royal William' seems to be

PEAUDOUCE. *The pale primrose yellow colouring illustrates a new tendency towards softer colours among Hybrid Tea Roses.*

WHISKY MAC, *a popular Hybrid Tea Rose.*

Left: JUST JOEY, *a Hybrid Tea Rose with long elegant buds.*

Right: GRANDPA DICKSON, *a Hybrid Tea Rose with giant flowers.*

167

the exception. It has excellent, hardy and vigorous growth with good foliage, while at the same time the flowers are very fine and of a good rich crimson. They also have a strong fragrance. Height 3ft. Kordes (Germany), 1987. See page 155.

SAVOY HOTEL (Harvintage). A charming rose of gentle shell-pink colouring. Its flowers are perfectly formed and the petals have a delicate luminosity. An ideal bedding rose of short and even growth — perhaps rather too short and even to be an ideal border plant. Apart from its other virtues, it is an excellent long-lasting cut rose. Fragrant. Height 3ft. Bred by Harkness (U.K.) introduced 1989. See page 154.

SILVER JUBILEE. Perhaps the finest rose bred by Alec Cocker in his short but highly successful career as a rose hybridist, whose work, it is good to know, is carried on by his wife and son. 'Silver Jubilee' is one of the most robust and reliable Hybrid Teas and has exceptionally large and plentiful foliage. The flowers are not very large, but they are well formed and of a lovely salmon-pink colour, shaded with peach and coppery-pink. They have only a slight fragrance, but are produced with exceptional freedom. Very healthy. Height 3ft. Named to commemorate the Queen's Silver Jubilee, the breeding was ('Highlight' x 'Colour Wonder') x ('Parkdirector Riggers' x 'Piccadilly') x 'Mischief'. 1978. See page 171.

SILVER LINING. Large, well-formed high-centred blooms of silvery-pink with a silvery reverse. It is fairiy vigorous and branching, 2½ft. in height, with glossy, dark green foliage. Very fragrant. A cross between 'Karl Herbst' and 'Eden Rose'. Bred by A. Dickson (U.K.), 1958.

SORAYA. I include this rose for its pleasing and unusual colour. This is bright orange-red, the reverse of the petals crimson-red, resulting in a pleasing effect. The flowers, which are held on long stems, are of medium size and tend towards a cupped formation. They have only a slight fragrance. The foliage is dark green, tinted crimson at first. Growth, vigorous and upright. Height 2½ft. ('Peace' x 'Floradora') x 'Grand'mère Jenny'. F. Meilland (France), 1955.

SUNBLEST ('Landora'). A reliable pure yellow rose ideal for bedding. The flowers are not large, hold their colour well, even in strong sunlight, and have a slight fragrance. The growth is bushy and compact. Seedling x 'King's Ransom'. Raised by Tantau (Germany), 1970.

SUNSET SONG. Medium-sized blooms of a pleasing golden-amber to copper colouring. It forms a vigorous, upright bush of 3ft. in height, with plentiful foliage. Slight fragrance. Parentage seedling x 'Sunblest'. Raised by Cocker (U.K.), 1981.

168

SUPER STAR ('Tropicana'). This is one of the most widely planted of all roses, largely because its colour — a bright vermilion — was new among Hybrid Tea Roses when it was first introduced in 1960. Although it has now to some extent been succeeded by certain of its numerous progeny, it is still a good rose, with medium-sized, well-shaped flowers and vigorous, branching, free-flowering, if somewhat top-heavy, growth. Roses of such brilliance should be planted only sparingly if they are not to dominate all else in the garden. Only a faint fragrance. Height 3ft. Unfortunately, 'Super Star' seems to have developed a susceptibility to mildew in recent years. (Seedling x 'Peace') x (seedling x 'Alpine Glow'). Tantau (Germany), 1960.

SUTTER'S GOLD. A beautiful Hybrid Tea with elegant slender buds of delicate appearance and without the heaviness of so many recent varieties. Its buds are of orange-red, developing into light orange-yellow flowers flushed with pink and veined with scarlet, becoming paler with age. The blooms have a strong and pleasing fragrance. The growth is robust, although of slender appearance in keeping with the flower. I have noticed that American roses are sometimes of more refined appearance than their European counterparts. The foliage is a glossy dark green and quite healthy. Height 3ft. 'Charlotte Armstrong' x 'Signora'. Bred by Swim (U.S.A.), 1950.

TROIKA ('Royal Dane'). Medium-sized flowers of a coppery-orange shade, occasionally veined scarlet. One of the strongest, most reliable and healthy roses of its colour. Glossy, medium green foliage. Little fragrance. Height 3ft. Breeding unknown. Poulsen (Denmark), 1971.

VELVET FRAGRANCE (Fryperdee). This is a rose that deserves to be more widely grown: perhaps it was unfortunate in being introduced in the same year as 'Royal William'. It is of a deeper and more dusky crimson than that rose and has a very strong fragrance. It is vigorous in growth and has good disease-resistance. Height 3ft. Bred by Fryer (U.K.), introduced 1988.

VIRGO. Beautiful white flowers frequently tinged with blush-pink. These can easily be damaged by rain and like 'Message', page 157, the growth is rather weak. It is also subject to mildew, and spraying may be necessary. Dark green, matt foliage. Slight fragrance. Height 2ft. Breeding 'Blanche Mallerin' x 'Neige Parfum'. Mallerin (France), 1947.

WENDY CUSSONS. It is difficult to describe the colour of this excellent rose, but it could be said to be a rose-red or very strong bright pink. However this may be, it is a most beautiful shade. The flowers are well

PRIMA BALLERINA, *a Hybrid Tea with beautifully shaped blooms.*

SILVER JUBILEE, *one of the most robust and reliable Hybrid Teas.*

formed and very fragrant. The growth is strong and bushy, about 2½ ft. in height, with glossy, dark green foliage. It is the result of a cross between 'Independence' and 'Eden Rose', the first parent being perhaps responsible for its unusual colouring. Gregory (U.K.), introduced 1963.

WHISKY MAC. This is not a very strong nor a particularly good rose by Hybrid Tea standards, and yet is is one of the most popular. The reason for this lies in its lovely clear amber-yellow colouring which contrasts so effectively with its dark green foliage. Very fragrant. Height 3ft. Parentage not known. Raised by Tantau (Germany), in 1967. See page 167.

YELLOW PAGES. Full flowers of golden-yellow flushed pale pink. These are not of the highest quality and there is little fragrance, but it is robust, reliable and easily grown, flowering freely and continuously. Good disease-resistant light green foliage. Height 2½ft. An unfortunate name, no doubt chosen for advertising purposes. 'Arthur Bell' x 'Peer Gynt'. McGredy (U.K.), 1972.

Floribunda Roses

The Floribundas share with Hybrid Teas the major position in modern gardens. Whereas the Hybrid Teas are notable for the size and quality of the individual flower, the purpose of the Floribundas is to provide a massed effect by the production of many flowers in large clusters. They were originally produced by crossing Hybrid Teas with Polyantha Roses. I shall be discussing the Polyanthas in the next chapter: it is sufficient here to say that they are a small class of very hardy and extremely free-flowering bedding roses, with numerous small rambler-like pompon blooms held in very large clusters. By combining the two groups it was possible to produce a class of hardy, free-flowering and colourful roses. This is exactly what the Floribundas are.

The credit for their origination goes to the firm of Poulsen in Denmark which, in the early part of this century, became interested in the development of hardy roses for the Scandinavian climate. P.T. Poulsen crossed the Polyantha 'Madame Norbert Levavasseur' with the Hybrid Tea 'Richmond' and produced a rose that he named 'Rödhätte' (or 'Red Riding Hood') with semi-double cherry-red flowers in large clusters. Distributed in 1912, this rose seemed to get lost in the turmoil of the war and little more was heard of it. After the war Poulsen's son, Svend, crossed the Polyantha 'Orléans Rose' with the Hybrid Tea 'Red Star', and the result was 'Kirsten Poulsen', a bright red rose, and 'Else Poulsen', which was pink. These were distributed in 1924. Both proved great successes.

These roses were followed by others, and it was not long before breeders were producing numerous varieties. At first the class was known as Hybrid Polyanthas but, in about 1950, this was changed to the less attractive name of Floribundas. Since then there has been a continual admixture of Hybrid Tea genes, with the result that the two classes draw closer together, so that at times it is difficult to know where to place some varieties. The flowers of the earlier Floribundas were often single or semi-double, opening flat, but more recently they have taken on the Hybrid Tea form, and indeed at one stage it seemed as though they might overtake the Hybrid Tea in popularity. However, this has not happened, for people still seem to want what they think of as a 'real rose', and at our nursery we sell about three Hybrid Teas for every two Floribundas.

I often feel it might have been better if breeders had concentrated more on the single or semi-double flowered Floribunda Roses, for such flowers provide a better and more natural massed effect. However, having said this, it cannot be denied that few other flowers of any kind have the capacity to produce so much colour over so long a period. It should also be remembered that the Floribundas are a mixed bag. Apart from the simple colour makers, there are roses for all tastes: single-flowered varieties like 'Dainty Maid'; varieties with flowers of almost Old Rose formation like 'Geranium Red', 'Rosemary Rose' and 'Plentiful'; those that have flowers of almost Tea Rose perfection such as 'Chanelle', 'English Miss' or 'Clarissa'; the near shrub-like growth of 'Iceberg', and the wild rose beauty of 'Escapade'.

Floribundas are on the whole hardier, more free flowering and have better disease resistance than the Hybrid Teas. They are therefore less demanding in their cultural requirements. Nevertheless, it is still worth while giving them the same generous treatment as Hybrid Teas, which they will repay with an even more plentiful and continuous display of colour. Pruning should be much less severe than for a Hybrid Tea, and it is only necessary to remove ageing, dead and diseased growth, as well as weak, twiggy branches, and then to cut back the remaining growth to about two-thirds of its length, taking care to leave a tidy, balanced bush.

ALLGOLD. A low growing Floribunda long valued for its unfading, clear, buttercup-yellow colouring. It has a depth and purity of colour that is still unequalled in this class. ('Korresia' is a better rose, but of a rather different shade.) The flowers are rather shapeless and the growth is not very strong, but the overall effect is dainty and pleasing. It has medium green, glossy, disease-resistant foliage. Slightly fragrant. Height 2½ft. Breeding 'Goldilocks' x 'Ellinor Le Grice'. Bred by Le Grice (U.K.), 1958.

AMBERLIGHT. This is one of a number of brownish shades bred by E.B. Le Grice. They are generally not very strong but have their uses, particularly for flower arrangers. This variety has large, semi-double flowers held on wiry stems in small clusters. Its colour is a pleasing clear amber. Fruity fragrance. Height 2ft. (Seedling x 'Lavender Pinocchio') x 'Marcel Bourgouin'. Introduced 1961.

AMBER QUEEN. Full-petalled, shapely buds of a lovely shade of amber-yellow. The colour is similar to that of 'Whisky Mac', and blends nicely with its dark green foliage. It has a low, spreading, bushy habit of growth. The fragrance is quite strong. Height 2 to 2½ft. Parentage 'Southampton' x 'Typhoon'. Harkness (U.K.), 1984. See page 175.

ANNE HARKNESS. Large sprays of apricot-coloured flowers on long stems. The growth is unusually tall and robust, and it might be used as a shrub. A good cut flower. 'Bobby Dazzler' x ('Manx Queen' x 'Prima Ballerina') x ('Chanelle' x 'Piccadilly'). Harkness (U.K.), 1980.

APRICOT NECTAR, *a Floribunda Rose with flowers similar to those of a Hybrid Tea Rose.*

APRICOT NECTAR. An attractive Floribunda with flowers of almost Tea Rose form and delicacy. These are apricot-yellow in colour and have a good fragrance. The growth is tall and angular, forming a rather open bush. Medium green foliage. This is one of those Floribundas that comes very close to a Hybrid Tea, with large flowers held in small groups. Height 3ft. Seedling x 'Spartan'. Boerner (U.S.A.), 1965.

ARTHUR BELL. A strong and reliable pale yellow Floribunda whose colour fades to a rather unattractive cream. The growth is tall, vigorous and upright, with leathery, medium green, healthy foliage. Good fragrance. Height 3ft. 'Cläre Grammerstorf' x 'Piccadilly'. Bred by McGredy (U.K.), 1965.

AUGUST SEEBAUER. An early Floribunda which is perhaps worth retaining as it is a little different from the general run of roses in this class. The flowers are deep rose-pink and have pointed buds opening to rather Old Rose flowers with quite a good fragrance. The growth is vigorous and it flowers profusely. 'Break o'Day' x 'Else Poulsen'. Bred by Kordes (Germany), 1944.

BEAUTIFUL BRITAIN. Shapely Hybrid Tea buds opening to form double

AMBER QUEEN, *a Floribunda Rose with shapely buds.*

flowers of a bright tomato-red colouring. It is very free flowering with medium green foliage, and has upright growth to about 2½ft. in height. Little fragrance. Breeding 'Red Planet' x 'Eurorose'. Dickson (U.K.), 1983.

BROWNIE. Flowers of an unusual shade of tan edged with pink, with a yellow reverse. They are large, cupped, opening flat and held in small clusters. Height 2ft. 'Lavender Pinocchio' seedling x 'Grey Pearl'. Boerner (U.S.A.), 1959.

CAFÉ. Another rose with brown colouring, usually described as 'coffee-and-cream'. The growth is short and stocky and the foliage an olive green colour. Fragrant. ('Golden Glow' x *Rosa* x *kordesii*) x 'Lavender Pinocchio'. Bred by Kordes (Germany), 1956.

CHANELLE. This is one of my favourite Floribundas. It is a charming and distinctive rose with pretty Tea Rose buds of a delicate shell-pink. The growth is vigorous and branching and it can, if required, be grown as a small shrub. It has a light fragrance. Height 2½ft. Breeding 'Ma Perkins' x ('Mrs. William Sprott' x 'Fashion'). McGredy (U.K.), 1958.

CHINATOWN ('Ville de Chine'). An exceptionally tall and strong Floribunda, often classified as a shrub. It has large, double rosette-shaped yellow flowers that are sometimes edged with pink. Although it has its uses where a large display is required and will grow in poorer soils, all in all it is a rather stiff and coarse rose. Good fragrance. Height 5ft. Breeding 'Columbine' x 'Cläre Grammerstorf'. Poulsen (Denmark), 1963.

CIRCUS. Quite large, very double rosette-shaped flowers that are cupped at first and have a spicy fragrance. Their colour is light yellow, marked with pink, salmon and scarlet. A strong, bushy plant with good, leathery foliage. 'Fandango' x 'Pinocchio'. Swim, (U.S.A.), introduced 1956.

CITY OF BELFAST. A reliable bedding rose, with medium-green, glossy disease-resistant foliage. The flowers are medium size, orange-red in colour and held in large sprays. Slight fragrance. Height 2½ft. Breeding 'Evelyn Fison' x ('Circus' x 'Korona'). Bred by McGredy (U.K.), 1968.

CITY OF LEEDS. Bud-shaped flowers of rich salmon-pink held in large sprays. A reliable and easily grown variety, with bushy growth and good dark green, disease-resistant foliage. Slight fragrance. Height 3ft. 'Evelyn Fison' x ('Spartan' x 'Red Favorite'). McGredy (U.K.), 1966.

CLARISSA. This is something a little different from the usual run of Floribundas, being a cross between the very strong growing 'Southampton' and the Miniature Rose 'Darling Flame'. The flowers are like very small Hybrid Tea Roses, similar to those of the much loved 'Cécile Brunner', although they do not quite have the delicacy of that rose. They are apricot in colour, with a slight scent, and held in many flowered clusters. The growth is upright with glossy foliage. Height 2 to 2½ft. A very welcome addition to this class. Named after Mrs. James Mason. Harkness (U.K.), 1983.

DAINTY MAID. A beautiful single Floribunda with large flowers that are clear pink on the inside, carmine on the reverse. They are held in small and medium-sized clusters on a plant of vigorous, bushy growth with healthy, dark green, leathery foliage. This excellent rose is one of the parents of 'Constance Spry' and thus plays an important part in the foundation of our English Roses. Slight scent. Height 3ft. 'D.T. Poulsen' x seedling. Le Grice (U.K.), 1938.

DAIRY MAID. Dainty pointed yellow buds splashed with carmine, opening to form single flowers of cream colouring eventually turning to white. These are quite large and borne on a bush of medium height. Breeding ('Poulsen's Pink' x 'Ellinor Le Grice') x 'Mrs. Pierre S. du Pont'. Bred by Le Grice (U.K.), 1957.

DEAREST. A beautiful rose of open, full petalled, rather Old Rose formation. The colour is a soft rosy-salmon, and the flowers are produced freely in large trusses on a vigorous bushy plant of about 2½ft. in height. They have a good fragrance for a Floribunda. Dark, glossy foliage. Unfortunately the blooms are easily damaged by rain and there is a tendency to mildew. Seedling x 'Spartan'. Dickson (U.K.), 1960.

DUSKY MAIDEN. An early Floribunda with large almost single flowers of dark red with deeper shadings and contrasting golden stamens. To me this is still one of the most pleasing of the crimson Floribundas, and all the better for being single. It has some fragrance. Breeding ('Daily Mail Scented Rose' x 'Étoile de Hollande') x 'Else Poulsen'. Bred by E.B. Le Grice, introduced 1947.

EDITH HOLDEN (Chewlegacy). Semi-double flowers of a unique russet-brown colour. Unlike most brown shades, it has strong and bushy growth. A very useful rose where the gardener may wish to work this shade into his colour scheme. It will also no doubt be an asset to the flower arranger. Height 3½ft. Bred by Warner (U.K.), 1988.

ELIZABETH OF GLAMIS ('Irish Beauty'). This once popular rose is not much grown now as, unlike the lady in honour of whom it was named, its vigour diminished not long after introduction. This is a shame, as it is a pretty little rose with nicely shaped open flowers of soft salmon-pink and given good soil it will grow quite adequately. It has a good scent. Height 3ft. Breeding 'Spartan' x 'Highlight'. Bred by McGredy (U.K.), 1964.

ENGLISH MISS. A charming variety producing large sprays of light pink, medium-sized flowers which start as pretty pointed buds and open to a camellia-like shape. Thus we have a good example of an ideal bloom — one that is beautiful at all stages. The growth is upright, rather short, and the foliage dark green with a purplish tinge. It has a good fragrance. Height 2½ft. Breeding 'Dearest' x 'Sweet Repose'. Bred by Cant (U.K.), 1977. See page 182.

ESCAPADE. The almost single flowers of this variety have a simple wild rose charm far removed from that of the typical Floribunda. The colour is a rose-pink with a hint of violet and the flowers are held in dainty profusion above the bush. The result of a cross between 'Pink Parfait' and the little purple Polyantha 'Baby Faurax', it is from the latter that it gains its originality, providing us with a hint as to what the breeder might do with Floribundas as a whole. It is vigorous, hardy, disease resistant and reliable. Light fragrance. Height may vary between 2½ and 4ft. Harkness (U.K.), 1967. See page 183.

EUROPEANA. A strong growing and exceptionally free flowering dark crimson Floribunda, which is a cross between 'Ruth Leuwerik' and

EYE PAINT, *a Floribunda Rose which is almost a shrub.*

EUROPEANA, *a Floribunda bearing huge clusters of flowers.*

'Rosemary Rose'. It relates back to 'Gruss an Teplitz' through both parents, and this shows up in its growth which is unusually strong, lax and spreading. It bears huge clusters of flowers that weigh down its branches to such an extent they have been known to break. The individual flowers are quite large, full of petals and of an informal rosette shape, but of modern appearance. Bronze-tinted, glossy foliage. Unfortunately 'Gruss an Teplitz' has handed down a tendency to mildew. Slight fragrance. de Ruiter (Holland), 1963.

EVELYN FISON ('Irish Wonder'). Unfading scarlet flowers of exceptional brilliance. The growth is strong and healthy with dark green, glossy foliage. This is a very reliable Floribunda providing a mass of colour, but perhaps a little ordinary in its overall appearance. Even so, it is a particularly good bedding rose for the production of colour. It produces numerous small to medium-sized flowers on a vigorous, bushy plant. Height 2½ft. 'Moulin Rouge' x 'Korona'. McGredy (U.K.), 1962.

EYE PAINT. A rose of exceptional vigour, with branching, bushy growth that would perhaps be better regarded as a shrub. Its parentage is an unnamed seedling x 'Picasso'. It thus relates back, rather distantly, to *Rosa pimpinellifolia*, and something of this species is still evident in its growth. It bears small scarlet flowers with a white eye and reverse in large clusters. The growth is tall, dense and bushy. Unfortunately it is rather subject to blackspot. Height 4ft. McGredy (New Zealand), 1976. See page 178.

GERANIUM RED. This has something in common with an English Rose, with flowers similar to those of an Old Rose, opening flat, full-petalled and rosette shaped. I do not quite know why it is called 'Geranium Red', for the colour is, in fact, a dusky red which becomes tinged with purple as the flower ages. It is not, in my experience, excessively strong, although it is a rose of considerable beauty. Good fragrance. Height 2½ft. 'Crimson Glory' x seedling. Boerner (U.S.A.), 1947.

GLENFIDDICH. Pointed buds opening to medium-sized flowers with a slight fragrance. The growth is bushy and of medium height, with healthy, glossy, dark green foliage. It is said to perform better in Scotland: perhaps the name may have something to do with this. In the south it is at its best in the autumn. Height 2½ft. Breeding 'Arthur Bell' x ('Sabine' x 'Circus'). Cocker (U.K.), 1976.

GOLDEN SLIPPERS. This variety has been popular in America where it was bred, but it has never received much attention here. It has a nice, airy, spreading growth and the flowers are quite small and of delicate appearance, their colour being Indian yellow flushed with vermilion, with golden-yellow at the centre. Moderate vigour. Height about 2ft. Slight fragrance. 'Goldilocks' x unnamed seedling. Von Abrams (U.S.A.), introduced 1961.

GOLDEN YEARS (Harween). Golden yellow, double flowers, suffused with just a hint of coppery-gold and held in sprays of three-seven. This variety blooms freely and continually – the flowers maintaining their quality until the end of the season. Height 2½ft. Harkness (U.K.), 1990.

GREENSLEEVES. One of the few roses with green flowers. They are, in fact small, semi-double and pale pink, but turn to green as they age, particularly in warm sun. Occasionally beautiful, but frequently dull and uninteresting. 'Rudolph Timm' x 'Arthur Bell' x ('Pascali' x 'Elizabeth of Glamis') x ('Sabine' x 'Violette Dot'). Harkness (U.K.), 1980.

HARVEST FAYRE (Dicnorth). Pure pastel apricot flowers of Hybrid Tea form, borne on an excellent bushy, branching bush and backed up with dense, glossy foliage. Fragrant. Height 2½ ft. Dickson (U.K.).

HONEYMOON ('Honigmond'). Medium-sized canary-yellow flowers of full-petalled rosette shape, but without the charm of an Old Rose. The growth is medium to tall, strong and upright, the foliage pale green and healthy. Slightly fragrant. Height 3ft. Breeding 'Cläre Grammerstorf' x 'Spek's Yellow'. Kordes (Germany), 1960.

ICEBERG ('Fée des Neiges', 'Schneewittchen'). This is probably the best rose ever to come out of the Floribunda class. The flowers are white, of medium size, double, opening wide, and held in large clusters. If we study both growth and flower, we soon notice it is no ordinary Floribunda. The growth is tall, very bushy and branching; the leaves glossy, light green and rather narrow; the stems smooth and slender. The fact is, it is not of typical Floribunda breeding, being a cross between a Hybrid Musk Rose, 'Robin Hood', and a Hybrid Tea Rose, 'Virgo'. Although 'Robin Hood' was a Polyantha on the one side, it is probable that its other parent was one of Pemberton's Hybrid Musks. This shows up in 'Iceberg' which, although it makes a first class bedding rose, is really more of a Shrub Rose. The whole plant has a Hybrid Musk appearance. Lightly pruned it will form an excellent shrub of 4ft. in height. It flowers early and late and is seldom without bloom in between. In the cool of the autumn the flowers have a distinct blush tinge, and are then particularly attractive. Undoubtedly, no Floribunda makes a better standard and grown thus it seems to flower even more abundantly, forming a large, well-shaped head of growth. It will also make a fine low hedge. Its only weakness is a tendency to blackspot as the season advances, but it seems to have the ability to outgrow this. All the same, spraying is advisable for the best results. It has a pleasing, light fragrance. Bred by Kordes (Germany), 1958.

ICED GINGER. Clusters of large Hybrid Tea-shaped flowers in an unusual blend of ivory, pink, yellow and copper. The growth is vigorous and upright, the flowers fragrant, and the foliage light green and disease resistant. It lasts well when cut. 'Anne Watkins' x unnamed variety. Height 3ft. A. Dickson (U.K.), 1971.

INTRIGUE. Neatly rounded, rather small flowers of an intense dark crimson which, unlike many dark roses, does not burn in the sun. The

ENGLISH MISS, *a Floribunda Rose with charming buds.*

ESCAPADE, *a good Floribunda with flowers of a wild rose charm.*

blooms are held in large, well spaced sprays. The growth is bushy and of medium height. 'Gruss an Bayern' x seedling. Kordes (Germany), 1979.

IVORY FASHION. This is a favourite of mine, although it is not particularly strong and somewhat subject to disease. It was bred from 'Sonata' x 'Fashion' and, like many Floribundas with 'Fashion' in their make up, the flowers tend to have an added delicacy. These are ivory-white, large and semi-double. They have some fragrance. Bred by Boerner (U.S.A.), introduced 1958.

JOCELYN. Flowers of an unusual matt mahogany tint that become a purplish-brown with age. They are very double and flat in shape, and held in clusters above shiny foliage. Le Grice (U.K.), 1970.

JOYBELLS. Unusual and attractive large rose-pink flowers shaped like those of a double camellia. The growth is strong and branching, about 2½ft. in height, with many thorns and glossy, medium green leaves. Worthy of attention by those who like something a little different. Slight fragrance. Breeding unnamed seedling x 'Fashion'. Bred by Robinson (U.K.), 1961.

KORRESIA ('Fresia', 'Friesia', 'Sunsprite'). This rose stands alone as the best yellow Floribunda. It is of a particularly pleasing shade, not quite so deep as that of 'Allgold', but equally unfading, making a good splash of colour across the garden. Its flowers are held in small clusters and are of average size, opening wide, with quite a good fragrance. The foliage is a glossy light green and has good disease resistance. It flowers well and repeatedly. Height 2½ft. 'Friedrich Wörlein' x 'Spanish Sun'. Kordes (Germany), 1974. See page 186.

LAVENDER PINOCCHIO. This is quite the most beautiful Floribunda among the lavender and mauve shades. The colour is a brownish-lavender, which may not sound very attractive but is, in fact, most pleasing. The flowers open to a full, slightly cupped formation and have a lot of character. The growth is quite vigorous and bushy. Slight fragrance. Height 2ft. 'Pinocchio' x 'Grey Pearl'. Boerner (U.S.A.), 1948.

LILAC CHARM. Single or almost single flowers of the clearest mauve colouring, with golden anthers and red filaments. This is not a very strong rose, but it is bushy and its single flowers and purity of colouring give it a dainty beauty. Dark matt foliage. Slight fragrance. Height 2ft. Le Grice (U.K.), 1962.

LILLI MARLENE. A standard variety that can always be relied upon to provide a mass of scarlet-crimson. It is, however, rather uninteresting and mechanical in the individual flower. The growth is vigorous, bushy and of medium height. ('Our Princess' x 'Rudolph Timm') x 'Ama'. Kordes (Germany), 1959.

MA PERKINS. Pale salmon-pink flowers of a deeply cupped formation unusual amongst Floribundas; a little like an old Bourbon Rose. It is strong, healthy and has rather upright growth. Light fragrance. Height 3ft. 'Red Radiance' x 'Fashion'. Bred by Boerner (U.S.A.), 1952.

MARGARET MERRIL. An excellent white rose of recent introduction. The flowers have exquisite high pointed buds, with just a tinge of blush, and eventually open wide. They have what is probably the strongest fragrance of any in this class. The growth is of medium height, about 3ft., and it has dark green foliage, with particularly good disease resistance. 'Rudolph Timm' x 'Dedication' x 'Pascali'. Harkness (U.K.), 1978. See page 187.

MASQUERADE. The rose that many gardeners love to hate. This I suspect is because it was at one time very much overplanted, and although it is a great performer its flowers are lacking in character. They are semi-double, quite small, and in various shades of colour — yellow at first, turning to salmon-pink and becoming red, with all these different tints to be seen at one time. They are produced very freely in large clusters, and continually if the hips are removed. The fact is, that when seen in the mass or featured in a mixed border, this can be quite an effective rose even if there is little to be said for the individual blooms. Its growth is very vigorous and bushy. It is more attractive in autumn when the red is less in evidence. Light fragrance. Height 3ft. 'Goldilocks' x 'Holiday'. Bred by Boerner (U.S.A.), 1949.

MATANGI. Semi-double open blooms of bright orange-red, with a distinct white eye and a white reverse. A good bedding rose of vigorous growth, with healthy dark green foliage. Slight fragrance. Height 2½ft. Seedling x 'Picasso'. McCredy (New Zealand), 1974.

MOUNTBATTEN. This is very nearly a Shrub Rose and only suitable for the largest rose bed. The colour is usually described as mimosa-yellow. It has many virtues: strong, very bushy growth, excellent disease-free foliage, and it flowers abundantly and continually. The individual blooms are large, fragrant and fully double, starting as nice buds and retaining their beauty when fully open. Height 5ft. Parentage 'Peer Gynt' x ('Anne Cocker' x 'Arthur Bell') x 'Southhampton'. Harkness (U.K.), 1982.

Left: KORRESIA, *best of the yellow Floribunda Roses.*

Right: VICTORIANA, *a Floribunda of most unusual colouring.*

NEWS. A cross between an Old Rose, 'Tuscany Superb', and the Floribunda 'Lilac Charm'. It thus has a similar origin to my English Roses, but whereas these lean towards the old type of flower, this rose is of typical modern character. However, it takes from its Old Rose parent a rich purple colouring which was not previously found in Floribundas or Hybrid Teas. A more exact description of the colouring is beetroot-purple. The flowers are large, semi-double, with contrasting creamy-yellow stamens. It has excellent strong, bushy growth and flowers freely over a long period. Medium green matt foliage. Slight fragrance. It is perhaps a little surprising that the parents mentioned above should have produced a repeat-flowering variety, and that this should be of typical Floribunda growth. It may well have been a second cross-back to a Floribunda. Le Grice (U.K.), 1968.

MARGARET MERRILL, *an excellent white Floribunda.*

OLD MASTER. A low growing, vigorous, bushy variety with glossy, dark green foliage. The flowers are quite large, semi-double, opening wide with about eighteen petals. Their colour is a deep carmine, becoming purple with age, with a white eye at the centre. The reverse of the petals is silvery-white. The whole adds up to an Old Rose effect. Slight fragrance. Healthy. ('Maxi' x 'Evelyn Fison') x ('Orange Sweetheart' x 'Frühlingsmorgen'). McGredy (New Zealand), 1974.

ORANGE SENSATION. Fairly large clusters of medium-sized, semi-double, bright orange-vermilion flowers on a vigorous, bushy plant. It has quite a good fragrance for a Floribunda. Light green matt foliage. Height 2½ ft. de Ruiter (Holland), 1961.

PADDY MCGREDY. A bushy, low growing Floribunda of little more than 2ft. in height, with deep pink flowers of almost Hybrid Tea shape and size. These are produced with exceptional freedom, covering the plant with bloom. There is usually a period when there are few flowers after the first flush, but a second good crop appears in the autumn. Slight fragrance. Breeding 'Spartan' x 'Tzigane'. Introduced by McGredy (U.K.), 1962.

PAPRIKA. An attractive Floribunda with a little more character than many of its kind. Its flowers are semi-double, of dusky brick-red colouring, with a bluish tinge towards the centre. It forms a vigorous, bushy plant of about 2½ ft. in height, with good, glossy, dark green foliage. Good disease resistance. Some fragrance. 'Märchenland' x 'Red Favorite'. Tantau (Germany), 1958.

PICASSO. A vigorous, branching bush, bearing large scarlet flowers with a white ring and yellow stamens at the centre, the reverse of the petals being white. 'Marlena' x ('Evelyn Fison' x 'Frühlingsmorgen' x 'Orange Sweetheart'). McGredy (U.K.), 1971.

PINK PARFAIT. Pointed Hybrid Tea buds of pink and cream, prettily shaped and held on slender stems. The growth is strong and healthy with abundant foliage and it is possible to grow this variety as a shrub. It is very free flowering and excellent in every way, except that it has no scent. Medium green foliage. Good disease resistance. Height 2½ ft. Parentage 'First Love' x 'Pinocchio'. Introduced by H.C. Swim (U.S.A.), 1960. See page 190.

PLENTIFUL. This rose is distinguished by the Old Rose formation of its flowers. These are of a bright, strong pink, with numerous petals in a full, quartered, shallow cupped shape. They are produced in large trusses and are, indeed, plentiful. The foliage is a shiny light green, but unfortunately rather subject to blackspot which can reduce the vigour of the bush. Little scent. Height 2ft. Introduced by Le Grice (U.K.), 1961.

PRISCILLA BURTON. One of McGredy's 'hand-painted' roses, having deep carmine flowers with a white eye when open; an attractive effect. The buds also are pretty and it repeat flowers well. The foliage is dark, shiny and plentiful. Slight fragrance. McGredy (New Zealand), introduced 1978.

PURPLE SPLENDOUR. The result of a cross between 'News' and

'Overture', with brighter and purer purple colouring than 'News'. The flowers are double and carried on erect growth. The foliage is dark green. Slightly fragrant. Le Grice (U.K.), 1976.

QUEEN ELIZABETH (the 'Queen Elizabeth Rose'). Every now and again a rose appears that will sooner or later be found in almost every garden. 'Queen Elizabeth' and 'Peace' are two varieties that spring to mind when we consider the period since the Second World War. Both have the quality of extremely strong growth and near indestructibility, particularly this variety. 'Queen Elizabeth' has more in common with the Old Roses than other Floribundas. The flowers are large, clear pink and deeply cupped in shape. Although the plant is on the whole a little coarse and of rather ugly, upright habit, the individual flowers are not without their beauty, particularly when cut. The bush or shrub grows to a great height, at least 4½ft., but often when lightly pruned it may be seen growing to 6ft. or more. It is ideal for the back of a large mixed border. When allowed to develop without restraint the flowers tend to perch on top of the growth where they cannot be seen properly. There is no other Hybrid Tea or Floribunda quite so accommodating as regards growing conditions, for it will grow anywhere that a rose can reasonably be expected to grow. It has few, if any, practical weaknesses. The foliage is large, dark green and very disease resistant. It flowers freely and continually. Faint fragrance. Breeding 'Charlotte Armstrong' x 'Floradora'. Raised by Dr. W.E. Lammerts (U.S.A.), 1954. See page 191.

ROSEMARY ROSE. This variety and the pink Floribunda 'Plentiful' were two roses frequently requested by our customers before the arrival of the English Roses. The reason lies in the fact that people were looking for recurrent-flowering roses of the old type, and these two fulfil this requirement better than any of the others. The flowers of 'Rosemary Rose' are large, rosy-red, full petalled, slightly cupped at first, opening flat, with something of the Old Rose charm. They are freely produced on a vigorous, branching, bushy plant of medium height, and have quite a good fragrance. Its parentage is 'Gruss an Teplitz' x unnamed seedling and, like other roses with the first of these parents, it has inherited a tendency towards mildew. Height 2½ft. de Ruiter (Holland), 1954.

SOUTHAMPTON ('Susan Ann'). A very robust Floribunda of up to 4ft. in height, with plenty of glossy, disease-resistant foliage. The flowers are large and apricot-orange flushed with scarlet. It will make a fine show when used as a bedding rose. Slightly fragrant. ('Queen Elizabeth' x 'Allgold') x 'Yellow Cushion'. Harkness (U.K.), 1971.

PINK PARFAIT, *a Floribunda Rose with nice buds.*

QUEEN ELIZABETH, *a Floribunda Rose and one of the most reliable of all roses.*

SWEET REPOSE ('The Optimist'). Well formed Hybrid Tea shaped flowers of creamy-pink, remaining attractive when open; the colour becoming deeper and shaded with crimson at the edges. Strong growth, of medium to tall height, about 3ft., with plentiful bronze-tinted foliage. Slightly fragrant. 'Golden Rapture' x seedling. de Ruiter (Holland), 1956.

THORA HIRD. A charming and unique variety with something of the character of an Old Rose. The flowers are fully double and of delicate pink shades with cream and white, providing a gentle and soft effect seldom found amongst Floribundas. Height 2ft. Bred by Bracegirdle (U.K.), 1988.

TRUMPETER (Mactrum). A vivid scarlet Floribunda which, for sheer brilliance of colour and productivity of form, is probably without equal in its class. It has very short, compact growth and glossy, disease-resistant foliage. Height 2ft. Bred by McGredy (U.K.), 1977.

VICTORIANA. Large, full, rounded flowers carried in clusters on a short, sturdy bush. They are of a most unusual mixture of colours — vermilion on the inside of the petal with a soft silvery reverse. The result is an attractive effect. Sweetly scented. Le Grice (U.K.), 1977. See page 186.

VIOLET CARSON. This rose has something in common with 'Pink Parfait', with small Hybrid Tea buds of a creamy-peach colour and a silvery shade on the reverse of the petals. The growth is vigorous and branching, with bronzy-tinted foliage. It is not, perhaps, quite so beautiful as 'Pink Parfait', but does have the advantage of a mild but pleasing fragrance. Height 2½ft. Breeding 'Madame Léon Cuny' x 'Spartan'. McGredy (U.K.), 1964.

YELLOW CUSHION. Not a widely grown Floribunda, but it does have attractive yellow cup-shaped flowers, unusual amongst Floribundas. It blooms freely in small clusters and has some fragrance. The growth is low and bushy, with glossy foliage. Height 2ft. 'Fandango' x 'Pinocchio'. Bred by Armstrong (U.S.A.), 1966.

An Afterword

Readers may have gathered that I favour the open flower and more shrub-like growth of the Old Roses, but this is not to say that the Hybrid Tea, with its shapely buds and bush-like growth, does not appeal to me. A perfectly scrolled bud of a Hybrid Tea can be a thing of great beauty. If the life of the flower in this form is of necessity short, this is unfortunate; it can, however, be of such perfection that it is still very worth while. It is not so much the type of flower that I dislike, but what the breeder has made of them.

There is nothing to be lost by a rose breeder — or anyone else for that matter — stating his ideas as to the proper development of roses, and I shall therefore take this opportunity of laying out a few of my own very personal opinions regarding the future of the Hybrid Teas and Floribundas.

To breed a really beautiful Hybrid Tea is a very difficult task. The early varieties were not strong in constitution, and after the Second World War breeders set to to give them more strength. In this they have succeeded admirably. New strains and species have been brought in to provide further health and vigour. The trouble has been that too little thought has been given to the quality of flowers, or even to the attractions of the plant itself. It has been assumed that any rose must be beautiful as of right; that this side of the breeding would take care of itself. This has not proved to be the case. Too often the flower has been clumsy and the growth without grace. To me the bud flower should be essentially one of delicate elegance, but when it is heavier due attention must still be paid to the qualities of refinement. Colour, too, has been considered something to be extended regardless of suitability, but the addition of a new colour or colour mixture is not necessarily a virtue. What we need are good colours. Why, too, must the Hybrid Tea always be of rigid growth? Its ancestors, the China Roses and the Tea Roses, were not so; could they not sometimes be more lax in growth, with finer stems and more natural and shrub-like habit? After all, roses today are seldom grown in beds; most are grown in borders, so it might be better to develop something a little more natural and suitable for such positions.

There is an assumption that so long as roses are pointed in the bud and of symmetrical form this is all that is required. I suggest that this is not really enough. If we take early Hybrid Teas like 'Madame Butterfly' or 'Madame Abel Chatenay', with all their weaknesses, we cannot but be impressed by the beauty of form and general character of their flowers. Perhaps it is from such roses that we should take our inspiration. The breeding of Modern Hybrid Teas has been affected by many outside influences, not least by *Rosa multiflora*, via the Floribundas. These influences, for all their beneficial effects on the performance of the plant, have done little to enhance the beauty of the flower; indeed the effect has been very much the reverse. *R. multiflora*, in particular, has flowers of so different a character that it is difficult to blend them satisfactorily with a Hybrid Tea. The genes of a rose are not infinitely flexible.

Happily, there are signs that a change is already taking place. Breeders are now more alive to the demand for more suitable colours.

One of the most recent developments is the Patio Rose (Chapter 5), and here we often find small bushes of a very satisfactory habit of growth. Perhaps with time breeders will also pay more attention to the quality and form of the flowers.

As for the Floribundas, these I would like to see in single or semi-double form, producing flowers in great profusion, but with a natural, almost wild rose appearance. Their purpose should be to produce colour, but without crudeness.

If anything, the Hybrid Teas and their close relations the Floribundas suffer from over exposure. They are seen with such frequency that it is easy to take them for granted. Moreover, no flowers have been so packaged, presented and promoted almost to the stage where they are regarded as something apart from other garden flowers, and hardly as flowers at all. They seem to survive only on the stimulus of a new injection of publicity. They are talked of and written about by the media, often in rather silly terms, frequently with more regard for the person or worse still the product after which they may be named, but seldom with much regard for the attraction of the rose itself. The rose nurserymen are not without blame for all this. Breeding roses is a costly business, and it is sometimes hard to resist the temptation to recoup some of the expenses by charging a fee for the name. This does not matter so long as it is a name that is going to help the rose as well as the nominee.

I cannot pass on without some comment on the trials, held in many countries throughout the world, at which new roses are tested and awards made to those considered to be of greatest worth. These trials are, no doubt, a very good idea. Hundreds of new roses are bred each year, and nurseries cannot grow them all; indeed many are not worth a place in their lists. Unfortunately these trials do have a negative aspect. They are enormously influential, and their decisions can mean life or death to new roses. They are conducted on a points system: so many for health, so many for freedom of flowering, so many for scent, and so on. The shortcoming of such a system is that these figures do not necessarily add up to a beautiful rose, and I suspect that those who judge at these trials do not have the question of beauty very much in mind. Their concern is for a bush that will grow well, be free from disease, etc. The trouble is that they think quantitively, not qualitatively: more colour, more flowers, indeed more of everything. Not only this, but they also have to be concerned with the maintenance of the status quo — they can only judge by the standards that are already accepted and these can sometimes be a hindrance rather than a spur to progress.

To be fair, judges do have an impossible task and, as these trials are planned at present, there is little else they can do. There are, I think, two ways that might help us out of this plight. The first is that nurserymen should not take trials too seriously; that they should be a little more adventurous and not take the easy route of growing just what they are told. They should think a little more of what might appeal to their customers. The second is that trials should be divided into two sections. The first should be devoted to judging the practical virtues, the second to the assessment of aesthetic appeal. Even then it would be necessary for those considering the findings to use their own judgement and assess for themselves what exactly is implied by the judges when they make their decisions.

CHAPTER 5
Some Small Roses

Having completed our survey of the two main classes of Modern Roses — the Hybrid Teas and Floribundas, we are left with three other modern groups. These are all either short with small flowers, or miniature with miniature flowers: Dwarf Polyantha Roses, Patio Roses and the Miniature Roses. All these are very free and continuous in bloom and ideal for the very small gardens we frequently find with today's new houses.

The Polyanthas and the Patio Roses are both strongly influenced by *Rosa multiflora* and have inherited much of the hardiness and floriferous nature of that species. The Miniature Roses are descendants of a miniature China Rose, but have felt the influence of many other roses, including species from the Synstylae* section to which Multiflora belongs.

* See Chapter 6.

Dwarf Polyantha Roses

For the origins of the Dwarf Polyantha Roses we have to go back to the year 1860, when the French breeder, Guillot, of Lyons, sowed seed of the climbing species *R. multiflora* which is, as we shall see, the parent of many Rambler Roses. The resulting plants turned out to have not single white flowers, as would be expected, but flowers of varying shades of pink, some double and others single or semi-double. Most of these were sterile, but one produced hips. Guillot sowed seeds from this rose and, to his surprise, some of the resulting seedlings were not Ramblers, but short, perpetual-flowering bushes. It is almost certain that his original *R. multiflora* had, by pure chance, been pollinated by a China Rose — in all probability the 'Old Blush China'. Guillot chose two of these seedlings and named one 'Paquerette', which he introduced in 1875, and the other 'Mignonette', which he introduced in 1880; both bore large sprays of very small pompon flowers like those of a Multiflora, and both were a soft rosy-pink fading to white with age. Thus it was a new class was born.

Like their *R. multiflora* parent, the Dwarf Polyanthas are extremely tough and hardy, and produce their flowers with the greatest freedom in large, tightly packed clusters. They also repeat with continuous regularity. No sooner has one branch of flowers come into bloom than another flower shoot appears just beneath it. This virtue, together with their toughness, was to have a profound effect on the development of the rose — an effect that has by no means yet run its course. Unfortunately Dwarf Polyanthas usually have little or no fragrance.

These roses cannot be said to have reached great heights of popularity and few varieties were bred. Indeed, not long ago they had all but been dropped from catalogues. Recently, however, there has been a revival of interest, and we ourselves sell them in quite large numbers. Dwarf Polyanthas are very different to other bush roses and are ideal for the edges of borders where something low growing is required, particularly if the soil is not of the best. In recent years one or two new varieties have appeared, but these are usually of taller growth, as, for example, 'Yesterday'.

Cultivation is less demanding than for any other comparable roses. Pruning consists merely of cutting off last year's flower heads and the removal of old and dead growth. They shoot continually from the base of the plant, and this can result in a mass of ageing growth which will require some thinning.

I include with this class a small group of roses that are so different as hardly to warrant inclusion here, except for the fact that one of their parents was a Polyantha. They are 'Cécile Brunner', 'Perle d'Or', 'White Cécile Brunner', 'Madame Jules Thibaud' and 'Jenny Wren', which are often included with the China Roses, where they probably have less right to be. We have to place these particularly charming roses here as they are so much out on their own and they do not really fit in anywhere else. They are like exquisite little miniature flowered Tea Roses, with perfectly formed scrolled buds.

BABY FAURAX. A short grower, no more than 12ins. in height, that might well be at home amongst the Miniature Roses. It is usually regarded as being as close to blue as it is possible to get in a rose. This I think is true, with the possible exception of 'Reine des Violettes' and 'Veilchenblau'. The colour is, in fact, reddish-violet. A very useful little rose with close sprays of tiny cupped flowers on a continuously flowering bush. Lille (France), 1924.

A BORDER *of miniature roses.*

CAMEO. Neatly shaped clusters of dainty salmon-pink, semi-double flowers, with a slight fragrance. 1½ft. de Ruiter (Holland), 1932.

CÉCILE BRUNNER ('Madame Cécile Brunner', the 'Sweetheart Rose', 'Mignon', 'Maltese Rose'). An exquisite little rose with buds no larger than a thimble. Each of these is of perfect pointed Tea Rose formation and retains its beauty even when fully open. The colour is a pale pink which deepens towards the centre of the bud. The flowers are borne singly on thin, wiry stems, and later in the season strong base shoots appear bearing open sprays of bloom. The foliage too is small, but otherwise like that of a Tea Rose. It usually grows to a height of 3ft. and repeat flowers throughout the summer. There is a faint perfume, and the bush is free of disease. One of its parents was the famous old Tea Rose

CÉCILE BRUNNER, *Dwarf Polyantha Rose, one of the most perfect of miniature-flowered roses.*

'Madame de Tartas'. Bred by Pernet-Ducher (France), distributed 1881.

Another rose, 'Bloomfield Abundance', is almost identical except that it is much taller. This variety does not have quite such perfect flowers, but it is worth while referring to Chapter 1 before deciding which variety to grow. There is also an excellent climbing version of 'Cécile Brunner'.

CORAL CLUSTER. Pure coral-pink flowers in large clusters. Its rich, glossy-green foliage has some tendency to mildew. Height 1½ft. R. Murrell (U.K.), 1920.

GLOIRE DU MIDI. A sport from 'Gloria Mundi', with small globular flowers of brilliant orange-scarlet which retain their colour well. This is a well formed bush with bright green foliage. Slight fragrance. Height 1½ft. de Ruiter (Holland), 1932.

JENNY WREN. A hybrid of 'Cécile Brunner', its pollen parent being the Floribunda Rose 'Fashion'. The flowers are of a creamy-apricot colour with the reverse of the petals a pale salmon-pink. They are rather too large to be compared with those of either 'Cécile Brunner' or 'Perle d'Or', and open more loosely, but are still small and prettily shaped in the bud. They are held in open sprays and have a strong fragrance. This is an attractive little rose and it is surprising more breeders have not attempted such hybrids. Height 3ft. Ratcliffe (U.K.), 1957.

KATHARINA ZEIMET. This rose and 'Marie Pavié' both have a pleasing delicacy of flower not often found in the Polyanthas, and it is interesting to note that 'Marie Pavié' was one of its parents. The flowers are small, fully double, pure white with a sheeny texture, and are held in large clusters. It has good short, bushy growth and smooth, rich green foliage. Sweet fragrance. Height 2ft. 'Etoile de Mai' x 'Marie Pavié'. P. Lambert (Germany), 1901.

LITTLE WHITE PET. See Chapter 1.

MADAME JULES THIBAUD. A peach-coloured sport from 'Cécile Brunner', otherwise identical.

MARGO KOSTER. A pretty little plant with branches of very cupped, almost bell-like flowers in a pleasing shade of salmon-pink. They are a little larger than is usual for this group and have a slight fragrance. The growth is short and bushy, about 16ins. in height. It is used as a pot plant in some countries.

This rose is the result of a quite extraordinary series of sports, starting with the Rambler 'Tausendschön' which sported to give a short bush called 'Echo'. This gave us 'Greta Kluis', which in turn gave us 'Anneke Koster', which produced 'Dick Koster', which finally resulted in 'Margo Koster'. There is little point in describing them all, as I think 'Margo Koster' is probably the best. All Polyanthas seem to have the capacity to sport and, indeed, to revert back again to their parent, so that we often find two different colours on one bush. Koster, 1931.

MARIE-JEANNE. An attractive variety, bearing very large clusters of small blush-cream rosette-shaped flowers on a bush of some 2 or 3ft. in height. The foliage is a glossy light green. Suitably pruned it will form a nice little shrub. It is almost entirely without thorns. Turbat (France), 1913.

MARIE PAVIÉ. A bushy, twiggy plant that grows well and bears dainty clusters of fresh blush-white flowers. One of the nicest roses in this group. Height 1½ft. Alégatière (France), 1888. See page 202.

MIGNONETTE. This, as I have said, is one of the two original Polyanthas. It bears small, soft rosy-pink flowers that pale almost to white with age. They are held in large clusters on a dwarf free-flowering bush. Height 1ft. Guillot Fils (France), 1880.

NATHALIE NYPELS ('Mevrouw Nathalie Nypels'). An excellent Polyantha bearing medium-sized, semi-double rose-pink flowers on a dwarf, spreading bush. It has rather unusual parents for a rose of this class: 'Orléans Rose', a typical Polyantha x (a seedling from the China Rose 'Comtesse du Cayla' x *Rosa foetida bicolor*). It is, consequently, not of a typical Polyantha character, the flowers being a little larger and showing signs of its China parentage. Quite a strong fragrance. Height 3ft. Leenders (Holland), 1919.

NYPELS PERFECTION. Open, semi-double flowers of hydrangea-pink with deeper shadings towards the centre. They are borne in large clusters on a vigorous bush of about 2ft. in height, with plentiful light green foliage. Leenders (Holland), 1930.

PAUL CRAMPEL. This rose, together with 'Gloria Mundi' and 'Golden Salmon', was the first to have the brilliant orange-scarlet or vermilion colour we associate with such modern Hybrid Teas as 'Super Star'. As such, these three Polyanthas represented an entirely new colour in roses when they were first introduced around 1930. 'Paul Crampel' is a typical Polyantha, with tight bunches of small flowers each with a tiny white eye at the centre. The growth is vigorous and erect, and the foliage light green. It has the unfortunate habit of sporting to flowers of a rather unpleasant crimson. Height 2ft. Bred by Kersbergen (Holland), 1930.

PERLE D'OR. Almost a replica of 'Cécile Brunner', with similar perfect, miniature Tea Rose buds. The flowers are a buff-apricot shade that deepens towards the centre, becoming tinged with pink as they open, finally fading to cream. They are of rather looser formation than 'Cécile Brunner' when fully open, but are equally, if not more, beautiful. Like 'Cécile Brunner' they are held on long, wiry stems and have a sweet fragrance, though the growth is perhaps a little stronger. Height 4ft. It is probably the result of a cross between a Polyantha and the Tea Rose 'Madame Falcot'. Rambaud (France), 1883.

THE FAIRY. See Chapter 1.

WHITE CÉCILE BRUNNER. A sport from 'Cécile Brunner'. Unfortunately it is not quite white but tinged with buff, giving it a rather dirty appearance. Nonetheless, it is a worthwhile rose for those who are

MARIE PAVIÉ, *a Dwarf Polyantha Rose bearing dainty clusters of flowers.*

particularly attracted to miniature flowers. Slight fragrance. Height 3ft. Discovered by Fauque (France), 1909.

YESTERDAY. A much more recent introduction, bred by Harkness and introduced in 1974. Its parents were ('Phyllis Bide' x 'Shepherd's Delight') x 'Ballerina'. Both 'Phyllis Bide' and 'Ballerina' have connections with *Rosa multiflora,* and 'Yesterday' therefore has a right to be included here. It forms a rather taller bush than the older varieties, being 3ft. in height. The flowers are small, flat and typically Polyantha, produced in graceful sprays and of a pleasant lilac-pink colouring paling a little towards the centre. They are sweetly fragrant. It has a natural bushy, branching habit of growth that fits easily into the garden scene.

YESTERDAY, *a Dwarf Polyantha Rose with a natural bushy branching habit of growth.*

PERLE D'OR, *a beautiful Dwarf Polyantha Rose, similar to 'Cécile Brunner'.*

YVONNE RABIER. Said to be a cross between *Rosa wichuraiana* and an unknown Polyantha, it is therefore surprising that this rose is so very perpetual flowering, as first crosses between once-flowering and repeat-flowering roses are almost always summer flowering only. It is a vigorous bushy rose of 3ft in height. As one would expect from two such parents, it is extremely hardy and disease resistant. The flowers, which are sweetly fragrant, are white with just a tinge of yellow and produced in abundance. It has long, slender, glossy-green foliage that shows signs of both parents. Turbat (France), 1910.

YVONNE RABIER, *a hardy and perpetual flowering Dwarf Polyantha Rose.*

Patio Roses

The Patio Roses do not form a clearly defined class, nor are they officially recognised as a class. It is, however, becoming increasingly necessary to place the roses I describe here in some sort of group. The name is not one I would have chosen, as it seems to have a rather artificial ring, but since no one has yet thought of a better one I shall continue to use it. It no doubt arose from the fact that these roses, being small, are rather suitable for growing in containers on patios; however, as they are also equally suitable for the garden in general, it seems an illogical name.

The Patio Roses are closely connected with the Dwarf Polyanthas and the Miniature Roses and are frequently the result of crossing these with Floribundas. It is, however, dangerous to be too dogmatic as to their origins for they are, in reality, the result of a variety of influences.

I regard Patio Roses as being one of the more satisfactory developments in present-day roses. They are usually small, bushy plants, rather like miniature Floribundas but much more compact, indeed some of them could be described as very small bushy or spreading shrubs. They have very numerous small flowers and repeat particularly well. The growth, though short, is often cushion-like or arching, and some varieties have flowers of attractive rosette shape. Others have small pompon flowers like those of a Polyantha. The foliage is often small and dark and there is little trouble with disease. If breeders will concentrate on beauty of flower, and not necessarily on a brilliant colour or a Hybrid Tea shape, I feel sure we could be hearing a lot more about these roses in the future, particularly if they can continue to develop a good bushy habit of growth. Unfortunately they tend to have little or no scent and it may be difficult to breed this into them.

Cultivation provides no problems, and pruning usually consists of little more than removing dead flower heads and a little thinning and reshaping of the bush.

ANNA FORD. An excellent spreading, bushy plant of 1½ft. in height, with shiny, polished foliage. This is covered with small mandarin-red, semi-double flowers that pale to orange-red with a touch of yellow at the centre and golden stamens. It is very free flowering, forming a mound of colour and repeating well throughout the summer. Its many small hips will have to be removed if further flowering is required. Slight fragrance. Harkness (U.K.), 1980.

BIANCO. Small creamy-white, rosette-shaped flowers, produced with great freedom in large clusters on a short, rather open and spreading bush. There is some fragrance. Height 1½ft. 'Darling Flame' x 'Jack Frost'. Cocker (U.K.), 1983.

BOYS' BRIGADE. Dwarf, bushy growth bearing single crimson flowers with a yellowish-white centre. Very free and continuous bloom. It bears many hips which should be removed before they develop. Height 1½ft. ('Darling Flame' x 'St. Alban') x ('Little Flirt' x 'Marlena'). Cocker (U.K.), 1984.

BRIGHT SMILE. Slightly larger flowers than is usual for this group, with deep yellow pointed buds, later opening wide to show their stamens, eventually fading. The growth is strong, neat and bushy with plentiful healthy, shiny, foliage; it is close to a Floribunda in general appearance. Free and continuous flowering. Slight fragrance. Height 2ft. Dickson (U.K.), 1980.

CAROLINE DAVISON. Fairly large pink flowers with a white centre. These are held in close bunches creating a Floribunda-like effect. Slight fragrance. Height 1½ft. Harkness (U.K.), 1980.

DAINTY DINAH. A bushy, spreading plant with numerous full-petalled, neatly-rounded flowers of a strong rosy-coral colour. The height is 2ft. and as much across. A charming little rose with an excellent habit of growth. Slight fragrance. 'Anne Cocker' x 'Wee Man'. Cocker (U.K.), 1981.

ESTHER'S BABY. Bright rose-pink flowers starting as pretty buds and opening to a semi-double star-like formation. It is very free flowering with low, spreading, bushy growth of 1¼ft. in height. Small, dark green foliage. Slight fragrance. Harkness (U.K.), 1979.

FAIRY CHANGELING. Attractive rosette-shaped flowers of Polyantha-like appearance, but of rather larger than usual size and in pleasing shades of very deep pink showing off well against a leafy background of dark foliage. A most satisfactory, spreading, cushion-like plant of 1½ft. in height. Light fragrance. Harkness (U.K.), 1981.

FAIRY DAMSEL. A nice, spreading bush bearing broad sprays of small Polyantha-like, rosette-shaped deep crimson flowers. It has plentiful foliage and is seldom without bloom. A pretty little rose. Slight fragrance. Height 1½ft. Harkness (U.K.), 1981.

HAKUUN. 'Hakuun' is Danish for a cloud, and this rose produces tightly packed trusses of small buff to creamy-white flowers in such quantities that they are, indeed, like a cloud. A tough, reliable and bushy plant of 2ft. in height. Slight scent. Poulsen (Denmark), 1962.

INTERNATIONAL HERALD TRIBUNE. A particularly fine variety with attractive, rather cupped semi-double purple flowers that pale a little but remain a good colour to the end. The centre of the flower is white with an occasional streak on the petals, and there are dainty stamens. The flowers are held in large sprays and produced with excellent continuity. The growth is robust but neat and compact, with ample foliage. Slight fragrance. Height 1½-2ft. Harkness (U.K.), 1985.

JEAN MERMOZ. This charming little rose has usually been classified with the Polyanthas, but I think it can now be moved to this group. It is, in fact, a cross between *Rosa wichuraiana* and a Hybrid Tea. It bears pretty, airy sprays of tiny, very double flowers on nice spreading growth. They are of a deep china-pink shade, and have a slight fragrance. An ideal rose for the edge of a border. Height 1½ft. Bred by Chenault (France), 1937.

KIM. An upright plant, but bushy and compact. The flowers are yellow lightly suffused with pink and are larger than is usual for those in this section. A good cut flower, lasting well in water. Height 1½ft. Harkness (U.K.), 1973.

LITTLE JEWEL. Attractive cup-shaped flowers of a bright rose-pink. Bushy, rather upright growth. Height 1½ft.

LITTLE PRINCE. Sprays of small orange-red flowers on a compact bush of

TOPSI, *Patio Rose.*

STARGAZER, *Patio Rose.*

KIM, *a compact Patio Rose.*

upright habit. It has many hips which must be removed for the benefit of later flowers. Height 1½ ft.

MARLENA. At the time of its introduction in 1964, this was a revolutionary rose. It was, in fact, the forerunner of this section. Growing to about 1½ ft. in height, it is covered with small semi-double, slightly cupped, crimson-scarlet flowers in clusters, forming a mound of colour. It is seldom without bloom. Bred by Kordes (Germany).

NOZOMI. See Chapter 1.

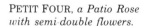
PETIT FOUR, *a Patio Rose with semi-double flowers.*

PEEK-A-BOO. A hybrid of 'Nozomi' which is a trailing or ground-cover rose. Although 'Peek-a-Boo' has not inherited this habit, it has taken on a compact cushion-like growth which is most satisfactory. It might be described as a perfect small — or perhaps I should say miniature — shrub. The flowers are apricot becoming tinted with pink and are held in graceful sprays. Attractive small foliage. Slight fragrance. Height 1½ft. and as much across. Dickson (U.K.), 1981.

PETIT FOUR. One and a half inch semi-double, clear pink flowers with white at the centre and an occasional white stripe. Neat, cushiony growth with plentiful foliage. Slight fragrance. See page 207.

PINK POSY. It is interesting to note that this is a hybrid of 'Trier', a rose I have already written about when discussing the ancestry of the Hybrid Musk Roses, Chapter 1. The outcome is a charming and unusual rose, close to a Polyantha in appearance. It bears bunches of tiny, double flowers of light rose-pink. We have not heard much about fragrance in this section, for the very good reason that there is not much to talk about; however, this variety does have a sweet fragrance, no doubt due to the influence of 'Trier'. It is the type of rose of which I should like to see more in this class. Height 2ft. Cocker (U.K.), 1983.

REGENSBERG. Light pink semi-double flowers mottled and edged with white with a white centre. These are rather larger than is usual and create a good massed colour effect. Neat, free, bushy growth of 1½ft. in height. Slight fragrance. McGredy (New Zealand), 1979.

ROBIN REDBREAST. Small, almost single flowers of dark crimson, with a yellowish-white eye and yellow stamens, creating a brilliant massed effect. Spreading, bushy habit, of about 2ft. in height. Ilsink (Holland), 1984.

STARGAZER. Almost single, bright orange-red flowers with a yellow centre of star-like formation. The reverse of the petals is pale yellow, giving something of the impression of *Rosa foetida bicolor*. Low growth of about 1½ft. Slight fragrance. Harkness (U.K.), 1977. See page 206.

SWEET DREAM (Frymincot). A charming little rose, growing to about 1½ft. in height and bearing plentiful small, neatly cupped double flowers of peachy-apricot in clusters on a compact plant. It has a slight fragrance. The most popular of the Patio Roses. Height 1½ft. Bred by Fryer (U.K.), 1988.

TOPSI. Semi-double blooms of unfading orange-red. Free flowering, slight fragrance. Somewhat subject to black spot. Height 2ft. 'Fragrant

Cloud' x 'Fire Signal'. Tantau (Germany), 1971. See page 206.

WEE JOCK. A well rounded cushion-like bush that has scarlet-crimson flowers with pretty buds like miniature Hybrid Tea Roses, but opening to a rosette formation. It has bushy growth with plentiful foliage and repeats well. Height 1½ft. Cocker (U.K.), 1980.

Miniature Roses

These are true miniatures, 5ins. in height in the case of 'Rouletii', but more usually from 9 to 15ins. in height, varying somewhat according to whether they are grown from cuttings or grafted on a stock — those from cuttings will be shorter. Miniature Roses are not only diminutive in height, but also in all their parts, having twiggy growth and tiny leaves and flowers. The flowers, when closely examined, can be very pretty, either in the form of little Hybrid Tea buds or as small Old Rose rosettes.

There can be little doubt that the original variety was a miniature form of a China Rose. The earliest example of this type of rose came to Britain from China at some time around the year 1800 and from here travelled to France. A number of varieties were raised which became popular in both countries, particularly as pot plants for the house. Later interest faded and they were almost entirely lost. In 1918 a Swiss Army Medical Officer named Roulet discovered plants of some of these varieties growing in pots in a Swiss village, where it was said they had been grown for a very long time; this rose became known as 'Rouletii'. The Dutch hybridist Van Vink and Pedro Dot of Spain used it as a parent, crossing it with various roses to found the modern race. After this a number of other breeders began to take a hand, and the popularity of Miniature Roses began to spread.

It is an odd fact that the Miniatures have received more attention in the land of the 'bigger and better' — the United States of America — than anywhere else. Space is usually not a problem there, while in Great Britain it frequently is. Even so, Miniature Roses have never been very popular here and their popularity in the United States must be in some degree due to the work of Ralph Moore of California. It is he who has done more than any other breeder to bring them to their present state of development. I had the great pleasure of visiting his most interesting nursery during the summer of 1985, where I had the opportunity of seeing the vast amount of work he has done and is doing in this field. He has numerous varieties on the market, but sadly many of the charming

STARS 'N STRIPES, *Miniature Rose.*   STARINA, *Miniature Rose.*

little roses he has bred have never been properly distributed. The problem seems to be the old one: the public, or perhaps more accurately the nurseryman, now demands small bud-shaped flowers like miniature Hybrid Teas. Nevertheless, at Ralph Moore's nursery I saw the most beautiful little rosette and cup-shaped flowers in good colours and in numerous varieties, including both mossed and striped roses. Moore is the only hybridist to breed Moss Roses since the time of the Old Roses.

The great problem with Miniature Roses is to know how to use them in the average garden. It would be easier if they were a little larger in growth, like the miniature Centifolias, with miniature flowers and leaves. As it is, they are useful plants for very small gardens. In larger gardens they are perhaps at their best in troughs, urns, window boxes, small raised borders and the like. Wherever they are used, it is necessary to place them where they can be seen at close quarters, otherwise their little flowers cannot be viewed with any real appreciation. There is also no reason why they should not be grown in pots and brought into the house when in full bloom, though they cannot, of course, be kept there, and must be taken outdoors at intervals so they can recover from the ordeal. One of the best ways to enjoy them is as cut flowers in posy bowls.

Miniature Roses will grow in any good garden soil, but where the soil is poor it will be necessary to improve it with a little manure. Pruning should consist of cutting back to about half the height of the plant, and removing dead and diseased wood.

ANGELA RIPPON. A compact, leafy plant, bearing full-petalled, coral-

GREEN DIAMOND,
Miniature Rose.

pink flowers in clusters. It is about 1½ft. in height, bushy in growth, and flowers very freely. There is some fragrance. de Ruiter (Holland), 1978.

BABY DARLING. Small orange-pink flowers with a slight fragrance. Growth dwarf and bushy. Height 8 to 12ins. 'Little Darling' x 'Magic Wand'. Moore (U.S.A.), 1964.

BABY GOLD STAR. This has rather large flowers for a Miniature Rose. Their colour is a bright yellow, but may be paler at times; the growth bushy, to about 15ins. in height. Little fragrance. 'Eduardo Toda' x 'Rouletii'. P. Dot (Spain), 1940.

Right: SHERI ANNE, *Miniature Rose.*

DRESDEN DOLL, *Miniature Rose.*

BABY MASQUERADE. This is the result of a cross between 'Tom Thumb' and the Floribunda 'Masquerade', and has the appearance of a very small version of the latter rose. The flowers are double, of star-like appearance and, again like 'Masquerade', the colour changes from yellow to pink, and then to a crimson that further deepens with age. Reliable but rather coarse. Height 18ins. Tantau (Germany), 1956.

BAMBINO. A sport from 'Perla de Alcanada', see page 215, and similar in every way except that it has rose-pink blooms. It has the same hardy, compact growth and pretty, shapely flowers. Height 6 to 10ins. Discovered by Pedro Dot (Spain), 1953.

CINDERELLA. A cross between the pretty little Polyantha 'Cécile Brunner' and 'Tom Thumb'. It has charming 1in.-flowers of satiny-white tinged with flesh-pink which, in spite of their small size, are made up of some forty-five tiny petals. Height about 10ins. Bred by de Vink (Holland), 1953.

CORALIN ('Carolyn', 'Karolyn'). A rather larger variety for the class, up to 18ins. in height, having comparatively large flowers with about forty petals. Their colour is turkey-red with an overtone of orange. 'Mephisto' x 'Perla de Alcanada'. M. Dot (Spain), 1955.

CRICRI. A dwarf, bushy plant of 12ins. in height. The flowers are well formed and very double, their colour salmon-pink shaded with coral. ('Alain' x 'Independence') x 'Perla de Alcanada'. Meilland (France), 1958.

DARLING FLAME. One and a half inch flowers of globular shape and vermilion-red colouring. A good garden plant of above average height. ('Rimosa' x 'Josephine Wheatcroft') x 'Zambra'. Meilland (France), 1971.

DRESDEN DOLL. A most interesting rose, the result of many years work by Ralph Moore of California, who has here managed to combine the attractive mossy buds of the Moss Roses with the small growth and repeat-flowering habit of the Miniature Roses. The growth is perhaps a little large for this class, but none the worse for that. The flowers are double, opening out into a rosette formation, and of a nice soft pink colouring, occasionally showing the yellow of their anthers. The buds are quite well mossed, and this provides a most charming effect. 'Fairy Moss' x unnamed Hybrid Moss seedling. Moore (U.S.A.), 1975. See page 211.

DWARFKING ('Zwergkönig'). Fairly full, dark red flowers of average size. The growth is bushy and of medium height. 'World's Fair' x 'Tom Thumb'. Kordes (Germany), 1957.

EASTER MORNING. Fairly large full-petalled ivory-white flowers. Growth medium-tall. Slight scent. 'Golden Glow' x 'Zee'. Moore (U.S.A.), 1960.

FIRE PRINCESS. Well-formed scarlet flowers on a rather tall, upright bush, with dark green foliage. 'Baccara' x 'Eleanor'. Moore (U.S.A.), 1969.

GREEN DIAMOND. There have been very few green garden roses, and most of these are rather disappointing. This is perhaps the most satisfactory example so far. The buds are tinted with rose-pink and the flowers a soft green when open, though at times they fail to open properly. It is of medium height and bushy growth. Unnamed seedling of Polyantha type x 'Sheri Anne'. Moore (U.S.A.), 1975. See page 211.

HAPPY THOUGHT. Full flowers of pink blended with coral and yellow. Growth vigorous and bushy; profuse bloom. (*Rosa wichuraiana* x 'Floradora') x 'Sheri Anne'. Moore (U.S.A.), 1978. See page 215.

JUDY FISCHER. Pointed buds opening into full-petalled, rose-pink flowers of medium size. Good low, bushy growth with dark, bronzy foliage. 'Little Darling' x 'Magic Wand'. Moore (U.S.A.), 1968.

LAVENDER JEWEL. Quite large, full flowers in a charming combination of pink and lavender. The growth is bushy, lax and of medium height. A good garden plant. 'Little Chief' x 'Angel Face'. Moore (U.S.A.), 1978.

LAVENDER LACE. Small, pointed buds of lavender colouring. Growth bushy and of medium height. Fragrant. 'Ellen Poulsen' x 'Debbie'. Moore (U.S.A.), 1968.

LITTLE FLIRT. Orange-red flowers with an orange-yellow reverse. Light green foliage and bushy growth of 12 to 14ins. The breeding is (*Rosa wichuraiana* x 'Floradora') x ('Golden Glow' x 'Zee'). It is interesting to note that *R. wichuraiana* is a giant Rambler; 'Floradora' a strong Floribunda; 'Golden Glow' a Climber, and only 'Zee' a Miniature. Moore (U.S.A.), 1961.

MAGIC CAROUSEL. This variety has quite large flowers with pointed buds prettily edged in red. The growth is upright and of medium height, the foliage small and glossy. 'Little Darling' x 'Westmont'. Moore (U.S.A.), 1972.

MR. BLUEBIRD. A charming little rose with semi-double flowers of a lovely bluish-lavender colouring. The growth is compact and bushy. In every way an excellent variety of considerable garden value. The breeding is recorded as 'Old Blush China' x 'Old Blush China'. I understand that self-set seed was sown and this resulted in a high

SNOW CARPET, *a creeping Miniature Rose.*

HAPPY THOUGHT, *Miniature Rose.*

proportion of Miniature seedlings. These must surely have been chance hybrids with a Miniature Rose. Moore (U.S.A.), 1960.

NEW PENNY. Moderately full flowers of coral-pink becoming pink as they age. Branching habit, dark green foliage. (*Rosa wichuraiana* x 'Floradora') x unnamed seedling. Moore (U.S.A.), 1962.

PEACHY WHITE. Pointed buds opening into small semi-double flowers. Their colour is white but tinted with blush. Growth upright and bushy. 'Little Darling' x 'Red Germain'. Moore (U.S.A.), 1976.

PERLA DE ALCANADA. Small, rosy-carmine flowers with fifteen to twenty petals. Growth very dwarf and compact, 6 to 10ins. in height, with dark, glossy foliage. 'Perle des Rouges' x 'Rouletii'. P. Dot (Spain), 1944.

POUR TOI. Creamy-white, semi-double flowers tinted with yellow at the base of the petals. Very short, only 6 to 8ins. in height, but with good, bushy growth. 'Eduardo Toda' x 'Pompon de Paris'. P. Dot (Spain), 1946.

RISE 'N SHINE. Comparatively large, shapely blooms of pure yellow on a good, bushy plant of medium height. 'Little Darling' x 'Yellow Magic'. Moore (U.S.A.), 1977.

SHERI ANNE. Pointed buds, opening to a flat flower of bright orange-red. The blooms are held in sprays and have quite a strong fragrance. An excellent variety. 'Little Darling' x 'New Penny'. Moore (U.S.A.), 1973. See page 211.

SILVER TIPS. Pointed buds, opening into small 1in.-flowers with very numerous petals. The growth is vigorous and bushy, and it flowers freely. Height 12ins. (*Rosa wichuraiana* x 'Floradora) x 'Lilac Time'. Moore (U.S.A.), 1961.

SNOW CARPET. An excellent little rose of a unique habit of growth. This is a miniature creeping variety that trails along the ground, slowly building into a small mound of growth. It has tiny short-petalled, star-like and very double flowers of pure white held in sprays against small glossy leaves. It may be grown in rock gardens, although the purist might not think it correct in such a position. It will also form an attractive Miniature Standard Rose. Repeat flowering. 'New Penny' x 'Temple Bells'. McGredy (New Zealand), 1980. See page 214.

STACEY SUE. Very full, soft pink blooms with up to sixty petals. It has an excellent lax, spreading habit, making it a good garden plant. 'Ellen Poulsen' x 'Fairy Princess'. Moore (U.S.A.), 1976.

STARINA. Rather large flowers of orange-red colouring on a comparatively tall, bushy plant. ('Dany Robin' x 'Fire King') x 'Perla de Montserrat'. Meilland (France), 1965. See page 210.

STARS 'N STRIPES. Another Moore innovation. This time he has used the old striped Hybrid Perpetual 'Ferdinand Pichard' to produce a charming little striped Miniature. The flowers are semi-double with white stripes on a red ground, and have something of the appearance of a diminutive 'Rosa Mundi'. The growth is bushy and lax, forming a small shrub of 2ft. in height, and should appeal to those who like Old Roses. 1980. See page 210.

TOY CLOWN. White flowers of pretty semi-double cupped formation with carmine at the edge of the petals. The growth is bushy and of medium height, with small, leathery foliage. Slight fragrance. Height 12ins. 'Little Darling' x 'Magic Wand'. Moore (U.S.A.), 1966.

YELLOW DOLL. Large blooms, starting as pointed buds, eventually revealing many petals of pale yellow to cream colouring. Good spreading growth to about 12ins. in height, with leathery, glossy foliage. 'Golden Glow' x 'Zee'. Moore (U.S.A.), 1962.

CHAPTER 6
Species Roses and their near Hybrids

Having looked at the Modern Shrub Roses, Climbing Roses and garden roses of the present day, and made a few suggestions as to their future, we must now return to the very first roses; the wild roses of many lands. It might quite reasonably be said that we should have begun at this point.

There are, however, certain advantages in placing them at the end of the story. We are concerned with the rose not principally from a historic point of view, intriguing though this undoubtedly is, nor from the point of view of a botanist, but as a garden plant. The Species and their hybrids are, generally speaking, quite different in character from those of horticultural origin, often occupying a different place in the garden. They are children of the wild, or, at least, close relatives of such roses, whereas the garden roses are very much the product of civilisation. The Species are all single flowered, double flowers being the result of selection by man.

Like the garden roses, the Species, too, have an interesting background, not so much from a human point of view — except perhaps for the often dauntless men who collected them — but because of the many lands and widely differing terrains which form their natural habitat. Although the cultivated rose has spread to virtually every country in the world, as a wild plant it is found only in the Northern Hemisphere. North America, Europe, across Russia, through China and into Japan — almost every country has its wild roses. China, in particular, is extremely rich in roses, as it is in many other plants. It is perhaps unfortunate for us, in this modern urban age, that wild roses tend to form rather large shrubs and are, therefore, not always ideal for our small gardens. Fortunately, there are many who have larger gardens, particularly those who live in the country, and for these there must always be a place for at least one or two wild roses. The Species, however, are not all large in growth; there are some that are entirely suitable for a place in the smaller garden.

The pleasure of wild roses lies not so much in their colourfulness or the showiness of their flowers, but more in their simplicity, as well as in the elegance of their growth, the daintiness of their foliage, and their often richly coloured fruit. Indeed, hardly any of the wild roses are lacking in beauty, but it is a beauty that has to be looked for. Through the long process of their evolution they have taken on many forms in order to deal with the vagaries of numerous different climates and terrains. Between Species there are to be found infinitely varying patterns of growth and leaf.

We may consider growing the Species in shrub borders or mixed borders, or perhaps more particularly in the wilder outer areas of the garden; even in fields, hedges and open woodlands. The Climbing Species, which I deal with in the second half of this chapter, may be encouraged to scramble over bushes and hedges and up trees — sometimes quite large trees. In fact, the Species include some of the best roses for these purposes.

Usually the Species will not require much in the way of attention. The occasional removal of old branches to encourage the new is generally sufficient, or perhaps a little cutting back to stop them becoming excessively large or smothering their neighbours. However, pruning should not be too heavy or it may promote growth at the expense of flowers and fruit, and perhaps destroy the natural grace of the plant. For this reason it is worth studying their ultimate size with some care before making a decision on planting. Where a Species Rose has been left unpruned for many years, and perhaps been a great source of beauty during that time, there is often a tendency for it to fill up with old and dead wood, thus becoming unsightly. This is nature's pruning, but not desirable from a garden point of view. In such cases it is sometimes best to cut the shrub hard back and begin again.

The Species Hybrids are usually hybrids between Species, although sometimes they are hybrids between Species and garden varieties. All of them have the nature of wild roses with certain exceptions, such as the Scotch Roses, which I place here more for convenience.

The Species are not the choice of man, but a development of nature, and as such they do not come as a conveniently standardised product to fit neatly into a book. Each Species may vary considerably, according to the area from which it was originally collected. With the more varied Species, such as *Rosa moyesii*, it is important to see that your nurseryman has a good form.

There are some two hundred and fifty different Species of roses; all have their beauty, as indeed do all plants, but some are more suitable for the garden than others. As has been my policy throughout this book, I describe only those that I consider to be of true garden worth.

ROSA CALIFORNICA PLENA, *Species Hybrid. An excellent free-flowering and entirely reliable shrub.*

Species Shrub Roses and their Hybrids

Rosa Alpina. See *R. pendulina.*

Rosa Altaica. See *R. pimpinellifolia* 'Grandiflora'.

Rosa Californica. A vigorous rose bearing 1½ in. deep pink flowers in clusters between mid-June and early July. These are followed by a good display of hips in the autumn. Height 8ft. It is a good shrub, with pleasing dark foliage of delicate appearance, but rather overshadowed by its double form described below. A native of the U.S.A.

Rosa Californica Plena. Opinions differ as to the origins of this rose. Some say that it is a double form of *R. californica.* Graham Thomas, however, suggested that it may be related to *R. nutkana.* The fact that it is double suggests to me the other parent was of garden origin, for it seems rather too much of a coincidence we should find a Species Hybrid that was also double. This is a very fine shrub and a better garden plant that its parent. Its semi-double flowers are deep pink, fragrant, and borne on long, pendulous branches in cascading abundance. The foliage is small, dark and plentiful, forming dense cover. It is hardy and grows vigorously, often suckering profusely, and would, I am sure, be very useful for municipal planting. Height 8ft. Introduced by Geschwind (Hungary), 1894. See page 219.

Rosa Canina. The Dog Rose of our hedgerows, and also to be found across Northern Europe and into Western Asia in varying forms. Although it will not require much description to people of the British Isles, for those of other countries it can be described as an open shrub of 10ft. in height, bearing 2-in. flowers either singly or in small clusters. Between different shrubs these may vary in colour from white to almost crimson, but are more often of a soft pink shade. It is unique among roses for its excessive variability, particularly in the colour of its flowers, but also in growth and leaf. In fact, if we study it in the wild, we seldom find any two plants that are the same. This is due to an unusual variability in its genetic make up, and not, as it may seem, to differences in soil conditions. The flowers have their own typical fragrance, and are followed by scarlet hips of long, oval shape. Those of us who have access to this rose will not perhaps consider planting it, although it is a beautiful shrub. Some people think it worth planting in hedgerows and wild places. I can well remember it on my parents' farm near Shrewsbury, in woodlands that had been cut some twenty years previously and where it was to be seen growing in great masses to a height of anything up to 20ft., providing an almost overwhelming profusion of bloom in season. I have come across few rose scenes to equal this since. See page 222.

R. *canina* has been the parent of a number of hybrids, most of which are excellent shrubs, often with larger flowers, but usually keeping close to it in appearance. These include R. *complicata* and R. 'Macrantha' which are described separately.

ROSA CANINA ABBOTSWOOD. A semi-double seedling of the Dog Rose showing little sign of hybridity. In spite of this I suspect it is a hybrid, as I have myself hybridized R. *canina* with other roses and obtained very similar results. This variety appeared in a hedgerow at Abbotswood in the garden of Mr. Harry Ferguson, of tractor fame, and was discovered by his gardener, Mr. Tustin, who gave it to Graham Thomas. It forms an 8ft. shrub with pink flowers of a sweet Canina fragrance followed by orange-red hips. 1954.

ROSA CANINA ANDERSONII. Probably a Canina x Gallica Hybrid with typically Dog Rose flowers but larger and of a richer, more brilliant pink, and blooming over an extended period. The leaves are long and downy on the underside. It has the bright red Canina hips. Fragrant. 6 by 8ft. First recorded by Hillier (U.K.), 1912. See page 223.

ROSA CANINA HIBERNICA. This rose has all the signs of being a Canina x Pimpinellifolia Hybrid. It forms a neat, bushy, twiggy, slightly arched shrub of medium size, with attractive pale pink flowers of about 1½ ins. across appearing late in the season. It will grow to approximately 8ft. in height, forming a dense bush, and has greyish-green foliage, midway between that of Canina and Pimpinellifolia. In autumn it bears brown-red hips. The original was discovered in 1802 by a Mr. John Templeton of Belfast who received a prize of 50 guineas from the Botanical Society of Dublin for a new indigenous plant. This was hardly an accurate description as it is, in fact, a chance hybrid. See page 222.

ROSA CANTABRIGIENSIS. See *Rosa hugonis* hybrids below.

ROSA COMPLICATA. Probably a hybrid of a Gallica Rose and R. *canina*. Indeed, it is often classified as a Gallica, although it is really very much a wild rose. It is one of the finest and most reliable of all the Shrub Roses. The flowers are large, about 5ins. across, slightly cupped at first, opening flatter, and of the purest bright pink paling to white at the centre, with a large boss of golden stamens. In mid-June the whole shrub is

ROSA CANINA HIBERNICA, *Species Hybrid. Probably a hybrid between* Rosa canina *and* R. pimpinellifolia, *with bushy growth and dainty flowers.*

ROSA CANINA, *Species Hybrid, the Dog Rose of our hedgerows. These two illustrations show the great variation of colour to be found in this rose.*

ROSA CANINA ANDERSONII, *Species Hybrid. A good garden shrub which is probably a Dog Rose hybrid.*

completely covered with a mass of over-sized Dog Rose blooms. The growth is extremely robust but quite compact, about 5ft. in height, with ample large foliage. It can be relied on to do well even under rather poor conditions — few roses are more fail-proof — and it deserves to be far more widely planted by municipal authorities. Nothing is known of its age, or origin. See page 227.

ROSA DAVIDII. A graceful, upright shrub of about 9ft. in height, bearing 2-in. mallow-pink flowers borne in large open clusters and elegantly poised along its branches. There is a pleasing fragrance, and the flowers are followed by slim, flagon-shaped hips of bright orange-red. The leaves are rough textured and of a greyish-green. It is one of the last of the Species to flower. This rose has shown a tendency to die back in my garden but soon renews itself. It grows wild in West China and Southeast Tibet, and was first collected by E.H. Wilson in 1903.

ROSA DUPONTII. This beautiful rose is probably a hybrid between *R. damascena* and *R. moschata*. It may have been raised at Malmaison, and appears in Redouté as *R. damascena subalba*. The flowers are about 3ins. across and single, with occasional extra petals. Their colour is white, sometimes tinged with blush, and they are held in nice Damask-like sprays of five or more blooms. They have a clean-cut shape and a purity which adds much to their attraction, particularly when viewed against their elegant, downy-grey foliage. It is a strong and rather loose-growing shrub of perhaps 7ft. in height and rather less across. There is a sweet fragrance. Late flowering. Circa 1817. See page 226.

ROSA ECAE. A compact shrub of about 5ft. in height and almost as much across, with slender, thorny, dark brown branches and small, dark green fern-like leaves, similar to those of *R. hugonis*. The flowers are small, no more than 1in. across, deep buttercup-yellow, and set all along its branches. A good shrub, but not always easy to establish. It is best in a warm, sunny position. A native of Afghanistan, it was first collected by Dr. Aitchison in 1880. The name derives from the initials of his wife, E.C.A.

ROSA EGLANTERIA (*R. rubiginosa*, the 'Sweet Brier'). A native of Britain and Northern Europe, this rose is greatly valued for the rich and spicy fragrance of its foliage which is emitted from glands on the underside of the leaves, and is particularly in evidence on a warm, moist day, when it can fill the garden around it. An even stronger fragrance can be obtained by crushing the leaves between the fingers. Graham Thomas wisely recommends that it should be planted on the south or west side of the garden to catch the warm, moist winds. This is a strong, easily grown shrub of 8ft. in height and across, with many thorns. It will form an impenetrable barrier where this is required, and may also be used as a hedge. The flowers are clear pink, about 2ins. across, and they too are fragrant. Later there is a mass of bright red, oval-shaped hips that last well into the winter. There are a number of hybrids, all with fragrant foliage, but never of quite such power as the original.

ROSA EGLANTERIA HYBRIDS INCLUDING PENZANCE BRIERS
During the years 1894 and 1895 Lord Penzance introduced a number of Sweet Brier hybrids that he had bred himself. These were mainly crosses between *R. eglanteria* and various Hybrid Perpetuals and Bourbons. They have a certain garden value, combining as they do a variety of colours with the fragrant foliage of the wild Sweet Brier. They are nearly all extremely robust, usually about 8ft. in height, though most of them are inclined to grow into what are, to me, rather coarse shrubs of upright growth. They all have aromatic foliage, but not to the extent of the Sweet Briers. Where space can be found for only one such rose it might be best

to plant *R. eglanteria* itself. It is probable that the Penzance Briers are the result of a very few crosses, with little selection.

I also include here three other hybrids — 'Janet's Pride', 'La Belle Distinguée' and 'Manning's Blush' — which come from different sources.

AMY ROBSART. Semi-double flowers of deep clear pink. Extra strong growth. Not very fragrant foliage. Good, scarlet hips. Height 9ft.

ANNE OF GEIRSTEIN. Single flowers of dark crimson with yellow stamens. Free-flowering. Many hips.

CATHERINE SEYTON. Soft pink single flowers. Orange hips. 8ft.

FLORA MCIVOR. Single flowers of rose-pink, fading to blush, with a white centre. 8ft. See page 227.

GREENMANTLE. Single, rosy-crimson flowers, white eye. 8ft. See page 227.

JANET'S PRIDE. ('Clementine'). This was distributed by W. Paul & Sons (U.K.) in 1892, but may have been in existence before. It is smaller than the Species, 6ft. in height, with scented, semi-double, cherry-pink flowers attractively veined with pale pink, the centre being almost white. The foliage coarser and less fragrant than the Species.

JEANNIE DEANS. Semi-double, bright scarlet flowers. Foliage with above average fragrance. 7ft.

JULIA MANNERING. Single, delicate pink flowers veined with darker pink. 6ft.

LA BELLE DISTINGUÉE. An old hybrid with very double crimson flowers that make a good show of colour. It grows to about 4ft. by 3ft. across. The foliage is not very fragrant.

LADY PENZANCE. An attractive shrub, the product of a cross between *R. eglanteria* and *R. foetida bicolor*. It bears dainty single yellow flowers that are flushed with coppery-pink towards the outer edges. Unfortunately it has inherited some of *R. foetida*'s susceptibility to blackspot. The foliage has only a slight fragrance, while the flowers have the scent of *R. foetida*. Height about 6ft.

LORD PENZANCE. *R. eglanteria* x 'Harison's Yellow'. Not so robust as the others, but with foliage that is quite strongly aromatic. The flowers are single, fragrant and of a soft rosy-yellow with pale yellow at the centre. Height 6ft.

LUCY ASHTON. Attractive single white flowers edged with pink. Foliage with above average fragrance. 6ft.

ROSA DUPONTII, *Species Hybrid. An attractive shrub with shapely flowers and beautiful, grey-green foliage.*

MAGNIFICA. A seedling from 'Lucy Ashton', and thus a second generation Penzance Brier, but it is, in fact, a much better rose than we would expect from this group. It forms a fine shrub of 6ft. in height, with large, fragrant, cupped, semi-double flowers of a purplish-red. Widely used in the breeding of modern roses, it was bred by Hesse of Germany in 1916.

MANNING'S BLUSH. An old variety of a date certainly prior to 1799. It is a much smaller shrub than *R. eglanteria*, about 5ft. in height, with pretty little full-petalled flowers which are pink in the bud and pale to blush when they open. The foliage has a slight fragrance. See page 231.

MEG MERRILLIES. Semi-double bright crimson flowers. The foliage has a good fragrance. Scarlet hips. 8ft.

ROSA COMPLICATA, *Species Hybrid. One of the most reliable and free flowering of all Shrub Roses.*

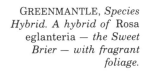

GREENMANTLE, *Species Hybrid. A hybrid of* Rosa eglanteria — *the Sweet Brier — with fragrant foliage.*

ROSA ELEGANTULA PERSETOSA (*R. farreri* 'Persetosa'). This rose was selected by E.A. Bowles from seed of *R. elegantula,* collected by Farrer from West China in 1915. It has deeper pink flowers than is usual for the typical Species which is now very rare in cultivation. Owing to the small size of its flowers, *R. elegantula* 'Persetosa' is often known as the 'Threepenny Bit Rose', a name that may soon have little meaning to future generations of gardeners. It is a dainty little shrub, with tiny, clear salmon-pink flowers lacing its arching growth, and with small leaves and many hair-like thorns. The foliage turns to a purple shade in autumn, and there are numerous small orange-red hips which persist well into the winter. Height 5ft.

ROSA FEDTSCHENKOANA. A large and very strong growing bristly shrub of 8ft. or more in height which, if grown on its own roots, suckers very freely, spreading far and wide — so much so that it can become a problem. Perhaps its chief virtue is its pleasing grey-green foliage, but it also has the distinction of being one of five wild roses that have a natural ability to flower throughout the summer, the other four being *R. rugosa, R. beggeriana, R. foliolosa* and *R. bracteata.* The flowers are white and about 2ins. across, but although they continue over a long period I have not found them to be very plentiful. The hips are long, pear shaped and bright red with persistent hairy sepals. The flowers are fragrant, some say rather unpleasantly so. A native of Central Asia, it was discovered by and named after a Russian in 1868/71, arriving at Kew in 1890. See page 230.

ROSA FOETIDA (*R. foetida lutea,* 'Austrian Yellow'). This rose is often, rather misleadingly, known as the 'Austrian Brier'. It is, in fact, a native of Iran and Kurdistan, and has been with us since the late sixteenth century. *R. foetida* was a very important Species in the development of garden roses, being the main source of yellow colouring in our Modern Roses through its variety *R. foetida* 'Persiana'. This has been a mixed blessing, as *R. foetida* suffers from blackspot and has passed something of this fault on to its progeny. Indeed, it frequently and rather unfairly receives the total blame for the problem. It bears 2½in. flowers of bright sulphur-yellow with a scent that does not appeal to everyone. The foliage is pale green and the stems brown with greyish coloured thorns. It forms a pleasing, rather sparse shrub of 5ft. in height. This Species and its varieties provide a most brilliant effect early in the season. If your garden is subject to blackspot it might be better to grow *R. pimpinellifolia* 'Lutea Maxima' which is less prone to this disease and has flowers of a similar colour, being probably a hybrid of *R. foetida.*

ROSA FOETIDA BICOLOR (*R. lutea punicea,* 'Austrian Copper'). A dramatic and intriguing sport from *R. foetida.* The upper surface of the petals has become a dazzling coppery-red, while the under-surface remains bright yellow. Otherwise it is identical to its parent. If we look at this rose, it is not hard to see how the Modern Rose arrived at its present state of often excessively bright colouring. This rose, however, is beautiful and well worth a place in the garden. It was grown in the Arab world as far back as the twelfth century. Height 5ft. See page 230.

ROSA FOETIDA PERSIANA ('Persian Yellow'). An attractive double form of *R. foetida* with flowers of similar bright sulphur-yellow colouring. It will achieve a slender 4ft. in height, although I understand that it will grow more strongly in a warmer climate. Its flowers are cupped in shape and have a rather Old Rose appearance. Introduced to England, probably from Iran, in 1838 by Sir Henry Wilcock. See page 230.

ROSA FORRESTIANA. A shrub of some 6 or 7ft. in height, and 6ft. across, bearing rosy-crimson flowers of about 1½ins. with creamy-yellow stamens. These are fragrant and borne in dense clusters, and have large, leafy bracts. The hips are flask shaped, bright orange-red and rather bristly, the green bracts persisting. An attractive shrub. A native of West China, first cultivated in 1918. See page 234.

ROSA GLAUCA (*R. rubrifolia*). A native of Central Europe usually grown for the beauty of its foliage. It is a shrub of some 7ft. in height, and nearly as much across, with smooth, almost thornless purple-red stems and glaucous coppery-mauve leaves which provide an excellent colour contrast in the border or in an arrangement of cut flowers. Its blooms are not very conspicuous, being light pink, quite small and held in rather tight bunches, but in spite of this they have a certain charm among the tinted colour of the leaves. The hips, which are small and globular, provide us with a further pleasing effect. See page 234.

ROSA GLAUCA CARMENETTA. A hybrid between *R. glauca* and *R. rugosa,* which is more robust and thorny, with larger leaves and flowers than *R. glauca.* As one would expect, it is a little coarser and lacks the elegance of *R. glauca,* but is otherwise similar with the same pink colouring. Height 7ft. by 7ft. across. Bred by the Central Experimental Farm, Ottawa (Canada), 1923.

ROSA HEMISPHAERICA (*R. sulphurea, R. glaucophylla,* the 'Sulphur Rose'). This rose has little claim to a place among the Species, but since it is difficult to know where to put it, I include it here. It bears large full-petalled, sweetly fragrant, deeply globular flowers of typical Old Rose

ROSA FOETIDA BICOLOR, *Species Hybrid. Brilliant colours with yellow on the back of the petals.*

Left: ROSA FEDTSCHENKOANA, *a Species Hybrid with attractive grey-green foliage and a natural ability to repeat flower.*

Right: ROSA FOETIDA PERSIANA, *Species Hybrid. A double form of this Species Rose with rich yellow colouring.*

MANNING'S BLUSH, *Species Hybrid. A fine example of an old Sweet Brier hybrid.*

appearance which are pale sulphur-yellow in colour. Indeed at one time it was, quite erroneously, known as the 'Yellow Provence Rose'. The growth is rather loose, up to 6ft. in height, the foliage a pale greyish-green and the blooms hang their heads from the branches: all of which sounds very attractive, and indeed it is, but unfortunately the flowers seldom open, and then only in the driest and most favourable seasons. A little rain, and they ball up and soon decay, although the plant itself is completely winter hardy. The protection of a warm sunny wall can be a help. This rose was a favourite of the old Dutch painters, and there is a particularly fine Redouté print which shows how good it can be. Unfortunately this happens only occasionally. Gordon Rowley has suggested that it is a double-flowered sport of the species *R. rapinii* which is found in Turkestan and Iran. It is known to have been in cultivation in Europe as early as 1625.

ROSA HUGONIS (the 'Golden Rose of China'). A shrub of 8ft. in height, with long, graceful branches, brown bark, many thorns and small, pale green fern-like foliage which turns a bronzy colour in autumn. It would be worthwhile for its growth and foliage alone, but in mid-May its branches are wreathed along their length with dainty, slightly cupped flowers of soft yellow colouring, each 1½ to 2ins. across. These are followed by small, round, maroon-coloured fruit. If it has a fault it is that the flowers do not always open completely, the petals tending to be crumpled. Although this is quite attractive, in some seasons it can be excessive. Possibly it may be due to our climate. *R. hugonis* is, however, the parent of some fine hybrids that are very similar and may be preferable; these are described below. They are all particularly good shrubs, with similar dainty foliage, flowering long before most other roses appear. *R. hugonis* probably grows best on its own roots. It was originally collected in West China by the missionary Hugh Scanlon (known as Pater Hugo) who, in 1899, sent seed to Kew where the original plants still thrive.

ROSA HUGONIS HYBRIDS

CANTABRIGIENSIS (*R. pteragonis* 'Cantabrigiensis'). An excellent shrub similar to *R. hugonis* but stronger in growth, easily achieving 10ft. in height. The flowers are saucer-shaped, rather larger, of a paler yellow, and more symmetrical in form than *R. hugonis*. They are produced in great profusion, providing a magnificent sight in mid-May. It has graceful growth and dainty foliage, similar to that of *R. hugonis*. There is a light fragrance. It was a self-sown seedling discovered at the University Botanic Garden, Cambridge, and was named in 1931. See page 235.

GOLDEN CHERSONESE. A comparative newcomer which is a hybrid between *Rosa ecae* and *R. xanthina spontanea* 'Canary Bird', and thus only one quarter Hugonis. It has very numerous, small, deep buttercup-yellow, sweetly scented flowers which are held closely along its branches. A good shrub, stronger and hardier than its parents, with flowers of a particularly rich colour. It is of unusually upright growth, a fact that gives it a certain added value in the garden, even though we are grateful that most species do not share this habit. Fragrant. 6ft. Bred by E.F. Allen, 1963.

HEADLEYENSIS. A seedling of *R. hugonis,* probably hybridized with *R. piminellifolia* 'Grandiflora', and one of the best of this group. It is very vigorous, achieving 9ft. in height and considerably more across. It thus requires space if it is to develop properly. Its broad, graceful, open growth carries ample fern-like foliage. The creamy-yellow flowers are particularly fine and plentiful, and are fragrant. Raised by Sir Oscar Warburg (U.K.), 1920.

HELEN KNIGHT. This is named after the wife of the former Director of the Royal Horticultural Society's gardens at Wisley, where I understand it is a great favourite. I have only grown it for a short time, however, and have not yet got a mature shrub. It is of unusual upright growth; some might think a little too stiff and upright, but we do not require roses to be all the same, besides which there are positions in the garden where a rose of this habit can be a definite asset. It is a seedling of *Rosa ecae,* probably hybridized with *R. pimpinellifolia* 'Grandiflora', and will grow to 5 or 6ft. bearing deep yellow flowers with dark stamens. F.P. Knight (U.K.), 1966.

HIDCOTE GOLD. Considered to be a hybrid of *Rosa hugonis* and *R. sericea pteracantha,* with the fine fern-like foliage of the first rose, and large, flattened thorns showing the influence of the latter. It forms a graceful shrub with long, hanging branches which are wreathed with canary-yellow flowers in May. Height 7ft. by 7ft. Thought to have been raised at Hidcote in 1948 from seed collected in the wild in China by Reginald Farrer.

ROSA MACRANTHA. A fine, arching shrub, sending out long, thin growth, to a width of 10ft. and 5ft. in height. The flowers are large and borne in small clusters from mid-June to early July. Their colour is pale pink, fading almost to white, with a good boss of stamens and a pleasant fragrance. They have something of the appearance of much bigger Dog Roses. Little is known of its origin. The rather dull, rough-textured

Left: ROSA MACRANTHA, *Species Hybrid. Large flowers on an elegant spreading shrub.*

Right: ROSA GLAUCA, *the colourful hips of this Species Hybrid.*

Opposite: CANTABRIGIENSIS, *Species Hybrid. One of the best of the* Rosa hugonis *hybrids, with typical dainty flowers and fern-like foliage.*

ROSA FORRESTIANA, *Species Hybrid. An attractive shrub with flowers of almost formal appearance.*

foliage and the form of its flowers seem to suggest a Gallica as one parent. *R. canina* is often suggested as the other, but cytological analysis rules this out, nor does the growth fit in with this theory. Its appearance points to the possibility of some trailing rose like *R. arvensis* in its parentage. However this may be, *R.* 'Macrantha' is a truly beautiful rose that is not only good as a shrub, but also very useful for covering banks, the stumps of old trees, or growing into other shrubs and over hedges. It has round, red hips, that persist well into autumn. See page 234.

ROSA MACRANTHA DAISY HILL. Very similar to *R.* 'Macrantha' but with semi-double flowers that are a little smaller in size. All other characteristics are very much the same, except that there is a particularly strong fragrance. 5ft. by 12ft. Raised by Smith of Newry (Northern Ireland), before 1912.

ROSA MACROPHYLLA. A very large shrub of 12ft. in height and as much across, possibly more under suitable conditions. This is one of the most magnificent of the Species, its exuberant growth and large leaves — which may be 8ins. in length and have up to eleven leaflets — forming a thick canopy. It has few thorns and dark red-brown stems. The flowers are a deep rose-pink, 3ins. across, and are held nicely poised either singly or in small clusters. In autumn it has long, bristly, bright red, flagon-shaped hips hanging elegantly from its branches. A common and widely varying shrub, found wild in an area spreading through North India, West China and the Himalayas. Introduced c.1888.

ROSA MACROPHYLLA MASTER HUGH. This rose illustrates the variability of *R. macrophylla*. It is a form collected in Nepal in 1966 and is similar to a typical example of that rose, although it seems to be taller, more upright and more open in growth. The chief difference with 'Master Hugh', however, is its exceptionally large hips which are rather more plump than those of *R. macrophylla,* and larger than those of any other rose. They hang like miniature lanterns, or small inverted pears. Height 15ft. Mason (U.K.), 1966.

ROSA x MICRUGOSA. A hybrid of *R. rugosa* and *R. roxburghii.* The latter was formerly known as *R. microphylla* — hence this variety's name. The foliage leans towards Rugosa in character, although it is a little coarse in texture. The growth is very dense and twiggy, forming a shapely shrub with plentiful foliage. The flowers are pale pink, about 4ins. across, opening flat. Individually they are among the most beautiful of single roses, nestling amongst the leafy growth and having a lovely silky texture. They are followed by round, bristly, orange-red hips. Flowering may not be plentiful in the early stages, but as it matures it does so more freely. It will, if required, form an impenetrable barrier. Height 5 or 6ft. A self-sown seedling found at Strasburg Botanical Institute in 1905.

ROSA x MICRUGOSA ALBA. An attractive second generation seedling from the above, bearing white flowers. The growth is more upright and the leaves paler. It has the ability to repeat flower. Height 5ft. Bred by Dr. Hurst at Cambridge.

ROSA MOYESII. Certainly one of the finest of the Species Roses. A native of North-west China, it was brought to this country by E.H. Wilson and introduced in 1903, when it caused a considerable stir in horticultural circles. This is not altogether surprising, as there was nothing quite like it among wild roses. The flowers are blood-red, 2½ins. across, with overlapping petals and a neat ring of contrasting pale stamens. They have no fragrance, but are followed by magnificent, long flagon-shaped, orange-red fruit which hangs down from the branch, providing an attractive effect from late August to October — or perhaps later. The growth is open, with long, sweeping, widely spaced canes to a height of 10ft. and 8ft. across. The foliage is dark green and attractive, with up to twelve leaflets. This is a useful shrub for the mixed border, as its tall growth can be encouraged to stand above other plants without smothering them. It should be noted that in the wild *R. moyesii* is more often of deep pink colouring. The rose we grow in gardens is a selected form. As with some other Species Roses it is extremely variable. If we grow this Species from seed it will usually revert to the pink type. It is therefore important, when purchasing a plant, to be sure that you obtain a red form. I have noticed that bees prefer *R. moyesii* to any other rose in our collection; indeed, they almost ignore the rest when it is flowering. It was named after the Reverend E.J. Moyes, who was a missionary in China. See page 238.

ROSA MOYESII FORMS AND HYBRIDS

EOS. This is a hybrid, *R. moyesii* x 'Magnifica', the latter being a self-sown seedling of the Sweet Brier 'Lucy Ashton'. It bears flat, almost single flowers of coral-red along its branches, providing a brilliant effect. The growth is rather gaunt and bare at the base. Height 12ft. There is rarely any fruit. Bred by Ruys (U.S.A.), introduced 1950.

FARGESII. Similar to *R. moyesii*, but with pink flowers. The hips are rather larger. Veitch (U.K.), 1913.

FRED STREETER. A seedling from *R. moyesii*, with more bushy

ROSA MOYESII, *Species Hybrid and one of the finest Species Roses, with bright red flowers followed by long pitcher-shaped fruit.*

HIGHDOWNENSIS, *Species Hybrid. A good form of* Rosa moyesii *with cerise flowers and rather fuller growth.*

GERANIUM, *Species Hybrid. The best form of* Rosa moyesii *for the small garden.*

growth and flowers of a bright cerise-pink. It has smaller flagon-shaped hips. Discovered at Petworth in Sussex, and introduced by Jackman (U.K.), 1951.

GERANIUM. This is probably the most useful form for the average garden, as it is a smaller shrub than *R. moyesii,* with more compact growth of about 8ft. in height. The flowers are bright geranium-red, the hips rather larger, with more plentiful bright green foliage. Raised by B.O. Mulligan at Wisley (U.K.), 1938. See page 239.

HIGHDOWNENSIS. A seedling from *R. moyesii,* selected by Sir Frederick Stern at Highdown in Sussex. It is a good shrub, with tidier, less open and more bushy growth than the typical Species. The light cerise-crimson flowers with a paler centre are borne in larger clusters. It is tall and vigorous, to about 12ft. in height, and bears particularly fine orange-red hips. See page 239.

HILLIERI (*Rosa* x *pruhoniciana*). The outstanding feature of this rose is the dark crimson colouring of its flowers, certainly the darkest to be found in this group, and as dark as any we might find in a Hybrid Tea or Hybrid Perpetual. A mystery surrounds its breeding; some say it is a *R. moyesii* x *R. willmottiae* cross, but we would not expect this to produce such a depth of colour. The growth is more arching and graceful than *R. moyesii,* the foliage small and rather sparse, and it does not flower quite so freely, but continues over a long period. It will grow to 10ft. in height by 12ft. across. The hips are large and flagon-shaped, but not always plentiful. Light fragrance. Long thin thorns. Introduced by Hillier (U.K.), 1920.

ROSEA (sometimes attributed to *Rosa holodonta*). A rose related to *R. moyesii* introduced from China in 1908, with deep rose-pink flowers and good hips. The leaves are larger and there are more thorns than on the typical Species. Height 10ft.

SEALING WAX. Notable for its particularly fine scarlet hips. The flowers are of a bright pink. A seedling from *R. moyesii,* it is otherwise similar. Height 8ft. Royal Horticultural Society (U.K.), 1938.

WINTONIENSIS. A vigorous hybrid, *Rosa moyesii* x *R. setipoda,* but close to *R. moyesii* in general appearance. It has bushy growth and ample foliage which has a Sweet Brier fragrance. Its flowers are deep pink. Fine bristly, orange-red hips. Height 12ft. Introduced by Hillier (U.K.), 1935.

ROSA MULTIBRACTEATA. A wide and gracefully arching shrub, with prickly stems and fragrant grey-green foliage of seven to nine leaflets. The flowers are plentiful, lilac-pink, 2ins. across, with prominent bracts along their stems which provide an attractive effect. They are held singly or in small clusters. The fragrance is unusual, similar to that of *R. foetida*. One of the parents of the beautiful 'Cerise Bouquet'. Height 7ft. by 6ft. across, more in favourable conditions. Collected by E.H. Wilson from West China, introduced 1908.

ROSA NITIDA. A low growing, suckering shrub of 2ft. in height which, once established on its own roots, will spread freely, forming a thicket of excellent ground cover. It sends up slender, twiggy growth, with many thin thorns and shiny green leaves of seven to ten leaflets which in autumn develop beautiful scarlet-crimson tints. The flowers are about 2ins. across and of an unfading deep pink, but its foliage is perhaps its chief asset. Hips, small, bright red, round, and rather bristly. A native of Canada and the North-east U.S.A., first cultivated 1807.

ROSA NUTKANA. A native of western North America, growing to about 6ft. in height by 4ft. across, with ample greyish-green foliage which turns to brown in the autumn. The flowers are lilac-pink, 2 to 2½ins. in width, and are followed by a good display of globular hips which persist well into the winter. Introduced to Britain in 1876.

ROSA OMEIENSIS. See *R. sericea* page 253.

ROSA PAULII (*R. rugosa repens alba*). *R. rugosa* × *R. arvensis* hybrid, bred by George Paul (U.K.), and introduced at some time prior to 1903. It is an extremely vigorous, procumbent shrub of about 4ft. in height, producing long stems that can gradually spread to as much as 12ft., although it can, of course, be restricted by pruning. The flowers are pure white, about 3ins. across, the petals being wedge-shaped, narrow at the base so that they do not overlap, and providing a rather star-like effect similar to that of a clematis. They have golden stamens, the petals are inclined to be crinkled and there is a clove-like fragrance. The foliage is rough textured, similar to that of *R. rugosa* in appearance, and there are many thorns. It is very tough, growing well under adverse conditions, and ideal where a large expanse of ground cover is required. See page 242.

ROSA PAULII ROSEA. This appears to be a hybrid of *R*. 'Paulii', from which it differs quite considerably in strength of growth. Although vigorous, it is much less so than its parent. It bears large clear pink flowers with a white centre and yellow stamens. The petals have a crinkled, silky appearance, and overlap in the more usual manner. A beautiful rose with a strong fragrance. Height 3ft. by 8ft. across.

ROSA PENDULINA (*R. alpina*). A native of the foothills of the Alpine regions of Central and Southern Europe, usually regarded as growing to about 4ft. in height, although in my experience it will easily achieve 5 or 6ft. under good garden conditions. The growth is erect and slightly arching, the stems are tinted with red and purple, and are smooth with few thorns. The foliage is finely divided, with anything from five to nine leaflets. The flowers are about 2ins. across, of a variable purplish-pink colouring with yellow stamens and are held singly or in twos and threes. They are followed by bright red pear-shaped hips of about 1in. in length, making a conspicuous show. This rose is sometimes difficult to establish, but seems to prefer light soil. An attractive shrub.

ROSA PIMPINELLIFOLIA. This rose was, until very recently, better known as *R. spinosissima,* but the botanists have now come down on the side of *R. pimpinellifolia.* It is more popularly known as the 'Scotch' or 'Burnet Rose'. A native of the British Isles, it is to be found growing in poor sandy conditions, often on seaside banks, anywhere from Cornwall to Scotland. It also grows in Europe and West Asia, and is occasionally to be seen

ROSA PAULII, *Species Hybrid. A large-spreading shrub with large flowers.*

ROSA PAULII ROSEA, *Species Hybrid, has large silky petalled flowers on a broadly spreading shrub.*

naturalised in North America. It is one of the hardiest, toughest and most reliable of roses. Its height will vary according to conditions. In the wild, in a windswept seaside position, it may grow to no more than 6ins. In the garden it may be about 3ft. in height, but in good soil it can reach up to 6ft. It forms a thicket-like growth, sending up slender stems with many bristles and small, fern-like foliage. In May and June it produces numerous creamy-white flowers of 2 to 3ins. across close along its branches. They have a distinct, refreshing fragrance. Later, there are round maroon-black hips. When grown on its own roots it will sucker far and wide, producing dense ground cover. This may be an asset, but can sometimes be a problem, and will not occur if the union of the stock and the rose is kept above the surface of the soil when planting. It is a particularly useful rose for large scale public planting, and for this purpose it is usual to use seedlings rather than budded stock. So grown it will cover big areas at minimum cost, producing a most satisfactory effect. See pages 246 and 247.

There are a number of good forms and hybrids, and these have been used with some success in the breeding of modern garden shrubs. There is also an old race of double-flowered garden varieties (see Old Garden Varieties of the Scotch Rose below). All are similar in foliage and general appearance and are equally hardy.

ROSA PIMPINELLIFOLIA FORMS AND HYBRIDS

ROSA PIMPINELLIFOLIA DUNWICH ROSE. I know very little about the origin of this rose. It was found at Dunwich in Suffolk, and David Clark of Notcutts Nurseries told me that it was still to be seen growing wild near the sea there in the late 1980s. What I do know is that it is an extremely beautiful shrub — one of the finest of this group. It is typically Pimpinellifolia in flowers, foliage, thorns and hips, but differs in the habit of its growth, which is its chief virtue. It spreads broadly, fanning out into a symmetrical dome of low, arching growth. My specimen has reached 3ft. in height and about 5ft. in width in four years. How much further it will grow I cannot say. The flowers are of a creamy-yellow, about 1½ins. across, and produced in great quantities along its long, elegant branches, covering the whole shrub with a mass of bloom. I feel it must be a hybrid, but of what I cannot say. See page 247.

ROSA PIMPINELLIFOLIA GRANDIFLORA (*R. pimpinellifolia altaica, R. sibirica, R. spinosissima altaica*). Commonly known as *R. altaica*. A native of West Asia, this is very similar to *R. pimpinellifolia* but grows rather taller, to about 6ft., and has larger flowers. These are pale yellow when opening, but quickly turn to creamy-white. The hips are globular and maroon-black. It has all the hardiness of *R. pimpinellifolia*. Fragrant. An excellent hardy shrub.

ROSA PIMPINELLIFOLIA HISPIDA. A variant from North-east Asia, usually growing to about 6ft. It is not so inclined to sucker as the typical species and the stems are covered with slender brown bristles. The flowers are of considerable beauty, being a soft creamy-yellow. Known to have been in cultivation in 1781.

ROSA PIMPINELLIFOLIA LUTEA MAXIMA. Almost certainly a hybrid of *R. foetida*, from which its flowers would have obtained their strong buttercup-yellow colouring — the brightest yellow in this group. The foliage is less typically Pimpinellifolia, being more plentiful and downy on the underside. The growth is less robust and it will usually reach a height of 4ft. Hips black and globular. The fragrance shows some similarity to *R. foetida*.

ROSA PIMPINELLIFOLIA ORMISTON ROY. The result of a cross between 'Allard' (an *R. xanthina* Hybrid) and *R. pimpinellifolia* has provided a nice compact shrub, bearing neatly formed bright yellow single flowers with attractive veining. These are followed by large maroon-coloured hips. Height 4ft. Doorenbos (Holland), 1938.

ROSA PIMPINELLIFOLIA ROBBIE BURNS. So far as I am aware there have been no Pimpinellifolia Hybrids bred in this century, unless we include Kordes's excellent 'Frühlings' series, which are some way removed from the Species. This variety, which was bred at our nursery in 1985, was the result of a cross between *R. pimpinellifolia* and the English Rose 'Wife of Bath'. It is of strongly Scotch Rose appearance. The flowers are small, neat and rather cupped, of a soft rose-pink at the outer edges shading to a distinctly white centre, and have a delicate beauty. The growth is quite tall, perhaps 5ft., and a little heavier than one would expect from these roses, but otherwise similar. Fragrant.

OLD GARDEN VARIETIES OF THE SCOTCH ROSE

These are double-flowered garden varieties of *R. pimpinellifolia*. I therefore have little right to include them with the Species, but place them here to avoid making too many divisions and thus causing unnecessary complication. They appear to have been largely the result of pure selection from the Species. We grow *R. pimpinellifolia* seedlings in large numbers, mainly for municipal authorities, and I have frequently noticed that there will nearly always be a few individual bushes with at least some sign of blush-pink in their flowers. I assume that this group is the result of selecting individuals of this kind. They were, as the name suggests, developed in Scotland, and indeed they are ideal roses for the more extreme climate of the North. It is difficult to say when Scottish interest in these roses began, but in the early 1800s, Dixon & Brown of Perth were probably the first nurserymen to grow them on any scale. Later the firm of Austin & McAslan of Glasgow listed 208 varieties, but there is no mention in their catalogues of those that we grow today. We may assume that a few of them at least survive under other names.

Although the Scotch Roses flower for a very limited period early in the season, and are not particularly showy, they do have certain virtues, not the least of which is the dense, bushy, compact nature of their growth. These bushes are covered with pretty little flowers in season, and the result is a charming picture. They are also extremely tough, and will grow under poor conditions, particularly on sandy soils. This gives them a special value which it would be difficult to replace with any other garden rose. They nearly all have their own pleasant perfume.

ROSA PIMPINELLIFOLIA, *Species Hybrid. The pretty flowers opposite are followed by these almost black hips.*

ROSA PIMPINELLIFOLIA DUNWICH ROSE, *Species Hybrid. Note the attractive mound-like growth.*

ROSA PIMPINELLIFOLIA, *Species Hybrid. A tough and reliable shrub which will survive poor conditions.*

ANDREWSII. Small semi-double, deep pink flowers of rather cupped formation. Dense, bushy growth of about 4ft. in height.

DOUBLE BLUSH. Blush-pink flowers, deepening towards the centre and paler on the reverse side. Height 4ft. A pretty little rose.

DOUBLE WHITE. An excellent shrub and the best known of these roses. It forms a fine, well rounded, dense and bushy plant of about 5ft. In May and early June it is studded with small, double, deeply-cupped flowers with a delicious fragrance.

FALKLAND. Semi-double, delicate pink flowers fading almost to white against a background of greyish-green leaves, provide us with a charming effect. Height 4ft.

GLORY OF EDZELL. This attractive rose is always particularly welcome, as it is one of the first of all to flower. It has single, clear pink flowers that pale towards the centre. A sprightly little shrub of 5ft.

HARISONII ('Harison's Yellow'). There is some doubt as to the origin of this rose, but it was probably raised by George Harison of New York in 1830. It is almost certain that it is a hybrid between a Scotch Rose and *Rosa foetida*. It forms a rather slender, upright shrub of 5ft., bearing bright sulphur-yellow double flowers which are cupped at first and open to a more flat formation, usually exposing their rather darker stamens. The foliage is of a slightly greyish-green. It provides a most satisfactory exclamation mark of bright colour in a border of Old Roses before most of them are in flower. Fragrant.

MARBLED PINK. Small semi-double, cupped flowers, opening wide with the outer petals turning back. In colour it is blush-pink at first, marbled darker, becoming almost white. It forms an attractive, low, dense but spreading shrub of 3ft. in height. See page 251.

MARY QUEEN OF SCOTS. I do not have this variety at present, but understand it is a charming rose. It has small, double flowers coloured a mixture of purple and lilac-grey, paler on the outside. There is a legend that it was brought from France by Mary Queen of Scots. Height 3ft.

MRS. COLVILLE. A shrub of 2½ft. in height, thought to be a hybrid with *Rosa pendulina*. The flowers are single, crimson-purple, white at the centre, with yellow stamens. The young wood is red-brown, and it bears elongated hips of darkest red.

SINGLE CHERRY. Small cherry pink flowers, with a lighter reverse and prominent stamens. Height 3ft.

STANWELL PERPETUAL. The first Old Rose I grew and still a favourite of mine. It was discovered in a garden in Essex, and introduced in 1838 by a nurseryman called Lee, of Hammersmith. It is highly probable that it was the result of a chance cross between *Rosa piminellifolia* and an Autumn Damask, as it is unique among Scotch Roses in that it is reliably repeat flowering. Its growth is more lax than is usual in these roses, and the foliage a rather greyish-green, but otherwise it is typical, showing little sign of the Damask parent. It is not so free-flowering as the others in this group, but this is made up for by a succession of later blooms. The flowers start as the most perfect little cupped buds of clearest blush-pink. These open to flat, semi-double, rather informal flowers of about 3½ ins. across, with quilled petals and a button eye. They have the most delicious fragrance. The height is about 5ft. Like all these roses, it is very tough and hardy. See page 251.

WILLIAMS' DOUBLE YELLOW ('Double Yellow', 'Scotch Yellow', 'Old Double Yellow', 'Scots Rose'). This is similar to 'Harisonii' and probably came from the same parents. It was said to be a seedling from *Rosa foetida,* raised in 1828 by John Williams who lived near Worcester, and must have been a chance cross with a Scotch Rose. At first sight it is easy to confuse it with 'Harisonii', but closer examination reveals it is much nearer in growth to its Scotch parent. It has pale green carpels, not stamens, in the centre of its small bright yellow double flowers that open to an informal formation. These have a strong fragrance, similar to that of *R. foetida.* In Scotland it is known as 'Prince Charlie's Rose'. Height 4ft.

WILLIAM III. A dwarf bush of no more than 2ft. in height, suckering freely when on its own roots and forming a dense thicket. The flowers are semi-double, purplish-crimson fading to lilac-pink, and are followed by small, round, maroon-coloured hips.

ROSA PRIMULA. This rose is similar to *Rosa hugonis,* to which it is closely related, having the same finely divided, fern-like foliage and dainty yellow flowers carried along its arching branches. These are of a delicate primrose-yellow, with a light scent, and it is one of the first roses to flower in mid-May. It is also known as the 'Incense Rose' for the fragrance of its foliage — a fragrance which will carry far on the air. It may be expected to grow to 6ft. and as much across. A native of the region

ROSA X RICHARDII, *Species Hybrid. Also known as the 'Sacred Rose of Abyssinia', this is a good shrub with large but dainty flowers.*

Left: ROSA XANTHINA SPONTANEA, *Species Hybrid. Commonly known as 'Canary Bird', the flowers are often a deeper yellow than here.*

Right: ROSA WILLMOTTIAE, *Species Hybrid. Dainty in growth, flower, foliage and hip.*

Opposite: MARBLED PINK, *a garden form of* Rosa pimpinellifolia, *and a good example of a Scotch Rose, both useful for poor conditions.*

STANWELL PERPETUAL, *a recurrent flowering hybrid between a Scotch Rose and an Autumn Damask.*

spreading from Turkestan to Northern China. First discovered near Samarkand by the American collector F.H. Meyer, 1911.

ROSA X RICHARDII. This interesting rose is also known as *R. sancta,* the 'Holy Rose' or the 'Sacred Rose of Abyssinia'. It was probably a natural hybrid between *R. gallica* and *R. phoenicea.* It forms a sprawling but shapely bush of 3ft. in height and 4ft. across, and bears large pale pink flowers in small clusters. It was introduced into Britain by Paul of Cheshunt in 1902.

Not only is it one of the most beautiful single flowered roses, but it also has a long and intriguing history. Dr. Hurst speculates interestingly on its origins. He suggests that St. Frumentius, who brought Christianity to Abyssinia, may have introduced it to that country in the fourth century, and that it was planted in the precincts of Christian churches and thus preserved throughout the centuries. He goes on to relate how in 1888 the eminent archaeologist, Sir Flinders Petrie, discovered the remains of this rose twined into garlands in tombs in the cemetery of the town of Arsione of Fayoum in Upper Egypt, near to the Labyrinth Pyramid. This would date them to a period between the second and fifth century A.D. He also tells us of Sir Arthur Evans's excavations at Knossos in Crete. Here Evans found a representation of a rose which Hurst felt bore a striking resemblance to the 'Sacred Rose'. This is probably the earliest picture of a rose. See page 250.

ROSA ROXBURGHII (*R. microphylla;* also popularly known as the 'Burr Rose', the 'Chestnut Rose', the 'Chinquapin Rose'). An unusual rose from China and Japan, it forms a vigorous shrub of about 7ft. in height and the same across, with stiff, angular branches and attractively flaking light brown bark. It has strong hooked thorns in pairs, just below the leaves. The leaves themselves are long, with up to fifteen evenly-arranged leaflets. The flowers are usually solitary, 4ins. across, and of a clear pink fading to white, with plentiful golden stamens, the stalk and calyx being covered with prickles. These are followed by large, round, bristly hips (hence 'Chestnut Rose'). The whole effect is that of an attractively gnarled shrub. In cultivation prior to 1814.

ROSA ROXBURGHII PLENA. This is a double form, probably of Chinese origin, and thought to be of great antiquity. The flowers are very full, giving the appearance of a beautiful Old Rose. They have large, pale pink outer petals, while the numerous shorter centre petals give a deep pink effect. They have a light fragrance. Height 2½ to 3ft. A curious and interesting rose. Introduced to Britain by Dr. Roxburgh, from Canton, 1824.

ROSA RUGOSA. This important species is the parent of the Rugosa Hybrids, and I have dealt with it in the companion to this volume, *Old Roses and English Roses.*

ROSA SERICEA (*R. omeiensis*). A vigorous, usually thorny shrub, occurring in a wide area extending over Northern India, the Himalayas, North Burma and Western China, and first collected in 1822. It is unique amongst roses in that its flowers have only four petals, although occasionally it is to be found with the normal five. These flowers are small, white or sometimes yellow, 1½ to 2ins. across, cupped, with the petals only just overlapping; they are held very closely along the branch early in the season in mid-May. The foliage is small and fern like with many leaflets; the hips are small, red and pear shaped. Height 10ft. *R. sericea* does not make a great show in the garden, although the growth and foliage are attractive. It has given rise to a number of forms and hybrids. The following three are worthwhile.

ROSA SERICEA HEATHER MUIR. The most beautiful form with creamy-white, scented flowers which are much larger than the species — about 3ins. across. These are produced with great freedom over a long period throughout the month of June. It will form a very large shrub of 10ft. by 10ft. or more. The hips are small and orange-red. It was named after the creator of the famous Kiftsgate Garden. Mrs. Muir obtained the original seedling from E.A. Bunyard, and it was eventually distributed by Sunningdale Nurseries in 1957.

ROSA SERICEA PTERACANTHA. This unique rose differs from *R. sericea* in the enormous size of its red thorns. These are triangular and flat, up to ¾in. wide at their base, and are the rose's chief attraction. When young, they are a translucent red-brown so that the sunlight shines through them, giving a brilliant effect. For this reason it is worth placing the rose where the sun can catch it, and cutting it hard back annually to produce new growth and, consequently, young thorns. Alternatively, it is sometimes useful as a barrier to halt both four-legged and two-legged intruders, for no rose has quite such a formidable armoury. The flowers are white, similar to *R. sericea,* with four petals, and not very conspicuous, although they have a certain quaint charm amongst the thorns. 8ft. by 6ft. Western China, 1890. See page 254.

ROSA SERICEA PTERACANTHA RED WING. A hybrid with *R. hugonis,* which has similar large red thorns, although they are rather smaller than those of its Pteracantha parent. The flowers are creamy-yellow, and it forms a graceful shrub with fine fern-like foliage. Height 8ft.

ROSA SERICEA PTERACANTHA, *a Species Hybrid with unusual four-petalled white flowers and huge colourful thorns.*

Left: ROSA SWEGINZOWII, *a giant Species Hybrid similar to* Rosa moyesii, *with the same flagon-shaped hips.*

Right: ROSA VILLOSA, *Species Hybrid. Good grey-green foliage and massive hips.*

ROSA SETIPODA. In every way a beautiful shrub: in flower, leaf, fruit and general demeanour. It will grow to about 10ft. in height and the same across. The foliage is very fine, the leaves being about 7ins. long, with nine neatly formed leaflets of a glaucous-green, and with a slight Sweet Brier fragrance. The flowers are quite large for a species, 2½ to 3ins. across, opening flat, the petals turning back slightly at the edges. They

ROSA SETIPODA, *Species Hybrid. A fine 10ft. shrub, beautiful in flower, leaf and fruit.*

are held nicely poised upon thin, bristly purplish stalks, have a light fruit-like fragrance and appear in the latter part of June. The hips are very large, orange-red, flagon-shaped and bristly, with persistent sepals. A native of Central China, brought to Britain by E.H. Wilson in 1895.

ROSA STELLATA (*Hesperhodos stellatus*). A native of the South-western U.S.A., from the west of Texas to Arizona, this is a wiry, thicket-like shrub of about 2ft. in height, with grey-green stems, pale sharp prickles and hairy, deeply-toothed leaves of three leaflets, rather similar to those of a gooseberry. The flowers are solitary, 2 to 2½ ins. across, soft rose-pink in colour, with deeply-notched petals and yellow anthers, having something of the appearance of a cistus. The hips are round, brownish-red and about ½ in. wide. It is very hardy, but likes sun and a well-drained soil.

ROSA STELLATA MIRIFICA ('Sacramento Rose'). Similar to *R. stellata,* but more vigorous, attaining 4 to 6ft. in the wild, usually with leaves of five leaflets. The flowers are slightly larger and it is more free flowering than *R. stellata.* It requires similar conditions. Both are roses of some charm.

ROSA SWEGINZOWII. A very vigorous shrub that is similar to *R. moyesii* in many respects, but larger, growing to 12ft. in height and the same across, with very large thorns and numerous bristles. The flowers are rose-pink, 1½ to 2ins. across, and held in small clusters. These are followed by long, bristly, flagon-shaped, orange-red hips. It is a native of North-west China. Introduced 1906. See page 254.

ROSA VILLOSA. Also known as the 'Apple Rose' for the exceptionally large size of its round hips which make a fine display in autumn. It is a vigorous, well-formed shrub of 7ft. by 7ft, with large, downy, grey-green foliage, against which its clear rosy-pink flowers show themselves to good effect. These are about 2½ ins. across, with slightly crinkled petals and a light fragrance. A native of Central Europe and Western Asia. See page 254.

ROSA VILLOSA DUPLEX ('Wolley-Dod'). This is a semi-double form or hybrid of the rose described above. Although it may be a little shorter in growth, it is otherwise similar. In spite of this, the chromosome count suggests that it is, in fact, a hybrid of a garden rose. The hips are less plentiful and perhaps a little smaller, the flowers rather larger, but we have the same attractive combination of flower and leaf. It is known to have been in existence prior to 1797.

ROSA VIRGINIANA. A dense, suckering shrub, notable for the varying colours of its foliage. This is bronzy when young, becoming green, and finally turning to autumn tints of red and yellow. The stems are tinged with red, and have few thorns. The flowers appear later than many other Species and continue from late June to early August. They are quite small, cerise-pink, paler at the centre, with pointed buds. The hips are small and bright red, persisting throughout the winter. It will grow to 4 or 5ft. in height, and sucker freely on its own roots. A useful rose for municipal planting or for the more natural areas of the garden. Many seedling strains of this rose have become rather mixed and show distinct signs of hybridity. A native of North America.

ROSA VIRGINIANA ALBA. A white-flowered form or hybrid of the rose described above, with green stems and pale green leaves which do not turn to autumn tints. Height 4 to 5ft.

ROSA VIRGINIANA ROSE D'AMOUR (St. Mark's Rose). There is a mystery surrounding the origins of this charming rose. However, I think it is safe to say that at least one of its parents was *R. virginiana*. Its flowers are small and double, with the most perfect high-pointed scrolled buds in the manner of a Hybrid Tea. They are deep pink at first, becoming paler at the edges as they open. The growth is robust, forming a large, wild Species-like shrub of perhaps 7ft. in height. Like *R. virginiana* it does not flower until mid-summer, but continues over a long period. It is similar in appearance to *R. virginiana,* although the leaves are rather less polished in appearance. It is a pretty, but not showy shrub.

It is interesting to speculate on its second parent: to produce double flowers, one would assume that this must have been a garden rose of some kind. Prior to 1759.

ROSA WARDII CULTA. *R. wardii* is a native of South-east Tibet and is not in cultivation. *R. wardii culta* is a form of this rose collected by Kingdon Ward and distributed in 1924. It is another Species of the *R. moyesii* type, being rather similar in growth and foliage. Its flowers are white, with a mahogany-red central disc surrounded by yellow stamens. In fact, it is sometimes known as the 'White Moyesii'. The growth is arching, the foliage light green, and it will grow to 6ft. in height and 5ft. across. There are very few thorns.

ROSA WEBBIANA. A pretty Species closely related to *R. willmottiae*. It is of dense growth, with slender, reddish-brown, twiggy stems in long, arching sprays, along which are borne pale lilac-pink flowers, each about 2ins. across, with a slight scent. These occur in early June. They are followed by narrow flask-shaped, scarlet-red hips of about ¾ in. long, making a particularly dainty display; indeed, few other Species can match it in this respect. The foliage is made up of up to nine small, finely-divided leaflets. It will grow to about 6ft. in height and 6ft. across. A native of the Himalayas, Afghanistan and Turkestan, it grows at from 6,000 to 18,000ft. First cultivated in 1879.

ROSA WILLMOTTIAE. Of all the Species, this is perhaps the most graceful in growth and foliage. It is a prickly shrub of 8ft. in height and rather more across, with arching growth bearing small, finely-divided greyish-green foliage, giving a dainty spray-like ferny effect. The flowers are small but pretty. They do not last for very long, but while they do they provide a pleasing picture. Their colour is lilac-pink with creamy stamens. Later, there are small pear-shaped orange-red hips. A native of Western China, collected by E.H. Wilson in 1904. See page 250.

ROSA WOODSII FENDLERI. *R. woodsii* is a variable shrub native to central and western North America. *R. woodsii fendleri* is the form usually seen in gardens, reputedly found in the southerly areas of this region — sometimes as far south as Mexico — although it is quite hardy. It forms a dense bush of 6ft. by 5ft, and has graceful growth, greyish-green leaves and small lilac-pink flowers with creamy stamens. These are fragrant and borne singly or in small clusters. In autumn the branches are hung with round, shiny, red hips that persist well into winter. These are perhaps its greatest asset. First cultivated in 1888.

ROSA XANTHINA SPONTANEA CANARY BIRD. One of the most popular and best known of the Species, mainly because of the deep yellow colouring of its flowers. Although it is a good shrub, I am not quite sure it deserves such pre-eminence. It has 2in. flowers, graceful growth, chocolate-brown bark and dainty fern-like, grey-green foliage. The hips are dark maroon, but not very conspicuous. An excellent rose, although not always very robust and it is inclined to suffer from die back unless on its own roots. Height 7ft. See page 250.

Climbing Species Roses

Apart from the shrubby Species, there are a number of good Climbing Species. In the wild these would climb over shrubs and into trees to find the light. The majority of them are of the Synstylae family (see below) and of very strong growth, producing large sprays of small, white flowers.

In addition there are a few Climbing Species of other families. These vary considerably and include some exotic roses of great beauty (see pages 265-268). Unfortunately, many of them are rather tender, but where this is the case they are usually well worth trying on a warm wall.

Nearly all the Climbing Species are best left to their own devices, with little pruning, at least in so far as space allows. They will require very little other attention.

Climbing Species of the Synstylae Family

Species of this family are so distinct as to make it helpful to include them in a section of their own. The name refers to the fact that all these roses have the styles of their flowers in one piece, and not separated and held individually as is the case with all other roses. This is the simple way in which botanists identify them. It is by crossing Species from this family

ROSA FILIPES KIFTSGATE,
Climbing Species. One of the
best Climbers for larger trees,
its growth can be massive
with enormous corymbs of
bloom.

with garden varieties that all our Rambler Roses have been developed.

A reader who is not familiar with the Synstylae roses might be excused if he complained that they seem to be all very much the same. They do, however, vary greatly in height, and as we get to know them better we find that they have many subtle differences which are hard to put into a few words. They usually have a strong, sweet fragrance, and flower with exceptional freedom. They include some dramatically tall and rampant roses ideal for growing in trees and over bushes, and indeed for covering any large structure.

ROSA ARVENSIS (the 'Field Rose'). A common rose of the British hedgerows, flowering after the Dog Rose and having rather smaller white flowers. It also grows wild over much of Europe. A climbing or trailing Species it is usually found scrambling over bushes. From a horticultural point of view it is mainly important as the parent of the Ayrshire Roses. The flowers are borne in small bunches along reddish stems, and are followed by ovoid, red hips. Contrary to what we often read in books, it is fragrant and is indeed the 'Sweet Musk Rose' extolled by Shakespeare and Spenser. This rose will grow to a great width if permitted — perhaps 20 by 10ft. in height. It is worth growing in wild places, and is sometimes used for roadside planting.

ROSA BRUNONII (*R. moschata nepalensis,* the 'Himalayan Musk Rose'). A variable Species and one of the most beautiful of this family. A native of the Himalayan region, extending into China, it grows extremely vigorously, to a height of 30 or 40ft., making it excellent for climbing into larger trees. The foliage is particularly fine, with very large, elegantly poised leaves of seven widely-spaced, long pointed leaflets. These are grey-green and downy on the underside. The flowers are creamy-white, about 1½ ins. across, with yellow stamens, and are held in very large clusters in late June and early July. They have a strong fragrance. This Species is not completely hardy and can be caught by severe frosts, but it is entirely worthwhile in most areas. First cultivated in 1822.

ROSA BRUNONII LA MORTOLA. A superior form of *R. brunonii* in almost every way, and should generally be grown in preference. It has larger white flowers of about 2ins. across, which are held in larger clusters. The leaves also are larger, more grey and more downy. In other respects it is as described in the Species above. Height 30 or 40ft. It was named after the famous garden in Italy, close to the French border, and was brought from there to England by E.A. Bunyard. It was introduced in the U.K. in 1954.

ROSA FILIPES. A strong and rampant climber that will grow to 30ft. The flowers are white and borne in large corymbs. They are of a pronounced cup-like formation, and each is held on a long, slender thread-like stem. They have a strong fragrance and are followed by very small oval hips. We do not grow this Species — it has been almost entirely superseded in the garden by *R. filipes* 'Kiftsgate'. A native of West China, first collected by E.H. Wilson in 1908.

ROSA FILIPES BRENDA COLVIN. A seedling from 'Kiftsgate' described below. It has all the strength of that massive rose, and small single flowers in large clusters. The difference lies in the colour: this is a soft blush-pink which quickly turns to white. Unfortunately, the pink is so indistinct as to be almost white in massed effect. There is a delicious fragrance. A chance seedling discovered by Miss Colvin, first distributed by Sunningdale Nurseries in 1970.

ROSA FILIPES KIFTSGATE. This is the form of *R. filipes* usually sold by nurserymen. It has become well known among keen gardeners as a climber for large trees and there is no better rose for this purpose. It is a prodigious grower and an astonishing bloomer. It can easily achieve 40ft. and bears enormous corymbs of bloom, sometimes with hundreds of flowers. Individually these are small, cupped and creamy-white with yellow stamens. They have a strong fragrance. It can at times be a little choosy as to the position in which it is grown, and refuse to live up to its reputation as a massive grower. The late Mrs. Muir of Kiftsgate Court, Gloucestershire, purchased this rose from E.A. Bunyard in 1938. Where he obtained it from we do not know, but it was eventually introduced by Murrell (U.K.) in 1954. Mrs. Muir's original plant is now some 60ft. in width, and over 40ft. high. See page 259.

ROSA HELENAE. A native of West China, collected by E.H. Wilson in

1907. It is a vigorous Climber that will grow to 18ft. in height. The flowers are small, about 1½ins., creamy-white and held in dense, well-rounded clusters of about 6ins. across. They have a strong fragrance. The hips are small, ovoid, orange-red and hang gracefully from the branch. The foliage is dark green with seven to nine leaflets, and there are strong, hooked thorns. This is a useful tree climber where R. *filipes* or R. *mulliganii* are too big; it may also be grown as a large shrub.

ROSA MOSCHATA (the 'Musk Rose'). Not, in fact, a wild Species, but a rose of ancient garden origin. It may have been brought to England in the time of Elizabeth I and has many romantic associations. Later, it had an important effect on the breeding of garden roses, being one of the original parents of the Noisette Roses. On a sunny sheltered wall it can be very fine, but in a less favourable position it may not be so impressive. The flowers are single (sometimes semi-double), creamy-white, and held in widely branching sprays. It has two important merits: its delicious musk fragrance, and the fact that it does not bloom until August, and then continues until autumn. Height about 10ft.

ROSA MOSCHATA PRINCESSE DE NASSAU. At one time known as R. *moschata* 'Autumnalis', this has semi-double flowers of creamy-buff. They are held in dainty sprays, appearing unusually late in the season (in August), continuing until autumn, and are exceedingly sweetly scented. This rose needs and deserves a sheltered position in full sun to hasten the blooms. We know nothing of its origin, but it has many similarities to a Noisette, which in fact it may be. Height 8ft.

ROSA MULLIGANII. For a long time this rose has been available from nurserymen as R. *longicuspis,* but according to Bean's *Trees and Shrubs,* it should properly be known as R. *mulliganii.* This is going to be rather confusing for a little while. R. *mulliganii* vies with R. *filipes* 'Kiftsgate' for the position as the largest tree-climbing rose. It is usually not quite so strong, but will reach 30ft., and has fine, glossy, almost evergreen foliage, with leaves of seven leaflets, the young shoots being tinted with brown. The flowers are creamy-white, almost 2ins. across, and are held in huge broad trusses of anything up to 150 individual blooms. They have a strong fragrance. In autumn there are small orange-red hips. It flowers late in the season, from the end of June to mid-July. A native of West China, it was collected by F. Kingdon Ward in about 1915. See page 263.

ROSA MULTIFLORA (R. *polyantha*). A vigorous Climber or shrub sometimes used as a root stock in this country, but more often on the Continent. For this reason it is frequently found surviving in gardens,

ROSA WICHURAIANA, *Species Climber, charmingly laced around a cottage window.*

long after the garden rose which was budded on to it has died away. However, this is not to say it is not a useful garden plant, although it is perhaps a little stiff in growth as a Climber, and there are better Species. It has considerable value for large-scale planting in municipal landscapes, as it grows very vigorously, forming a great mass of tall growth. For this purpose it should be grown from seed. It bears tight clusters of small, 1-in. creamy-white flowers with golden stamens in late June and early July. These have a strong fruity fragrance which carries extensively. There are small, oval, red hips in autumn. Its dimensions as a shrub are 7ft. high by 10ft. across; as a Climber it will grow considerably taller, and may reach 20ft. or more in a tree. It was one of the ancestors of the Multiflora Ramblers and the Polyantha Pompon Roses, eventually influencing the Floribundas. It is thus one of the most important ancestors of our Modern Roses. A native of North China, Korea and Japan. Known to have been in Britain before 1869.

ROSA POLYANTHA GRANDIFLORA. This is usually known as *R. gentiliana*, but it is more likely that it is an *R. multiflora* Hybrid, as no one seems to have any knowledge of it in the wild; and more conclusively by the fact that the styles of its flowers are separated, indicating it is not a pure member of the Synstylae family. In late June to mid-July it bears

ROSA MULLIGANII, *one of the most massive of the Species Climbers, and ideal for growing in a tree.*

masses of small, single white flowers in rather small clusters. These have orangy-red stamens, a strong fruit-like fragrance, and are followed by light red hips which last well into winter, making a fine display. It flowers freely and has plentiful, glossy foliage, which is tinted with bronze at first. Height 15 to 20ft. It is thought to have been brought from China, and introduced in 1886.

ROSA RUBUS (*R. ernestii*). A vigorous Climbing Rose closely related to *R. helenae*. The flowers are 1½ ins. across and are borne in tight clusters of up to forty. These are creamy-white at first with a tint of yellow at the base of the petals and attractive orange stamens at the centre. They have a particularly strong Multiflora fragrance, and appear from late June to early August. The blooms are followed by a good display of small orange-red hips. The leaves are made up of five of more leaflets which are downy beneath and have a purplish colour when young. Height 20ft. A native of Central and Western China. First discovered by Dr. Henry about 1886.

ROSA SEMPERVIRENS. This Species is a native of Southern Europe and North Africa and is best known as the parent of the beautiful Sempervirens Hybrids. It is, in fact, an attractive Species in its own right, with larger flowers than others of this family and of pleasing individual character. These are borne in small clusters on long, graceful, trailing growth. They have a slight fragrance. The foliage consists of five to seven leaflets and is almost evergreen. Not entirely hardy in the British Isles.

ROSA SETIGERA (the 'Prairie Rose'). There is some doubt as to whether this should be regarded as a shrub or a Rambler. It is so large that I think for most garden purposes it is best treated as a Rambler, when it will climb to 15ft. In late July and early August it bears small sprays of 2-in. rose-pink flowers that fade almost to white. These are followed by small, round, red hips. The foliage is of an attractive dull green colour. It is a useful rose for growing in a small tree or over bushes, and has the added attraction of coloured flowers which are unusual in this section. Where space can be found it is also an excellent shrub, sending out long, trailing stems and forming a mound of sprawling growth. It is a native of the Eastern United States, and has been used in the breeding of Rambler Roses, more notably 'American Pillar' and 'Baltimore Belle'.

ROSA SINOWILSONII. This rose has the most magnificent foliage of all the Species, and it is grown mainly for this reason. The leaves are of a dark, glossy green, very large, and may be up to 1ft. in length. They are deeply corrugated, tinted with purple beneath, and have seven leaflets.

The flowers are not outstanding, being white, 1½ins. across, and borne in small sprays. Most unfortunately, it is not completely hardy. I am not sure how tall it will grow, as the frost has always cut it short in my garden. I notice *Modern Roses* states 50ft. It was brought from China to Britain in 1904 by E.H. Wilson, who was responsible for bringing so many good Species from that country, so much so that he became known as 'Chinese Wilson'.

ROSA SOULIEANA. A very strong, loose-growing Climber or shrub, with long, arching stems, distinctly greyish leaves, and hooked yellow thorns. The flowers are pale yellow in the bud, opening white, about 1½ins. across, and freely produced in clusters. There is a fruity fragrance. Bunches of small, ovoid orange hips make a good show in autumn. As a Climber it will grow to 12 or 15ft. without difficulty. As a shrub it will create a mound of growth 10ft. high and the same across. It is excellent for wild areas, where it can be grown as a shrub or into trees and over bushes. In the British Isles it may be cut back by cold frosts. Collected in West China by Père Soulié, and sent to France, arriving at Kew in 1899.

ROSA WICHURAIANA. A vigorous, trailing rose, native to Japan, East China, Korea and Taiwan. Best known as the parent of the Wichuraiana Ramblers, it is a useful garden plant in its own right. It will make excellent ground cover where space permits, sending out trailing growth of great length which will keep close to the ground or climb into bushes and trees with the help of its hooked thorns. It does not flower until August, when it has attractive pyramid-shaped clusters of small white flowers shading to yellow at the centre. These have a strong fruit-like fragrance. The foliage is a bright, glossy green and almost evergreen. Later we have small, ovoid, dark red hips. It is also a most attractive Climber, growing to 20ft., its long shoots hanging gracefully from their support. There is also a less robust, semi-variegated sport – *R. wichuraiana variegata*. See page 262.

Other Climbing Species

ROSA BRACTEATA (the 'Macartney Rose). A most beautiful and exotic rose, but unfortunately not completely hardy in the British Isles. It will, given a warm and sheltered wall, survive most winters, certainly in the warmer parts of the country. The flowers are large, up to 4ins. across, pure white, with a silky texture and a large boss of orange-red stamens;

ROSA RAMONA, *Climbing Species. A hybrid of* Rosa laevigata, *this is one of the most beautiful of single roses, but rather tender.*

they are fragrant and borne singly on short stalks, with attractive, large, leafy bracts around the buds. The fruit is globular and orange-red. It has fine, smooth, dark green leaves with up to nine leaflets, and is almost evergreen. The growth is bushy, to about 12ft. in height in a suitable position, and it will in warmer climates form a good shrub. Unusually among Species it continues to flower until autumn. It is a native of Eastern China, collected by Sir George Staunton, and brought to this country by Lord Macartney in 1793. In the warmer regions of the Southern U.S.A. it has become naturalized and is regarded as something of a weed in certain areas. It is one of the parents of the beautiful 'Mermaid'.

ROSA GIGANTEA. The most splendid of the wild Species Roses. Sadly, it is too tender to be grown in the British Isles, except in the very warmest areas, but even then it seldom blooms. In its native habitat of South-west China and Upper Burma the flowers are very large, 5 or 6ins. across, and may be pale yellow, cream or white, with large, overlapping petals and a boss of golden stamens. The fragrance is similar to that of Tea Roses. It has huge, 9-in. glossy dark green leaves, and will make massive growth to as much as 50ft., even 80ft. in warm climates. The hips, too, are very large, about 1½ins. across, and globular. Indeed, it is in every way gigantic. Gault and Synge, in their *Dictionary of Roses,* tell us how the giant hips are sold for eating in the bazaars of Manipur State. Discovered by Sir George Watt, 1882, introduced by Sir Henry Collet, 1889.

R. gigantea is of particular interest to us as one of the great influences in the development of Modern Roses, and this has been discussed at some length in Chapter 4 and in the companion to this volume, *Old Roses and English Roses*. It was this rose, above all, which was responsible for the transition of Old Roses to what we now call Modern Roses. It is so huge and so different that it was certain to change the whole character of garden roses.

ROSA LAEVIGATA (*R. sinica, R. cherokeensis*). A vigorous Climber or shrub, with dark green leaves which are unusual in that they each have only three coarsely-toothed leaflets. It has 4-in. creamy-white, deliciously fragrant flowers borne singly or in pairs in late June. This is another beautiful but tender Rambling Species. It will flower well in this country, but requires a warm wall if it is to survive. A native of China, it has adapted itself to the wild in south-eastern North America, where it has become known as the 'Cherokee Rose'. Growth 20ft. Introduced 1759.

ROSA LAEVIGATA HYBRIDS

ROSA ANEMONE (*R. anemonoides, R. sinica* 'Anemone'). This is a hybrid of *R. laevigata*, probably with a Tea Rose. It is more delicate in appearance than the former, with sparse growth, less foliage and finer stems. The flowers, however, are very similar to those of *R. laevigata*, and are of supreme beauty, being a clear shell-pink, lightly veined with deeper pink and paler on the reverse side. In spite of its refined appearance it is hardier than *R. laevigata*, but still requires a warm wall. It starts flowering in early June and, although not repeat flowering, continues over an extended period. It will grow to 15ft. in a suitable position. Slight fragrance. Bred by J.C. Schmidt (Germany), 1895.

ROSA LAEVIGATA COOPERI ('Cooper's Burmese Rose'). This is a

Species closely allied to *R. laevigata,* and a native of Nepal, North Burma and South-west China. Its flowers are large, about 4ins. across. They are held singly and are of glistening pure white, with a large boss of yellow stamens. It has fine, very glossy foliage, with three (occasionally five) leaflets. Unfortunately it is tender and has failed to flower in my garden, although at Sissinghurst Castle it flowers freely early in the season on a sunny wall. In England it will grow to about 12ft., although in its habitat it is a giant. We have a plant under glass where it flowers freely and would no doubt grow to a great length. It was first brought to this country by Mr. R.E. Cooper, and grown at the then National Rose Society's Trial Ground at Haywards Heath, in 1931. Our stock was brought to us by Mr. and Mrs. Cooper-Willis from Nepal, where they saw valleys of it growing to the tops of tall trees, and sweeping in long, trailing stems almost to the ground. This must be the most wonderful rose spectacle in the world.

ROSA RAMONA. A sport from *R. anemonoides,* discovered by Dietrich and Turner of California in 1913. It is similar in every way, except for the colour of the flowers. This is cerise-crimson with a greyish tint on the reverse. A very beautiful rose. See page 266.

Hulthemia

This is a sub-genus that was previously classified by botanists as part of the genus *Rosa.* It is closely related to the rose, as is illustrated by the fact that the two have been successfully hybridized.

HULTHEMIA PERSICA (*Rosa persica, R. berberifolia,* 'Rose of Persia'). This is an interesting shrub that occurs in the semi-desert conditions of Iran, Afghanistan and neighbouring U.S.S.R., where it is a common sight. It forms low, twiggy, spiny growth of about 2½ft. in height, spreading by means of runners. The foliage is silvery-grey. The flowers are small, about 1½ins. across, of deep golden-yellow with a red-brown blotch in the centre. No rose is of quite such a brilliant yellow. Later, there are small, bristly hips. In its native territory it is extremely hardy and persistent, and I understand it has been known to push its way up through concrete. It is not easy to grow in a northerly climate, but not impossible if given a warm, dry position. First introduced to Europe around 1790. See page 267.

x HULTHEMOSA HARDII (*Rosa* x *hardii*). This is a bigeneric hybrid;

268

reputedly *Hulthemia persica* x *R. clinophylla*. It has larger and finer flowers than *H. persica*. These are bright golden-yellow with a bright red-brown eye at the centre. I have never seen it in flower, but understand it is beautiful. It is a rather straggly plant and somewhat subject to mildew, but will grow to about 6ft. with the protection of a warm wall. Raised at the Jardins du Luxembourg, Paris, 1836.

MODERN HYBRIDS OF HULTHEMIA

As early as 1880, Thomas Rivers, the famous rose specialist of the time, predicted that *Hulthemia persica* would probably be the parent of an entirely new group. He, of course, saw it as a species of *Rosa*, and was not to know that it might not be quite so simple as that. Nonetheless, there are signs that his prediction may well be about to become true. In 1964 Alexander Cocker obtained seed of *Hulthemia persica* from Iran, and gave some of it to Jack Harkness who grew the Species and hybridized it with a number of true roses. Attempting to hybridize between two separate genera is no easy matter, but Jack Harkness succeeded in doing this with a number of roses and states in his book *Roses* that he had successfully hybridized *H. persica* with 'Ballerina', 'Buff Beauty', 'Canary Bird', *R. chinensis* 'Mutabilis', 'Cornelia', 'Fru Dagmar Hastrup', 'Margo Koster', 'Mermaid', 'Perla de Alcanada', 'Phyllis Bide', 'Roseraie de l'Hay' and 'Trier'.

It was the bright central 'eye' of *H. persica* that appealed to him, and no doubt the bright yellow colouring and extremely tough growth, but there is more to his hybrids than this. They form appealing small shrubs of unrose-like appearance. Their growth is bushy and rather sprawling, with flowers of distinct character. I would like to see them bred further, not just as an improvement on the rose, but as something quite different. Here are two varieties Harkness has introduced. Unfortunately they have proved difficult to propagate and stock is not plentiful.

EUPHRATES. Sizeable clusters of single reddish-salmon flowers, each with a prominent scarlet eye at the centre. These are produced freely on an excellent spreading bushy plant of 2ft. in height. The leaflets show considerable variation in shape, which is a feature of the Persica hybrids. *H. persica* x 'Fairy Changeling'. Harkness (U.K.), 1986.

TIGRIS. Attractive semi-double, canary-yellow flowers with red centres. The growth is lax, dense and spreading, with many thorns and light green foliage providing a gooseberry-like effect. It flowers in June and July with occasional blooms appearing later. *H. persica* x 'Trier'. Harkness (U.K.), 1985.

CHAPTER 7
Rose Cultivation

Rose growing is not difficult. It is easy to surround it with a mystery that is not warranted. Good results can be achieved with little more than common sense and a minimum of attention. In fact, many who grow roses do so with no more than this. To insist on more would be to bar the majority of people from growing roses in their gardens. In spite of this a little extra skill, care and knowledge will help us to achieve better results. One thing is certain, the more we put into our roses, the more pleasure we shall get out of them.

Choice of Site

The choice of position for roses depends in part on aesthetic, and in part on practical considerations. There are certain conditions that roses do not like. They do not like shade, not even partial shade, although, as we have already seen, there are some roses that will withstand this better than others. They do not like competition from tree roots, nor do they like the drip from the outer edges of trees. Both English and Old Roses look particularly well when mixed with other plants and shrubs, but it is very necessary to take care that these others are not such as might compete too strongly with the roses. This is particularly important when the roses are first planted; once they have risen above their neighbours it is rather less crucial. The soil should be of reasonable depth and in good condition. It should also be well drained. It is not possible to grow roses in waterlogged soil.

Soil Preparation

Usually the gardener does not have much choice as regards soil type. He has to make the best of what is there. Without doubt most roses are happiest in a heavier soil where they will grow far larger and more strongly than in other soils. With adequate manuring, good results should be easily obtained. If you have an exceptionally heavy clay this may cause some difficulty at first, but it can be overcome by mixing in liberal quantities of humus and by using a planting mixture around the roots of the rose.

Light soils and medium loams are entirely suitable, but the roses will require more generous treatment, particularly if the soil is very light.

The real problems arise in limy or chalky soils. Roses do not like too much lime. They prefer a soil that is either neutral or very slightly acid. As a nurseryman, I am sometimes a little dismayed when I meet our customers — so many of them seem to have chalk gardens, and I cannot help wondering how our roses are faring. Fortunately this is a problem that can be overcome, but it does require some expenditure and effort. Large quantities of humus should be mixed with the soil, particularly immediately around the rose, although it is better if this does not actually touch the roots. The humus will neutralize the alkalinity and help retain moisture.

Peaty soils are the most difficult of all. Here, the only solution is to import soil and place it in the area around the rose to a depth of 1ft.

Care in the preparation of the soil is very worthwhile. A rose, if it is a Hybrid Tea, will thrive for ten years or more. If it is a Shrub Rose it may well continue for much longer. We are therefore making a long term investment, and it will certainly pay dividends if we do the job thoroughly. If the soil can be dug some weeks before the roses arrive, so much the better. Thorough cultivation to a spade's depth, together with the careful mixing of soil and humus, will make a great difference. In addition to this, it is worth breaking up the subsoil with a fork as you dig; this will help drainage and enable the deep tap roots to go well down. If you dig up an old rose bush you will usually find that there are few roots in the first foot of soil; most of the growth is deep down. In spite of this, the humus should only be mixed with the top 12ins. of soil; beneath this it will be unable to work effectively.

The reader will have noticed the emphasis I place on humus. I regard this as crucial in growing good roses. Its use is not really necessary with very strong roses such as the Species, but with repeat-flowering roses it is essential if we are to get the best results, particularly later in the year. The humus may take various forms: well-rotted farmyard manure, compost, one of the various proprietary brands, or peat. The first two are best, but peat is a good alternative. It is not a bad plan to use peat together with the other forms of humus. It is long lasting and has a good effect on the condition of the soil, but has little nutritional value.

If you are unable to apply humus, at least use a proprietary rose fertilizer. Indeed, a dressing of fertilizer early in the spring after planting will be desirable in any case. Potash is vital for roses, particularly on light soils which tend to be deficient in this. Heavy soils often lack phosphates. Sulphate of potash is a good source of potash, and bone meal an excellent natural source of phosphates.

Replanting Roses in the Same Ground

There is one point above all I would like every rose grower to heed. When the soil has had roses grown in it for any length of time, say five or six years or more, it should not be replanted with roses. Such soils will be what is usually known as 'rose sick'. This does not mean the existing roses will not thrive in it indefinitely, but when the ground is replanted with new roses, it is quite probable that they will fail to grow properly. This is true even when extremely healthy and robust roses have been taken out. The exact nature of the problem is not fully understood; it is almost certainly due to microscopic organisms known as nematodes, but poisons from the roots of the previous roses may also be involved.

Fortunately this only concerns the area immediately around the bush or shrub. If it is possible to move even a little way to one side of the previous rose, there should be no problem. Where this is not practical the answer is to remove the soil from the area where the original rose has been, to a width of about 2 to 4ft. across, and 1ft. in depth, according to the size of the rose, and replace this with a mixture of one part humus to three parts good soil from another area of the garden. Where rose beds are involved, it will be necessary to remove all the soil and replace it. This may seem a little extreme, but I think it is worthwhile. Far better, if you can, to move your new roses to a different part of the garden. Another more simple method is to sterilize the soil before planting. It is possible to obtain chemicals especially for this purpose from your garden centre.

For those who do not feel inclined to go to these lengths, the problem can be mitigated by the use of large quantities of humus. The problem of rose sickness is greater in light soils that tend to lack humus and, in my experience, much less in humus-rich soils.

Purchasing Roses

There are two ways in which roses can be purchased — bare rooted or in containers. There is now a generation of gardeners which tends to know only the latter, or to think there is something rather risky about the former. This is quite wrong; both have their virtues, but on balance I would favour the bare rooted. Roses are not very happy in containers, and unless the garden centre has looked after them well, there is a danger they may be poor specimens.

If you require roses that are in any way out of the ordinary, it will be necessary to buy through mail order — unless you are lucky enough to live near to a suitable rose specialist. It is not practical for the average garden centre to carry any more than a very limited range. When buying from a rose specialist it is advisable to order well in advance. The grower has to plan his crop some two and a half years ahead, and it is not always possible to predict what the demand will be. Varieties will inevitably become sold out.

Planting

I will deal with the bare-rooted roses first. These may be planted at any time between November and March. If they are not purchased locally, they may arrive either at a time when you are not able to plant them immediately, or when the weather or soil conditions are not suitable. In this case, they should be temporarily heeled into the ground by digging a small trench and covering the roots with soil. They will then be quite safe for many weeks. If the soil is frozen when the roses arrive, they will be all right in their packet for three or four weeks, so long as they are kept in a cool but frost-proof building.

Planting should be at such a depth that the joint at which the rose has been budded on to the root stock is just beneath the surface of the soil. Make a hole of adequate size to take the roots, spread the roots out evenly, and fill in with soil, treading it down gently with the feet, being careful not to get the soil too solid. It is very worthwhile using a special planting mixture for this purpose. This can be made up of half peat and half best garden soil, together with a sprinkling of bone meal. Alternatively, a ready-made mixture may be bought. This will give your rose a much better start and, incidentally, if your mixture is kept dry, make it possible for you to plant when the soil and weather conditions are less than perfect.

If you wish to move established plants, this is entirely possible providing they are not too old and gnarled. Roses often seem to relish this treatment. Before doing this, it is vital to prune the bush very severely, removing all old and dead wood, and cutting it almost to the ground. This will mean that the roots of the plant, which will have inevitably been badly maimed, will not have to maintain too much growth in the early stages.

The planting of container-grown bushes is very much the same as for those with bare roots, except that it is important to avoid breaking up the soil when removing the bush from the pot. It is best to cut away the plastic with a knife, or, if the container is a solid pot, to knock the bush and soil out whole. The advantage of a container rose is that it can be planted at any time of the year. Having said that, it has to be pointed out that such roses, when planted later than June, will by the following year usually be little further ahead than a bare-rooted rose that has been planted the following winter.

If we are planting late in the season, say late March or early April, it is advisable to keep an eye on soil moisture. The ground can easily become dry before the roses have had time to make roots. In such cases give a heavy watering that will go deep. This is doubly important in the case of container roses that are planted out of season. It is easy to think that they are quite safe in their little ball of soil, but this can quickly dry out.

Climbing Roses require special consideration when they are planted against a wall. It will frequently be found that the soil here is very dry, even in a damp period. For this reason there are more failures with Climbing Roses than among any other type. The plant is unable to get a start in life without sufficient moisture and will not grow strongly for two or three years, until the roots have been able to move away from the wall. To alleviate this problem, plant the rose at least 1ft. from the wall, and instead of arranging the roots in the usual circular manner, spread them away from the wall towards the more moist soil. Even then, a regular soaking of water is often necessary for the first year.

Pruning

Pruning is not difficult, and much latitude is possible. It is something of an art and it can be interpreted, in some degree at least, according to the type of growth that is required. Used in this way, it becomes an interesting and enjoyable task. I have from time to time, while progressing through the various classes of roses, made notes on the subject, but it would perhaps be convenient to summarise it here in a more general way.

SHRUB ROSES. Pruning Shrub Roses is quite simple – they can usually be allowed to develop naturally at first. They require very little pruning in the first two or three seasons. After this, it is necessary to remove some of the older growth to encourage new growth. It may also be necessary to trim the shrub generally to keep it shapely and prevent it from invading other roses or plants nearby. Some varieties have the habit of growing upwards so that if this allowed to continue, most of the flowers will be so high that we do not see them and the lower part of the plant will be bare and unsightly. The aim should always be to develop an attractive and shapely shrub.

CLIMBING AND RAMBLING ROSES. Climbing Roses, which are in the main repeat flowering, should be pruned during the winter. Pruning them is quite simple. A Climber consists of the main long stems which do the climbing, and short side stems from these which produce the flowers. All we have to do is to remove some of the main stems each year where they can be spared. These will be those that are becoming weak and unproductive. Having done this, we cut back the smaller side shoots to about 3ins.

Rambling Roses are even more simple to prune. It is only necessary to remove some of the older growth from the plant to ensure renewal and to avoid it getting out of hand. Where the area for growth is more or less unlimited, as on trees or over large structures, the plant can be given its head for a few years. In this way, a more natural effect will be achieved. In fact, I would go so far as to say that with most Ramblers, the less we interfere with the growth, the better. In the case of the Multiflora Hybrids it is necessary to remove more of the basal wood, as they tend to become choked with growth at this point. There are certain exceptions to these rules. Banksian Roses should be left unpruned as should 'Mermaid' — all it requires is an occasional thinning.

SPECIES ROSES. These are wild and natural roses and require little pruning other than the removal of old and spent wood once the shrub begins to mature. This is best done during the winter. Do not allow the shrub to become too full of dense and dying growth.

HYBRID TEAS AND FLORIBUNDAS. New bushes should be pruned back to within 5ins. of the ground at planting time. Thereafter their stems should be cut to about half their length. Weak, twiggy growth is cut away, as are dead and diseased branches. As the main growth ages, some of it should be cut harder to encourage strong new stems from the base. Pruning is probably best done in March, although it can be done earlier. Early pruning encourages early flowers so long as the young shoots are not damaged by late frosts.

Mulching, Feeding and Watering

This is not necessary on the largest and most robust of shrubs such as the Species Roses. Nor is it entirely essential for once-flowering roses, although these will be greatly improved by such attention. With repeat-flowering Shrub Roses and the Hybrid Teas and Floribundas it becomes very necessary if we are to have quality and continuity of flowering. It is true that acceptable results can be achieved without such care, but a little extra assistance in this direction yields results out of all proportion to the effort involved. This is particularly true with soils that are less favourable to roses: light sands, chalk, limestone, and so on.

Mulching is most important. If roses are given a good mulch each year, or even every other year, most other cultural considerations fade into insignificance. Mulching helps to maintain the moisture in the soil through drier periods, and this makes continual flowering possible. It provides plant food, it reduces susceptibility to black spot, and has a smothering effect on weeds. Various materials can be used. Rotted compost is excellent. It is worthwhile gathering your garden and household waste for this purpose, but it should be given ample time to rot down. Perhaps the simplest method is to use bought materials such as peat or forest bark. These are free from weeds and easy to handle. The feeding value will be less, but this can be corrected by the application of fertilizers.

When growth begins in the spring, a dressing of one or other of the various proprietary rose fertilizers should be applied. This should be repeated in June or July as the first flush of flowers is passing in order to encourage the next. A good general fertilizer is suitable, but it should contain a high proportion of potash, particularly on light land. Roses demand large quantities of potash, more than most other plants.

Many people who grow repeat-flowering Shrub Roses are disappointed to find that their plants frequently fail to make a second crop. Obviously we cannot have repeat flowering without growth, and growth is entirely dependent on the availability of moisture. It is of little use applying fertilizer to a rose if there is not the moisture to make it available to the plant. Even in a climate like our own, there is rarely sufficient rain to maintain moisture at the necessary levels throughout the summer. I am certainly not going to suggest that watering is anything like essential in Britain, but it can contribute considerably to the performance of our roses. In drier climates it is of course vital. There are excellent automatic watering systems available which will make the task very simple, and they are not expensive. If you do decide to water, give a good soaking. In this country, even one or two such soakings in the course of an average summer will make all the difference. This is particularly important after the first flush of flowers.

Suckers and Dead Heading

Most roses are budded on to root stocks and this inevitably means that from time to time there will be suckers, that is to say growth from the stock. Suckers are not difficult to detect, as their leaves are usually very different from those of the garden variety. A great deal of trouble will be saved if suckers are removed early on; it is much easier at this stage, and little of the energy of the plant will have been wasted. A knife is the best tool for this purpose — try to cut away a little of the bark together with the sucker, otherwise the sucker will quickly re-emerge from the same point.

The removal of dead flowers is not essential, but the plant retains a much tidier appearance if this is done. Roses are by nature single flowered, but man has made them double flowered. For this reason the petals tend to stay intact even as the flower dies, and they are often unsightly.

Dead heading is more important in the case of repeat-flowering shrubs and Hybrid Teas and Floribundas, for if these produce hips they will take up the energy of the plant and inhibit further flowering. Of course, where hips are to be desired, as with the Species, no dead heading should be done.

Diseases and Pests

Considering how widely the rose is grown it cannot be said that it is particularly subject to diseases and pests. By and large, the rose is able to live with most of them. They become more of a problem when many roses are grown in close proximity. This is, of course, true of nearly all plants. We hear a great deal about elaborate spraying, but this is not always essential, although it is more important with the repeat-flowering roses.

Perhaps the biggest problem is blackspot. Few roses are completely resistant to this disease, and it might be said to be the greatest single drawback of the rose. Anyone who can breed roses that will resist blackspot will be doing a great service. Unfortunately in the breeding of such resistance we can lose many other desirable characteristics.

With modern sprays and equipment, control both of diseases and pests is not too much of a hardship. The important point is to start spraying early in the season. Most problems start in quite a small way but quickly mutliply. If you can halt them at an early stage, treatment will be much easier and more effective.

DISEASES

BLACKSPOT (*Diplocarpon rosae*). The symptoms of this disease are just as the name suggests — black patches appear on the leaves, with yellow at the edges. These will grow and multiply and may, if left unattended, defoliate the whole plant. Blackspot is worse in the country or in any area where the air is clean, but some varieties are much more susceptible than others.

The most effective spray at present is one which contains bupirimate-triforine. This should be applied as directed both on leaves and stems, at the time when the leaves are emerging. This early spraying is most important. It is then recommended that spraying should continue at ten to fourteen day intervals, but this is a counsel of perfection. With most roses, a further two sprayings at the normal rate in late May, June and July will keep the disease sufficiently in check.

Good cultivation will help in the avoidance of blackspot. Adequate feeding and mulching is important, but avoid the excessive use of nitrogen. Poor drainage and the shade of trees will also encourage this disease.

POWDERY MILDEW (*Sphaerotheca pannosa*). A white powdery mould appears on the leaves and buds. The leaves may turn yellow and purple and eventually wither and drop prematurely. The buds may fail to open. Use a spray containing bupirimate-triforine as soon as the disease appears, and continue as suggested for blackspot. Do not allow mildew to develop too much before spraying.

Here again, good cultivation encourages healthy growth. Mulching, watering and feeding will help to prevent the problem in the first place. Excessive nitrogen provides soft growth which mildew thrives upon. Climbing and Rambler Roses are particularly susceptible.

ROSE RUST (*Phragmidium tuberculatum* and other species). This is one of the worst diseases, but fortunately is not common. Orange swellings appear both on upper and lower leaf surfaces in spring. Later in the season, rust-like patches appear on the underside of the leaf and eventually turn black in August.

Normally you will not have to worry about this problem, but where it does occur it is important to catch it early. Spray in mid- to early May, when the first infection appears. An effective spray is one which contains oxycarboxin. It is vital to spray the underside of the leaf — the upperside is not important.

Rose rust occurs most frequently on hot, dry soils and where the soil is deficient in potash. It occurs more often in a wet season, or where there is a prolonged heavy dew. Certain varieties of rose are much more subject to it than others. Most Shrub Roses are immune.

PESTS

APHIDS. These may be green, orange, reddish or black. Most gardeners will be familiar with them. They feed off young shoots, starting in the spring, and multiply rapidly if not checked. Eventually they will cause distortion of the leaf. Excreted honeydew dropped on the leaves often grows a black fungus known as 'Sooty Mould'.

Control is not difficult, and numerous systemic sprays are available. Spray when the insects first appear. When purchasing, make sure that the chemical is not a hazard to bees or other useful insects.

LEAF-ROLLING SAWFLY. The leaflets become tightly rolled and a greyish-green grub may be found inside. This problem chiefly occurs where roses are in the shade of trees.

It is only possible to spray for prevention before the curling of the leaf occurs. When you have this problem it will be necessary to wait until the following year and spray in May with a spray containing fenitrothion.

Having provided this short list of troubles, it is important to stress that we should not regard rose growing as a continual battle with diseases and insects. Often these will not occur. We only need to treat them where they show signs of becoming a real problem. We ourselves do minimal spraying in our nursery garden.

Glossary

ANTHER. The part of the flower which produces pollen; the upper section of the stamen.

ARCHING SHRUB. A shrub in which the long main branches bend down towards the soil, usually in a graceful manner.

BALLED, BALLING. The clinging together of petals due to damp, so that the bloom fails to open.

BARE-ROOT ROSES. Roses bought without soil, not in a container.

BASAL SHOOT. The strong main shoot that arises from the base of the rose.

BICOLOUR. A rose bloom with two distinct shades of colour.

BOSS. The bunch of stamens at the centre of a flower.

BRACT. A modified leaf at the base of a flower stalk.

BREAK. New growth from a branch.

BUDDING. The usual method for the propagation of roses by the grafting of a leaf bud on to the neck of a root stock.

BUD-SHAPED FLOWER. I have coined this term to describe rose blooms that are in the form of a Hybrid Tea, i.e. flowers that are of high-centred bud formation and mainly beautiful in the bud (as opposed to those of Old Rose formation).

BUD UNION. The point on the root stock where the bud of the garden rose was inserted.

BUSH. I use this word to describe closely pruned bedding roses, as for example a Hybrid Tea.

BUSHY SHRUB. A rose of dense, rounded growth.

BUTTON EYE. A button-like fold of petals in the centre of a rose.

CALYX. The green protective cover over the flower bud which opens into five sepals.

CANE. A long rose stem, from the base of the plant, particularly as in a Rambling Rose.

CHROMOSOMES. Chains of linked genes contained in the cells of plants and animals.

CLIMBING SPORT. See Sport; the climbing form of this phenomenon.

CORYMB. A flower cluster that is flat-topped, or nearly so.

CROSS. See Hybrid.

DIE BACK. The progressive dying back of a shoot from the tip.

DIPLOID. A plant with two sets of chromosomes.

FLORE PLENO. Double flower.

FLUSH. A period of blooming.

GENE. A unit of heredity controlling inherited characteristics of a plant.

GENUS. A group of plants having common characteristics, e.g. *Rosa*.

HEELING IN. Temporary planting of roses when conditions are not suitable for permanent planting.

HEIGHT. The heights given for individual varieties are only approximate. Much will depend on soil, site, season and geographic area. The breadth of a rose bush or shrub will usually be slightly less than the height.

HIPS OR HEPS. Seed pods of a rose.

HYBRID. A rose resulting from crossing two different species or varieties.

LEAFLETS. The individual section of a leaf.

MODERN APPEARANCE, ROSE OF. Rose that usually has high-pointed buds and smooth foliage, similar to a Hybrid Tea Rose.

MUTATION. See Sport.

OLD APPEARANCE, ROSE OF. Rose with bloom of cupped or rosette shape, rather than the pointed bud and informal flower of a Modern Rose; the plant usually having rough textured leaves, i.e. Gallica, Centifolia, etc.

ORGANIC FERTILIZER. A fertilizer made from natural materials rather than chemicals.

PERPETUAL FLOWERING. A rose that continues to flower in the same year after the first flush of bloom, though not necessarily continually.

PISTIL. Female organ of a flower consisting of the stigma, style and ovary.

POLLEN PARENT. The male parent of a variety.

POMPON. A small rounded bloom with regular short petals.

QUARTERED. A flower in which the centre petals are folded into four quarters.

QUILLED PETALS. Petals folded in the form of a quill.

RAMBLER-LIKE. I use this term to describe roses bearing large sprays of small blooms similar to those of a small flowered Rambling Rose, particularly a Multiflora Rambler.

RECESSIVE GENE. A gene that is dominated by another, rendering it ineffective.

RECURRENT FLOWERING. See Perpetual Flowering.

REMONTANT. See Perpetual Flowering.

REPEAT FLOWERING. See Perpetual Flowering.

ROOTS, ROSES ON THEIR OWN. Not budded on to a stock; grown from cuttings.

ROOT STOCK (STOCK). The host plant on to which a cultivated variety is budded.

RUGOSE. Leavs with a wrinkled surface.

SCION. A shoot or bud used for grafting on to a root stock.

SEEDLING. A rose grown from seed. In the context of this book, the offspring of a variety.

SEPAL. One of the five green divisions of the calyx.

SHRUB. A rose that is normally pruned lightly and allowed to grow in a more natural form, as opposed to a bush which is pruned close to the ground.

SPECIES. A wild rose.

SPORT. A change in the genetic make up of the plant, as for example when a pink rose suddenly produces a white flower.

SPREADING SHRUB. A shrub on which the branches tend to extend outwards rather than vertically.

STAMEN. The male organ of a flower, consisting of the filament and anther, which produces pollen.

STIGMA. The end of the pistil or female flower organ.

STYLE. The stem of the pistil which joins the stigma to the ovary.

SUCKER. A shoot growing from the root stock instead of from the budded variety.

TETRAPLOID. A plant with four sets of chromosomes.

TRIPLOID. A plant with three sets of chromosomes.

UPRIGHT SHRUB. A rose in which the growth tends to be vertical.

VARIETY. Strictly speaking, a naturally occurring variation of a species. The popular meaning, so far as roses are concerned, is a distinct type of rose.

Bibliography

American Rose Society's *Annuals,* from 1917.

Beales, Peter, *Classic Roses,* Collins Harvill, London, and Harper & Row, New York, 1985.

Beales, Peter, *Twentieth-Century Roses,* Collins Harvill, London, and Harper & Row, New York, 1988.

Beales, Peter, *Roses,* Harvill, London, 1992.

Bean, W.J., *Trees and Shrubs Hardy in the British Isles,* 8th edn. revised.

Bois, Eric and Trechslin, Anne-Marie, *Roses,* 1962.

Dobson, B.R., *Combined Rose List. Hard to Find Roses and Where to Find Them,* Beverly R. Dobson, Irvington, New York 10533, 1985.

Fletcher, H.L.V., *The Rose Anthology,* Newnes, 1963.

Foster-Melliar, Rev. A., *The Book of the Rose,* Macmillan, 1894; 1910.

Gault S.M. and Synge P.M., *The Dictionary of Roses in Colour,* Michael Joseph and Ebury Press, 1970.

Griffiths, Trevor, *The Book of Old Roses,* Michael Joseph, 1984.

Griffiths, Trevor, *The Book of Classic Old Roses,* Michael Joseph, 1986.

Harkness, Jack, *Roses,* Dent, 1978.

Harkness, Jack, *The Makers of Heavenly Roses,* Souvenir Press, London, 1985.

Hillier's *Manual of Trees and Shrubs,* 4th edn., 1974.

Hole, S. Reynolds, *A Book about Roses,* William Blackwood, 1896.

Jekyll, G. and Mawley, E., *Roses for English Gardens,* Country Life, 1902; reprinted Woodbridge 1982.

Kordes, Wilhelm, *Roses,* Studio Vista, 1964.

Krussman, G., *Roses,* English edn., Batsford, 1982.

Lawrance, Mary, *A Collection of Roses from Nature,* 1799.

Le Grice, E.B., *Rose Growing Complete,* Faber & Faber, 1965.

McCann, S., *Miniature Roses for Home and Garden,* David & Charles, London, 1985.

McFarland, J.H., *Roses of the World in Colour,* Cassell, 1936.

McFarland, J.H., *Modern Roses,* 8th edn., McFarland Co., U.S.A., 1980; 9th edn. The American Rose Society, Shreveport, 1986.

Paul, William, *The Rose Garden,* 10th edn., Simpkin, Marshall, Hamilton, Kent & Co., 1903.

Pemberton, Rev. J.H., *Roses, Their History, Development and Cultivation,* Longmans Green 1908; rev. edn. 1920.

Rose Growers' Association, *Find that Rose.*

Ross, D., *Shrub Roses in Australia,* Deane Ross, 1981.

Royal National Rose Society's *Annuals,* from 1911.

Shepherd, R., *History of the Rose,* Macmillan, New York, 1966.

Swain, V., *The Australian Rose Book,* Angus & Robertson, Sydney, 1983.

Thomas, G.S., *Shrub Roses of Today,* Phoenix House, 1962.

Thomas, G.S., *Climbing Roses Old and New,* Phoenix House, 1965.

Warner, C., *Climbing Roses,* Tiptree Books.

Willmott, Ellen, *The Genus Rosa,* Murray, issued in parts 1910-14.

Index